# My Beloved

## THE STORY OF A CARMELITE NUN

# My Beloved

## THE STORY OF A CARMELITE NUN

by

### Mother Catherine Thomas

OF DIVINE PROVIDENCE, D. C.

McGRAW-HILL BOOK COMPANY, INC.

New York    Toronto    London

NIHIL OBSTAT

Fr. John Emmanuel of the Cross, O.C.D., Censor Librorum

IMPRIMI POTEST

Fr. Evarist of St. Cecilia, O.C.D., Provincial Feast of the Solemnity of St. Joseph, 1954

IMPRIMATUR

✠ Eugene J. McGuinness, D.D.,
Bishop of Oklahoma City and Tulsa
August 10, 1954

The Nihil Obstat and Imprimatur are official declarations that a book or pamphlet is free of doctrinal or moral error. No implication is contained therein that those who have granted the Nihil Obstat and Imprimatur agree with the contents, opinions or statements expressed.

*Published by the McGraw-Hill Book Company, Inc.*
*Printed in the United States of America*

To

## CHRIST JESUS, THE BELOVED

*My Beloved is my Bridegroom*
*And my Lord—O what a joy!*
*I will henceforth all the powers*
*Of my soul for Him employ;*
*And the flock that once I tended,*
*Now I tend not as before*
*For my only occupation*
*Is to love Him more and more.*

*I have gone away forever*
*From the haunts of idle men*
*And a sharer in their follies*
*I will never be again.*
*They may say, and say it loudly,*
*I am lost; but I am not;*
*I was found by my Beloved,*
*O how blessed is my lot!*

St. John of the Cross

## ACKNOWLEDGMENT

*Our deepest gratitude is due to Father John F. Donovan of Maryknoll for his indispensable help in preparing the manuscript for publication. May God reward him as only He can!*

# Contents

# Illustrations

# Chapter 1

# The Lamb Who Was Slain

† APOC. 5:12

THE LAST week of 1927 I was in New York City to do some shopping and to take care of a few business matters. I stayed at my sister Anna's apartment on Grand Avenue and 176th Street.

Long before dawn on New Year's morning I arose to attend five o'clock Mass at nearby St. Margaret Mary's Church. As I hurried down the stairway from my sister's apartment, I heard the sound of many laughing voices in the foyer of the main floor. A gay New Year's party was noisily breaking up, and I hesitated a few moments while the young couples scrambled out the door.

A carefree young man, who evidently had no partner to escort home from the party, gallantly held the door while the others filed through, giving him a parting "Happy New Year" as they left.

Seeing me approach the exit, he courteously held the door until I, too, had passed. I nodded a mumbled "Thank you" in his direction and quickened my steps in the misty darkness toward St. Margaret Mary's. In a few seconds I heard a voice behind me.

"May I see you home?"

It was the young man who had been holding open the door.

1

"I'm not going home," I replied as I nervously fingered my gloves. The darkness and the stillness made me doubly afraid, and I shivered noticeably in the cold dampness.

"Well," he insisted as we hurried along, "may I see you where you are going?"

"I'm going to church."

"Then, may I see you to church?" he said, with just a trace of doubt in his voice.

At a loss for anything else to say, I replied, "Of course, if you wish."

Then I asked, as casually as I could under the circumstances, "Are you a Catholic?"

He told me that he was, but I was not convinced. "Let me hear you recite the Act of Contrition," I said, half in fun, never dreaming that he could. But he recited the prayer perfectly, and I was somewhat reassured.

Then he confessed that his intention had been to go home after the party and spend the day in bed. I turned toward him and said, "You mean without going to church? And it is Sunday, too! . . . What a terrible way that would have been to start the New Year!"

In the basement church of St. Margaret Mary's he knelt beside me and fingered a black rosary during Mass. When Communion time came, he made way for me by stepping into the aisle. I glanced up into his face then and noticed how very dissipated and forlorn he looked, and I felt very sorry leaving him behind in the pew as I went up to the altar rail; so I took him, in spirit, with me. If only I were able to share with him some of the overwhelming happiness I felt when I returned to my place carrying within me Our Blessed Lord Himself! At that moment I was united with all the members of Christ's Mystical Body in a very special way—even with my anonymous escort kneeling drowsily at my side. Maybe it would be easier for him to believe, to hope, to love because of my believing, and hoping, and loving.

After Mass he asked if he might see me back to the apartment. I had no objection. It was drizzling, and he held my umbrella over both of us. I explained to him that it was not my apartment, that I was from Monticello, visiting my sister.

He told me that he lived on the Grand Concourse in an apartment with his mother. He said, "She will be waiting for me to get home." Then he added a bit sadly, "She'll be happy to hear that I have been to Mass. . . . You know, I hate to admit it, but I'm a great worry to her."

I could readily believe it.

Before taking his leave at the entrance of my sister's apartment, he gave me his business card—he was, I noticed, connected with a brokerage firm in Wall Street—then he said, "You have told me that you are from out of town visiting your sister here; but you have not told me your name. May I have your name and address? And may I write to you?"

I gave him my name, but not my address.

"It will do you no good to have my address," I said, "for you will never be able to hear from me or see me again. In three weeks I am entering the Carmelite cloister. . . ."

This seemed to startle him. He stared at me incredulously, and a shadow crossed his face.

I fidgeted a bit, smiled, and said, "But I shall always remember you, and when I am a nun, I will pray for you, I promise."

"Gee," he said with a grin, "this is like a story you'd read in the *Messenger of the Sacred Heart*."

These were the last words I heard as I turned away, laughing, and hurrying through the door which an hour before he had held open for me, while I passed through in fear and trepidation.

When my sister and her husband heard the story of my predawn adventure, they looked at each other, nodded knowingly, then tried to convince me that this was a sure sign I was not meant for the convent. "Things like that just don't happen to girls called to the cloister."

I laughed and said, "Well, it happened to this one."

Later that New Year's morning, I went to keep my appointment with the Mother Prioress at New York City's Carmelite monastery. During the interview I told about my early morning adventure and repeated the comments of my sister and her husband. Mother Prioress was greatly amused at their ability to interpret signs.

My entrance day had already been fixed for January 21. New Year's night I returned to Monticello for three final, busy weeks with my family.

But before I take you with me into the strict enclosure of the Carmelite monastery, and before I attempt to tell you about our hidden life of solitude, let me go back somewhat so that you may better know who it is that speaks to you and better understand how it came about that I found myself a contemplative cloistered nun behind the walls of one of the strictest religious orders in the Catholic Church.

Many influences bear on a vocation to the religious life, although there is often one soul-stirring event which stands out so clearly that we are justified in tracing the beginning of our vocation to that time.

There is, of course, a sense in which everyone has a vocation. God has a role for each person to whom He gives life, and the discovery of that role is the discovery of a vocation. If God called me to the religious state, He also called my sisters to the married state. All of us had to try to discover what God wanted of us; each of us had to decide whether or not to consent to God's demand.

But when Catholics speak of vocation, they are ordinarily thinking of the special call which some receive to devote themselves wholly to the service of God in the priestly or religious state. How did I come to discover that I had this special call? In what circumstances did the heavenly vocation first awaken an echo in my soul? In what way did I first become conscious of the possibility that God might ask me to belong to Him alone?

If I gave you a thousand guesses, I am sure you would never guess where I "found my vocation."

It is true that, like many little girls, I was thinking of the convent in my very early childhood. I can still see myself raising my hand, year after year, whenever Sister would ask the girls in school, "How many would like to become nuns?" And for one reason or another my eager response always brought forth an outburst of ridicule from my friends in the classroom. One such day my best friend, Sadie, said to me after class, "Celia, how long are you going to keep this thing up? You know you will never enter a convent in a million years."

Never having made a wager in my life before—or since—and not realizing exactly what I was saying, I shouted, "How much do you bet?"

Sadie said, "One dollar." Although there was not fifty cents in the whole group, several of our classmates who heard the conversation echoed the wager, which I proceeded to forget completely until it was brought to my attention at a farewell party a few days before I entered Carmel. Each of the girls paid up.

Even in my early years of grammar school I felt that to become a nun was the best thing any girl could do, and there never was a time when, in theory at least, I did not want the very best of everything. So despite the fact that I was far from nunlike in my conduct, I was nevertheless sincere in raising my hand as I always did. After all, "I should *like* to be a nun" was not quite the same as saying, "I *will* be a nun." However, I am not referring to this hand-raising period of my life when I speak now about where I got my vocation.

My vocation came to me in a slaughterhouse.

Before I was born, Papa and Mama moved to Monticello, New

York. Papa, who had become rather prosperous in his hotel business at Virginia Beach, was forced to retire after a serious injury to his leg. No doubt this was providential because it is possible that we would not have been a large family of thirteen had we remained in the city. And I, who was the tenth child, might never have been born. Mama often said it was easier for her to raise her large family in the country than it is for the modern big-city mother to raise a family of three.

The village slaughterhouse was a dilapidated barn with a cattle pen on one side, a deep well on the other, and a pigsty in the rear. Whenever a butcher's truck filled with livestock would come by, the boys and a few curious girls, like myself, would run pell-mell to witness the slaughter.

Very often Rabbi Betowsky would be there, and his solemn presence gave a decidedly religious aspect to the proceedings. He was a dignified, silent, patriarchal-looking gentleman with a long white beard and small blue eyes. He always reminded me of Michelangelo's magnificent Moses or someone's conception of the Heavenly Father.

On the occasions when Rabbi Betowsky officiated at the slaughterhouse he carried, firmly under his arm, a long, narrow leather case, nicely lined, from which he drew a quite lethal-looking knife, with a sharp, shiny blade. Despite the reverence we felt toward Rabbi Betowsky and despite our eager curiosity, we always retreated a few steps when he pulled out that knife.

In the slaughterhouse the oxen always put up the fiercest struggle. They seemed to sense exactly what lay ahead for them and literally had to be dragged to execution. We used to think the expression "dumb as an ox" should be changed to "dumb as a cow," for the cows could be led to the block without much trouble.

One day the Jewish butcher came down the road with some lambs in his wagon, heading for the slaughterhouse. Rabbi Betowsky was walking with mute dignity alongside the wagon. My brother Tommy and I left our unfinished chores and ran to the scene. We were the only spectators that day. I always loved lambs, and though I shuddered to think of seeing one killed, my natural curiosity triumphed and in silence I watched.

The dear little things were roughly taken from the cart and lined up on the floor. Not one of them seemed to move a muscle; they just looked at Tommy and me, trustfully, without the slightest suspicion of what was in store for them. Their innocence almost made me cry, and I was wishing we might buy them all from the butcher and put them with our own little flock.

As I stared through misty eyes at the scene before me, the picture of the spear-pierced lamb on the classroom wall and the story of the Lamb of God began to run through my mind. In class, Sister Geraldine, the Dominican nun whose name I took at Confirmation, had explained the whole symbolism to us. How Saint John the Baptist had greeted Christ, "Behold the Lamb of God. . . ." How the prophet foretold about Our Lord's death, "He opened not His mouth: He shall be led as a sheep to the slaughter, and shall be dumb as a lamb before his shearer, and He shall not open His mouth. . . ." And somehow the story Sister told us about Saint Agnes—whose name means "lamb"—ran through my excited mind —how she was martyred for the Faith when she was only thirteen years old. . . .

But my musings were cut short.

It was time for the first lamb to be slaughtered. Rabbi Betowsky readied his knife, and the butcher reached for the animal. I expected to see the usual tussle between victim and butcher; but to my utter amazement the poor silent lamb, with merely a suggestion from the butcher and with absolute trust and meek obedience, confidently got down on its knees and actually raised its little head for execution. I turned my head. It was impossible to look. Weeping, I ran home and hid myself in the attic.

Lamb of God. The true Lamb that was stricken for our transgressions. God's only begotten Son came down from Heaven and by becoming the Son of David was made the Lamb of God. Innocent, gentle, guileless, as befits the Truth, He opened not His mouth when led to the slaughter. And on Calvary the Lamb was sacrificed. In a vague imperfect way the idea of sacrifice began to dawn on my childish mind. Our Lord showed His love for His Heavenly Father and for us, by laying down His life; then I should be a lamb also and do likewise. . . . The "I should *like* to be a nun" had taken a definite advance. From this time on the thought was "I *ought* to be a nun." But the will to be a nun was still far off. In His own sweet and gentle way God was leading me and preparing me for Carmel, though at the time the name Carmel would have been less likely to suggest a cloister than a candy or a pie!

When this first stirring of the grace of vocation took place, I was in the eighth grade. And it was at this time that a newly ordained priest was assigned assistant pastor at St. Peter's in Monticello. Father FitzGerald, in the providence of God, was destined to play a large part in my spiritual formation, though it was two years before I was able to open my soul fully to him. During those years it was only on the occasions when I had been a particularly good girl that I would go to confession to him. Not fully realizing it, I was like the proud souls about whom Saint John of the Cross speaks in his book *The Dark Night.* "They are too embarrassed," he says, "to confess their sins openly, lest their confessors should think less of them. . . . And sometimes they seek another confessor to tell the wrongs that they have done, so that their confessor shall think they have done nothing wrong at all. . . ."

It used to be my supreme delight to have Father, when he visited our home, compliment me on my childish sketchings and water-color paintings. In the winters when the evenings were long, painting was a hobby in which all the family indulged. We copied everything we could set our eyes on. I liked most of all, in those days, to copy Nell Brinkley's pictures in the *New York American*. Her girls reminded me of my sisters, especially Sally and Catherine.

I kept at my art lessons all through school, and before I entered Carmel, Mother Prioress had me take an additional art course in New York. Later this was of some practical help to the community.

I once did an oil painting of Cardinal Hayes, who spent part of his summers in Monticello, and whom we knew quite well. The painting was very large, and I became so absorbed in doing it that often my night's sleep was completely lost. Somewhat like Francis of Assisi, who used to admire a jug he had carved, I was always waking up and putting touches on my "masterpiece"—the difference between Saint Francis and me was that the Saint, in reparation, threw his masterpiece into the fire. I like to think my delight in the work was a faint reflection of the Creator's delight in the beauty of the world when He beheld it and "saw that it was good."

Later when I saw the Cardinal, I mentioned the fact that he had a very difficult nose and that it caused me considerable trouble in painting his picture. His Eminence said, "Yes, I know; famous painters have told me that."

The Cardinal always took a fatherly interest in my work, and he was most anxious that I improve. Later on, when I was in our New York Carmel, he sent Sister Mary Andrew, the artist from Mount Saint Vincent College, to our cloister to help me. She was an invaluable teacher.

During my freshman year at Monticello Public High School, I drew an illustrative poster in connection with an English essay. My poster was entitled "Steppingstones to Success." And nothing I ever attempted with pencil or brush, before or since, gave me the vain thrill that came to me when my poster was displayed on the school bulletin board. It was a child's conception of Saint John of the Cross's *Map of Perfection*, though at that time I had never heard of St. John of the Cross. Like him, I pictured a Mount of Perfection, with Heaven at the summit as the goal. At the base of the mountain was a worthless marshland, and there were rocky cliffs up the side of the ascent. The marsh and various cliffs each had its name—laziness, avarice, impurity, and other imperfections; all of which had to be overcome before one reached the summit. There were also intermediate heights to be reached— justice, fortitude, charity, and prudence. My ascent was a purely human effort, for I made no mention of the need for God's grace in the arduous and difficult climb. Two students appeared in my sketch: a boy in the marshland and a girl approaching the summit. I always thought that girls should aim at and reach higher perfection than boys—even then I knew that boys become what girls want them to be.

Not all my free time during high-school days was spent with the brush and easel. Far from it. I was a true daughter of the "roaring twenties" and had my share of the special madness of that era. After school hours I dashed to the gymnasium to play basketball, or to play the piano for couples to dance, or—which I liked still more—to dance myself. In fact, I was having so much fun in school that I often (Lord forgive me) begged God to change His mind about wanting me to be a nun. It made me feel somewhat better later on to hear two or three other nuns here in Carmel say that they, too, had had the same thought at one time.

While it was true that I had formed an intention of becoming a nun after I had seen the lamb slain in the slaughterhouse, my vocation had never taken definite form. Like many young people, I thought one had to "feel pious" to have a vocation to the religious life. At that high-school age, so far from "feeling pious," I was becoming more and more attracted to selfish pleasure and vanity. Christ, the rising sun, was calling me, and I preferred looking to the West.

I was too young then to know that theologians are not agreed whether or not I would have sinned in refusing to follow the invitation I felt Christ was extending to me. I was too young to understand the difference between a counsel and a command or to realize that when God invites us to a higher life, He ordinarily does not back up the invitation with a threat. He leaves us free to accept the invitation or reject it. This is clear from our Lord's own words: "He that can take it let him take it." It is also clear from the way He worded His invitation to the rich young man; the opportunity of following Jesus more closely was given him, but Christ still loved him even after he refused. But for all such ideas I was then too young. I thought that it would be sinful for me to refuse the call; for me it *would* have been sinful. And I knew that there would be no rest for me if I refused; and theologians will not quarrel with me here. The young man "went away sad."

It is possible that God permitted me during my high-school years to live my life fully in order that my body might grow strong and vigorous. Not that exceptional physical health is an absolute necessity for the contemplative life; I have seen delicate women experience little difficulty in living the life of Carmel. But they were women of great fervor. To a cloistered nun, strong nerves are far more important than a strong body. Under the austerities of the cloistered life—the fasts, the penances, the long hours of prayer, the unvarying routine—an athlete may give way, while a frail girl with a sound personality will thrive.

It is also possible that God allowed me to enjoy these years of my youth in order to demonstrate that the contemplative life is not a refuge for those not at home anywhere else. There would be little merit in leaving a world one was incapable of enjoying; there would be no sacrifice if one entered a cloister to escape the life outside, or if one had a natural distaste for the joys of life.

My father curbed my pleasure-seeking somewhat by securing a

part-time job for me in a stationery store in town. It was difficult at times, but it proved a worthwhile experience. And it did reduce considerably my social activities after school hours.

It would have struck any of my friends in those days as utterly impossible were I to have told them that, despite my gay exterior, I was tormented by a host of horrible scruples.

It seems to me now that, like most scrupulous people whom I have since known, I had, in a sense, two minds. One was a common-sense mind which saw things the way other people saw them and which, fortunately, was the mind I was always able to use when I examined myself seriously or when I did my work in school. The other mind was the scrupulous one. It made moral mountains out of molehills; mere imperfections or slight faults appeared as horrible mortal sins. This was the mind that tormented and upset me; it was constantly changing and leading my soul to the very brink of despair.

I used to wish that my older sisters—incidentally, there were eleven girls in our family—would talk to me about my problems. But it never occurred to them, apparently, that I so much as had a problem. I recall saying to myself at that time, "When *I* grow up, I am going to remember how girls of my age feel, and I'm going to talk to them and let them ask me questions."

At that critical stage of my adolescence, I did not know that a girl could ask a priest *anything*. However, when I made this wonderful discovery and finally steeled myself to open my soul to my confessor, my troubles, thank God, were at an end—or almost at an end. Actually it was not until my feelings had been brought completely under control, through the rigid discipline in Carmel, that I finally knew perfect peace of soul.

Fortunately my case of scruples was not deeply rooted, and Father was able to straighten out my problems with apparent ease. Later he confided to me that many souls tormented by the disease of scrupulosity require long, painful treatment and that there are few people more deserving of prayer and sympathy.

It is with a smile now that I look back on those days before I was cured of my scruples. I recall one day finding myself alone in the church. I went up as close as I dared to the tabernacle, and I whispered there, "Jesus, if I am going to be separated from You for all Eternity, You will remember that I tried to get as close to You as I could in Time." Knowing Our Lord as I do now, it is a wonder He didn't appear to me from out the tabernacle!

What tormenting ideas I had about God's justice! There seemed little hope for me. Now that I know God better, I can get as much consolation from the thought of His justice as I can from the thought of His mercy. Saint Thérèse of Lisieux says it is precisely because He is just that He is "compassionate and merciful, long-suffering and plenteous in mercy. For He knoweth our frame, He remembereth that we are dust. As a father hath compassion on his children, so hath the Lord compassion on them that fear Him." In the entire Psalter, the psalm from which Saint Thérèse quotes these words strikes the deepest chord within me, and today I find myself looking forward to Saturday's Compline with keen antici-pation, when Psalm 102 is recited in the Divine Office.

Shortly after my soul was rid of its scruples, I received a very special grace. God does not work in troubled waters, but as soon as the muddy depths of my soul were stilled, He clearly and sud-denly manifested His will to me. It was March 25, Feast of the An-nunciation, that I received this grace. Afterward a conversion seemed to take place within me, a turning from the love of self to the love and service of God; a sort of putting away of the things of a child and the words and thoughts of a child, a decision to make God the end of and reason for all my activity. I no longer prayed that God would not ask me to be a nun.

Mama had a way of making sure we did not remain children for long. She gave each of us responsibilities which she knew would prepare us to face the world. Mama's way of teaching us to be good housewives was to give each of us a turn at managing the house during the summer vacation. We had to do all the buying and cooking and most of the housework. Papa used to say, "God forbid that any of my daughters should ever be delicatessen wives."

The vacation following my sophomore year in high school was to be my turn at "running the house." I loved the work and all the responsibility and despite the heavy toll it took of my time, I was able occasionally to go up into the attic to read my prayer book. Sometimes, I recall, I would just say the Our Father very slowly, trying to think of all the meaning in each word I said. Perhaps it was at this time that the tremendous truth of God's presence came home to me and I wanted everyone, everywhere, to know about it.

The cloister was a word about which, at that time, I probably knew nothing; yet, as I see it now, my visits to the solitude of the attic were preparing me for the life which I eventually embraced. And once I even asked myself, "Why shouldn't God, who is our wonderful Father, have friends that are completely devoted to thinking about Him and adoring Him and serving Him?"

Mama was a strict disciplinarian, and her household rubrics had to be followed exactly. She had specific hours for each chore, and she often scolded me for running off to the attic during worktime. She was neatness and orderliness personified; and I learned that summer the value of time and the necessity for a schedule in one's daily life. These lessons were arranged to prepare me for married life, but I have found them of equal value in the cloister.

# Chapter 2

# Go Up to Carmel

† 1 K. 25:5

Fᴏʀ some people in Monticello the elopement of Attorney Cooke's secretary afforded a choice bit of gossip; but for me it afforded an opportunity to put to practical use the business education I had been acquiring in high school for two and a half years.

Mr. Cooke approached my father with the suggestion, and I was thrilled when the arrangements were settled for me to have a tryout during the Christmas vacation. Mr. Cooke apparently was pleased with my efforts because he asked me to remain with the firm, working full time. This meant leaving high school and the associations I had enjoyed there, but it also meant a realization of an independence that at the moment outweighed the loss of high-school fun. It was not easy to convince my father and mother that they should permit me to discontinue my schooling, but I finally won out. I was to do the typing for the three lawyers in Mr. Cooke's law office. Plain typing gave me no trouble at all. It was dictation that froze my fingers and made my heart quicken its beat.

One of my fondest recollections is the atmosphere of absolute honesty and humble simplicity that reigned in Mr. Cooke's of-

15

fice. There were no impatient outbursts because work was not done on time; never any of that "mightier than thou" attitude. In fact, the first day I was in the office Mr. Cooke asked me how to spell the word "separate." I was flattered.

I am quite aware that the conduct and principles of our law office were not those which, unfortunately, prevailed in many places even then. God, in His goodness, spared me from any such pagan atmosphere.

Mr. Cooke somehow found out about an embarrassing mistake I made the day I was first sent to the bank with a check to be certified. So that I would not forget the word "certified," I kept repeating "certified milk, certified milk." When I arrived at the teller's window in the bank, my mind for a moment went blank; then I stammered, "Will you please pasteurize this check?"

Perhaps to ease somewhat my uneasiness, Mr. Cooke told me the story of a stenographer in a neighboring firm. The girl was inexperienced and correspondingly nervous taking her first dictation. In his petition, the lawyer had said, "Wherefore plaintiff demands that the defendant pay the sum of $8,000 (we'll take $800 if we can get it) plus the costs of this action." The poor girl included the parentheses in the transcription. The lawyer never checked her work, and the remark he made under his breath was read out in the courtroom!

While I had to return to school three years later to complete my high-school studies before entering Carmel, I found the business world fascinatingly interesting and an exceedingly fertile field in which to practice all the virtues one should acquire. How pleased I was with myself the day I refused to satisfy my natural curiosity and did not read data I saw in the files pertaining to people I knew! I have since learned that inordinate curiosity can be a serious obstacle to perfection, inside as well as outside the cloister.

My work and modified social life did not distract my mind from the vocation I knew I would ultimately follow.

I was quite certain now that God wanted me to become a nun. But to which religious order I was called, or to what special type of religious work I should devote my life, or when I should apply —these were questions to which at this time I could not give the answers.

However, after I had been out of school about three months, a priest gave me a wonderful book which I literally devoured. It was the *Autobiography* of Saint Thérèse, the Carmelite nun of Lisieux, France, popularly known as the Little Flower. A remarkable thing about the particular copy that Father gave me was the fact that the Prioress of the Carmelite monastery in New York City had given it as a Christmas gift to Miss Casey, the convent's faithful organist, who in turn gave it to Father and he to me. So it came to me indirectly from the very convent that God had destined me to enter.

Up to this time, I had heard little or nothing about the Carmelite Order, and less about Saint Thérèse. How the clear, heroic phrases of this simple, childlike nun struck the mind! While I could not then appreciate, as I do so well now, what her life of superhuman courage really was, still I could see in her something far more virile than a "Little Flower." For sheer heroism sustained during every moment of her short cloistered life, there are few heroines of fiction and indeed few saints who could surpass her.

"I will spend my heaven doing good on earth. . . ." What supreme generosity toward and love for everybody everywhere and forever! "O my Spouse, whence these desires to make known the secrets of Thy Love? Is it not Thou alone who has taught them to me, and canst Thou not likewise reveal them to others? I know that Thou canst, and I beseech Thee to do so. . . ." Could Saint Thérèse have had me in mind? Could God teach *me* the secrets of His love?

I read in the Little Flower's *Autobiography* that a novice once went to Saint Thérèse's cell and found the Saint absorbed in prayer. "What were you thinking of just now, Sister?" the novice asked the Saint. With tears in her eyes, Thérèse replied, "I was meditating on the Our Father. . . . It is so sweet to call God 'Our Father.' "

Wasn't that precisely what I had been doing at home when I went off to the attic to pray?

That incident in the life of Saint Thérèse convinced me that the life she had lived in the Carmel of Lisieux was the life I was longing to lead here in America.

No sooner had I finished the *Autobiography* of Saint Thérèse than I searched out and read with my customary enthusiasm everything I could find about the religious order of Carmel.

The name Carmel, I discovered, meant literally "garden" or "beautiful hill"; its mystical meaning—"sacrifice"—was far more significant.

I learned that Carmel was a small mountain, one of a chain of high hills that ran across Palestine, and that it was to Mount Carmel that the prophet Elias retired, to seek God in solitude, and to pray for his people. And this, nine hundred years before Christ was born. This same Elias was actually, according to the Carmelite tradition, the founder of the religious order to which Saint Thérèse of Lisieux belonged. I never dreamed it possible that a religious order in the Catholic Church could trace its origin to a date before the coming of Christ. The beautifully impressive statue of Saint Elias, the prophet, that stands in the Vatican alongside the saintly founders of other religious orders is inscribed *Elias, Founder of the Order of Mount Carmel.*

Carmel was called the Order of Mary, and the early members of the society were called the Brothers of the Blessed Virgin Mary of Mount Carmel; they were charged with the "blessed duty of honoring her, and spreading devotion to her."

As I read on, I learned that after the Black Death of the fifteenth century the Holy See mitigated the original austere rule of silence, fasting, prayer, and penance. It was thought the health of the people in fifteenth-century Europe could not stand such a rigorous discipline.

Then in the following century, at Avila in Spain, appeared the great organizer and mystic of Carmel, Saint Teresa of Jesus. After living as a nun for twenty years under the mitigated rule, she felt impelled to bring back to the Order all its primitive penance and prayer. When she hesitated, because of her sex and weakness, to attempt the restoration of the original rule of Carmel, Our Lord spoke to her: "It is because men and theologians will not listen to Me that, despised by them, I come like a beggar to talk of what I want with humble women and to find rest in their company."

How I admired the great Saint Teresa and her courageous confidence in God! Church dignitaries and ministers of state conspired against her. But once God's will became clear to her, there was no obstacle she could not overcome.

It was because Saint Teresa, with her irrepressible determination, succeeded in restoring the Primitive Rule of Carmel, the Rule followed throughout the world by all discalced (or shoeless) nuns, that I was thinking of Carmel. I discovered that monasteries of the Reform were established all over Europe. And, most exciting of all, I learned that in our own country the very first religious order of women to found a convent in what was then the United States was the Carmelite Order.

Four nuns, one an Englishwoman from the Antwerp Carmel and three Americans who had gone to Europe to enter the Carmelite cloister at the English convent in Hoogstraeten, Belgium, reached Port Tobacco, Maryland, on July 10, 1790.

Father Charles Neale of the Society of Jesus is called the Founder of the Carmelites in America, for it was through the untiring efforts of this zealous Jesuit priest that Monsignor John Carroll, later Archbishop of Baltimore, succeeded in bringing the Carmelite nuns from Belgium to establish a monastery in the United States.

As soon as the War of Independence was over, the message winged its way to Belgium: "Now is your time to establish in this country, for peace is declared, and Religion is free."

What surprised me most as I read of the history of Carmel in the United States was that so many young women from early American families left their homes of relative luxury, braved the arduous sea voyage from the colonies to enter Carmelite cloisters in Europe, and there embraced a life of solitude, silence, and prayer for the salvation of souls.

Once established in America, the Carmel in Maryland received many eager vocations, and Archbishop Carroll took a paternal interest in its beginnings. "I am exceedingly pleased at the increase in your most religious family. Every addition to it I look upon as a new safeguard for the preservation of the Diocese. Be so good as to request your virtuous community to be assiduous in their petitions to Heaven, that the faithful may increase in number and piety, and the Pastors in zeal, useful knowledge and truly Christian prudence."

From the original Maryland foundation, which moved from Port Tobacco to Baltimore in 1830, many Carmelite monasteries trace their beginning. Of special interest to us is the convent founded in New York City in 1920. Cardinal Gibbons gave his blessing to the little group as they set out, and Cardinal Hayes welcomed the nuns into his teeming diocese. A good friend of Carmel, Mrs. Clara B. McGinnis, made her home available as temporary quarters for the community. Later, a pious benefactor in the city, who desired to remain anonymous, provided for the nuns a more spacious abode on Gun Hill Road and then finally a permanent monastery on University Avenue. It was Mother Teresa, the same intrepid nun who later founded the Carmel in Oklahoma, who pioneered this establishment in New York City.

Saint Teresa says that one way of keeping close to God is by keeping close to His friends.

About this time I used to visit almost daily, during my lunch hour, one of God's favorite spouses, Sister Winifred, a Sister of St. Joseph from Brentwood. She was a young novice dying of tuberculosis. This extraordinarily holy novice was loved by everyone who came in contact with her. She will always be remembered fondly and prayerfully by me, not only because she thrilled me one day by asking me to dress myself in her beautiful habit; but also, and particularly, because she taught me in her silent, heroic manner how to suffer.

Shortly before she died I received this sweet, brief note written in her failing hand: "Be very faithful to grace, Cecelia, for God has great work for you to do."

Up to this time I thought that only nuns and priests made annual spiritual retreats, but one of my friends informed me of the fact that retreats were conducted for lay people, too, and very frequently—among other places, at the St. Regis Cenacle on Riverside Drive in New York City.

Lay retreats usually last two or three days and are held ordinarily at the end of each week. During these days the retreatant "retreats" from the noise and the problems of the world and enters a religious house, or convent, to think about God and her soul and to rest and pray. A noted priest speaker acts as Retreat Master; he gives three or four conferences on spiritual matters each day, and at other times he is available for private consultation and direction. It is good to hear that these invaluable spiritual retreats for lay people are far more popular today and far more widely attended than they were in the twenties. More and more people are learning to heed Our Lord's friendly invitation, "Come to Me all you who are weary and heavily burdened and I will give rest to your souls."

A great peace came over me the moment I entered the Cenacle

for my first retreat. The wonderful religious of the Cenacle, in their gentle, mild way, inspired everyone with inward joy and calm.

The Jesuit Father who conducted the retreat gave us four inspiring conferences on each of the three days. I memorized many of his expressions, like: "We came *from* God; we are here *for* God; we are going *to* God." And:

> *"Live Jesus, live. So live in me*
> *That all I do be done by Thee.*
> *And grant that all I think and say*
> *May be Thy thought and word today."*

The priest made everything about the spiritual life and the life of perfection lucidly clear. I felt at the moment that there could be little more to learn. However, I soon found out that there was much more to learn, and also—which is much more important—I discovered that knowledge was easily acquired, but not in itself a virtue; it was carrying out the knowledge that really mattered, and this was painfully difficult.

On Sunday evening I formed in line for my private interview with the Retreat Master. When the girl directly in front of me came out, I asked, "How is he?" Very jauntily she whispered, "Just wonderful."

Father's searching, steel-gray eyes watched me carefully as I nervously told him a bit about myself. He seemed to be reading my mind.

"What do you intend to do in life, Cecelia?" he asked.

"I intend to enter Carmel, Father. Please pray that it may be soon. Very soon."

There seemed to follow an eternity of silence. Then . . .

"Child, you are too thin to think of doing anything like that— at least for the time being. . . . What is more, I'd never approve a girl entering the austere order of Carmel until she was twenty-six."

Uneasily I counted on my fingers—eight more long years.

Father asked a number of questions and finally concluded that I knew altogether too little about life and said that I should go around more, accept dates with boys, go to dances and "socials." I told Father that I had seven older sisters and that I had seen a great deal of their social life.

"That is not enough," he said. "You must become more mature."

Although the priest's learning and holiness impressed me deeply, I could hardly believe he understood completely my yearning and my qualifications for Carmel. He was taking the bottom out of my small world. I was crushed.

In the Chapel I poured out my confused and broken heart to Jesus. It seemed certain that this man who had directed many young people to the religious life did not think seriously of my call to Carmel. Could his voice possibly be the will of God in my regard?

I had little heart for the colorful outdoor procession closing the retreat. The singing seemed far away, and the varicolored torches looked hazy to my misty eyes.

Later I learned that one of the boys from our dramatic society was watching the procession through the wrought-iron railing along Riverside Drive and was mystified by my tears. He told me later that he had been praying that the retreat would change my mind about the convent!

That quiet night there was no sleep for my disturbed mind. "Too thin . . . not before you are twenty-six . . . learn more of the world." I arose and sat on the broad window sill in my room on the top floor high above the sparkling Hudson, my gaze wandering off into the starry space beyond the Palisades. Father's discouraging words kept echoing in my tormented heart. I kept reminding myself that God's will was all I wished. In my imagination I went over my conversation with the Retreat Master and spent the sleepless hours trying to convince him that he was mistaken. . . . "Father, I assure you, my health is quite robust," I'd repeat and add, "I am never tired; besides my work in the law office, there is the Catholic Charities' typing before and after work, and the almost nightly rehearsals for the various plays performed by our dramatic society. How could I do all that if my health were poor?" Still it was of no use. Father was adamant, and the peace and joy I had hoped to receive from my days of recollection were changed to agitation and despair. At the end of the retreat I joined my parents, who happened to be in New York City on their way back home from their "second honeymoon."

"There's a man who knows what he's talking about" was my father's curt comment when I told my parents about my interview with the priest at the conclusion of the retreat.


One evening shortly after we returned to Monticello, I was kneeling at the altar rail in church when Mathilda Rice (one of former Senator Rice's daughters) came in and knelt beside me. She was sobbing inconsolably, and I put my arm around her. She whispered, "My little sister is dying."

I said, "Don't cry, Mathilda; everyone knows your little sister is an angel, and she will go straight to Heaven. If any of my relatives were as ready to go to God as your sister is, I'd be only too happy to let them go."

Little did I realize when I made that brave and consoling statement that within two days—even before the Rice girl died—God was to call my dear father.

It is true that Papa had been under the doctor's care for some time; still his end came with shocking suddenness. As I watched him during his last hour, his face reminded me of a picture of Our Lord on the Cross.

While his embalmed body lay on the undertaker's cot before the coffin came, I rested my head on his stilled heart and wept long, bitter tears. Every act of thoughtlessness, every moment of concern I had caused my father came rushing into my mind—how I had shown annoyance sometimes at the dry, piercing cough that was so frequent at night; how I might have eased in many ways the strain on his heart; how seldom I had expressed to him the deep love I had for him. My sorrow and anguish pierced the very bottom of my soul, and I promised him to carry on and do all I could for him and the family and so to conduct myself that he could always be proud of me.

We were all deeply touched to know that the shops were closed in town the morning of Papa's funeral, and the church was filled. "We have lost our peacemaker," they said.

Mama tried, through her tears, to remind us that actually we had not lost Papa. "Remember," she sobbed, "the words in the Preface of the Mass: 'Life is but changed, not taken away.' "

Recalling the admonition given to me by the Retreat Master at the Cenacle, I saw and heard regularly from two boys who belonged to our dramatic society. Selden and Steve came often to the house, and the family did what they could to encourage a budding romance. My mother showed a preference for Steve, perhaps because he came from her old neighborhood in Greenwich Village.

Steve and Selden were part of the "imported talent" which our coach, Mr. Castle, a retired Broadway director, used for our shows. They would spend their week ends at Monticello and also their summer vacations; and since a number of us girls spent our winter vacations in New York, we saw a good deal of each other.

Selden, whose mother was an opera singer, had an exceptionally fine tenor voice and was at his best—in fact, indispensable—for the Chauncey Olcott plays.

Steve, more versatile, could act almost any part but was particularly good in musical comedies, for he, too, had a fine voice and was a clever tap dancer. He was one of the most popular actors in the *Wall Street Follies* each year.

One seldom knows what is going on in another's mind.

I recall one night during our performance of *The First Year*, I was in my stuffy, powdery dressing room in the Lyceum Theater, awaiting my cue to appear on stage. At that particular moment in the play I was supposed to enter in tears. During rehearsals I found that all I had to do to make myself weep was to think of the emptiness and vanity of the life of glamorous pleasure I was leading in Monticello and New York and contrast it with my future solitude in Carmel. So the night of the performance I longed more intensely than ever for the silence and oblivion of the cloister, and I wept copious tears.

A business associate of Mr. Castle's, also a Broadway director, was on hand that night and spoke flatteringly to me after the show. He was particularly impressed with the ease with which I could force myself to shed tears!

My years in Carmel have taught me one thing: when God asks us to sacrifice the normal joys of living, it is only that He may give us a higher and holier joy. Living with God alone in the solitude of Carmel has proved sweeter far to me than all the pleasure and fickle applause of the world.

It was a delightful surprise to learn that Selden's sister, Virginia, was a Carmelite nun. She was, at the time, Prioress of Carmel-by-the-Sea in California, and he graciously brought me some of her letters to read. I was fascinated by the nun's simple stories of life within the enclosure and by her gay, gentle humor.

Selden told me of his parents' reactions to Virginia's entrance to Carmel. "Hoping to distract her thoughts from the convent," he said, "they sent her to a finishing school in Paris." Nevertheless, on her return to America she entered the Boston Carmel and shortly afterward departed, with four other nuns, to found at Santa Clara the first convent of Carmelite nuns in California.

At the first opportunity, I wrote eagerly to her and plied her with questions about the religious life and about my own calling to Carmel. Her letters were masterpieces of beautiful and practical spirituality, and they did me much good.

While I enjoyed Steve's and Selden's pleasant company (Steve's more eagerly and more often, perhaps because he was younger) and while each of them had used various arguments to show me that my life was never meant to be wasted in a cloister, still their words had little effect on me. No matter how attractive I found them and the world, my heart still longed for Carmel.

In fact, I was praying that my eighteenth birthday would be spent as a postulant in the convent. But would I be able to secure my mother's consent? And would they accept me without it before my twenty-first birthday?

Father FitzGerald, my spiritual adviser, promised to get the answers for me the next time he was in New York City. He called at the Carmelite monastery and had a long talk with Mother Teresa, the Prioress.

Not long after his visit I received this letter from the Prioress:

*"My dear Child:*

*"Your good confessor, Reverend Father FitzGerald, has told me of your desire to be a Carmelite. . . .*

*". . . first of all let me say, don't worry. When the Good God gives a vocation He gives all the graces and helps necessary to follow it, enabling the soul to triumph over all obstacles. If the obstacles prove insurmountable, that is sufficient evidence that the soul's desire is not inspired by Our Lord. So cultivate a great spirit of confidence in God and perfect abandonment to His will, and pray fervently and constantly for the accomplishment of His will in you. . . . Never forget that He is omnipotent.*

*"Write and tell me about your vocation—how long you have desired to be a religious and why you wish to be a Carmelite, your age, education, employment, etc. As the life of a Carmelite is*

*one of prayer and penance, good health is essential for admission. . . .*

*"In the meantime, we shall pray for you and trust that you will give us a little share in your good prayers. You will have a place in the novena to Our Lady of Mount Carmel, which we are now making. . . . May this dear Lady and Mother take you under her protection and make your love for Jesus grow more ardent every day.*

> *Very sincerely yours in the Sacred Heart,*
> *Teresa of Jesus, D.C.u."*

Mother Teresa had my answers immediately, and within a week she invited me to visit the monastery.

My heart missed a beat when for the first time the cross-mounted tower of Carmel came into view. As I approached the main door of the convent a great peace came over my soul and somehow I was sure that soon I was to live under that cross in solitude with my Beloved Master.

In my first interview I was, for a time, bewildered by the mystery of talking to a voice, the owner of which I could not see. It was like talking to a stranger over the telephone. But the soft, gentle, motherly voice behind the iron grille and black cloth shutter soon put me completely at my ease. The main features of my life and family background I briefly described for her.

I hesitatingly told Mother Prioress about my relations with Selden and Steve—how I had followed the advice of the Retreat Master at the Cenacle. Convinced that by now I had seen enough of the "other side" of life, Mother, with great common sense, said, "To continue going with young men, Cecelia, when you find your heart inclined to go out to them, would be toying with a temptation against the vocation which you feel, and which I feel God has given you."

It was not as easy as I had hoped when it came time to tell Steve that our outings must come to an end, that I would not be able any longer to accompany him to the beach, to dances and parties. I did not, until that moment, realize how attached I had really become to him. However, I asked Our Lord for the strength I needed, and at the first opportunity I reluctantly explained to Steve (and later to Selden) what Mother had said. And there the matter ended.

(Several years after I entered Carmel, Selden lay dying in Bellevue Hospital in New York, and he sent his brother one night to the monastery to ask us to pray for him. By morning he was dead. May Our Lord be very good to him. Steve is now a Jesuit.)

Now that Carmel seemed certain, Reverend Mother told me that one of the requirements for choir nuns was a complete high-school education. Because halfway through my junior year my schooling had terminated abruptly with the elopement of Mr. Cooke's secretary, Mother Teresa suggested that I leave the law office and resume my education in a Catholic High School.

Toward the end of my first visit with Mother Teresa she said with feigned seriousness, "Now, Cecelia, my dear child, there are three things I should like you to renounce as soon as possible."

Expecting to hear her speak of some deep, dark faults of character, I stammered, my heart in my throat, "And what are they, Reverend Mother?"

With a smile in her sweet voice, she answered, "Gee, gosh, and golly!"

# Chapter 3

# The World Is Mine

† PS. 49:12

THERE was no Catholic high school in Monticello in those days.

Mother Teresa had written, "When God gives a vocation He gives all the graces and helps necessary to follow it, enabling the soul to triumph over all obstacles. If the obstacles are insurmountable, that is sufficient evidence that the soul's desire is not inspired by Our Lord."

In my mind there were no insurmountable obstacles, there was no doubt that God called me to a life of contemplation; therefore I was quite confident that somehow He would arrange for me to attend a Catholic school to complete my education.

After considerable "shopping around" for a suitable school, Monsignor Snyder, a good friend of the family, finally got in touch with the superior of Ladycliff Academy, a private boarding school for girls on the west bank of the Hudson, beautifully located about sixty miles from home. Several Monticello girls went there and I was thrilled at the prospect of attending what I knew was an excellent school. However, I was quite unfamiliar with life in a boarding school, and I was somewhat apprehensive.

On the train the day I left Monticello for Ladycliff, I wrote a

30

letter to Father FitzGerald, my confessor. Years later he brought
the letter to Carmel and gave it to me.

"*My dear Father:*

"*Remember my telling you, Father, about that tall pine tree on
the hill. . . . Well, I was thinking about it again as I passed it this
morning. I think I'm going to become more and more like that
tree. I told you it was all alone on that big hill at the bottom of
which were many others—skimpy and frail, many of them lop-
sided because they were weak or too close together. The beautifully strong, tall one at the top was alone, and so could raise its
branches to Heaven unhindered. Well, now that I am going away,
I hope my soul will expand and grow stronger and more beautiful
like that tree.*

"*All this to someone else's eyes might look boastful and in no
way resembling a Carmelite nun, but actually it helps me to think
of myself as a big tree instead of a little flower, for example; because if the wind blew and the rain fell upon a little flower, its
petals would drop off and then what would become of it? A big
tree can stand a lot more. . . . So I'm going to try to live like that
lone pine. You be the Forest Ranger and keep watch over me. . . .*

"*Don't ever think, Father, that I'll ever forget all you've done
for me. Each day now I'm going to realize more and more how
good you were to me.*

"*It was sad pulling out of Monticello. I love that little place.
. . . Sometimes, Father, when you are out walking, I'd love you to
go down to Papa's grave for me. . . . I used to like to kneel there
when I was sad.*

"*I want to say some rosaries now because I may not get a chance
at school the first day.*

"*Keep happy and peaceful. I will too.*

*Gratefully,*
*Celia*"

Shortly after my arrival at Ladycliff I was moved from my original roommate, a quiet, excellent student named Marion Steiner, to live with Helen Williamson. Helen was a vivacious, somewhat mischievous girl, in the advanced stages of what Papa used to refer to as the "crazy age." She had pictures of Ben Lyon all over the room, even under her pillow! She had a habit of doing "tightrope" dancing on the bedstead and of waving her towel out the window at the Albany night boat.

But for all that, she was a wholesome, congenial girl—and oddly enough rather gullible.

One night, observing me as I looked sadly at a picture of my sister Mary's little baby son, who had recently died, she asked, "Celia, why do you look so sorrowfully at that baby's picture?"

"Can you keep a secret?" I asked.

She promised me she could and would.

"That's my child," I said while pretending to sob.

Helen almost fainted. Bewildered, she looked from me to the baby's picture.

"Yes," I continued sorrowfully, "I lost my husband a few months ago—killed in a plane crash—and to distract me from my grief my mother sent me here to finish my schooling. But, please, Helen, remember, you promised not to tell."

She ceased her outlandish antics immediately and seemed in that brief moment to have matured ten years. Comforting me in my affliction brought out the heretofore completely submerged motherly instincts in my friend Helen.

Because of the unexpectedly good effects the impish joke had on Helen, I decided to wait a day or so before disillusioning her. However, in the excitement of making new acquaintances, and in the fervor of wanting to do well in my studies, I utterly forgot about undeceiving her.

About a week later one of the Sisters called me out of the art studio. Very seriously she wanted to "get to the bottom" of the story of my marriage and motherhood that was circulating among the girls.

Now the joke was on me.

In great embarrassment I explained to Sister about the hoax and my failure to enlighten Helen about the deception. Sister failed to see anything particularly amusing in my deceit, and I confess I could find no justification for the lie even though it was uttered in fun and not maliciously to deceive.

I apologized to Helen but she thought it was a great joke, and for some time all the girls called me "Widow Walsh."

My roommate and I teased each other a great deal about the "game of sacrifices" we played during Lent, though she thought it was going a bit too far when I began to give her the "opportunity" to win points by fetching me drinks of water from the other end of the corridor.

The Franciscan nuns who conducted Ladycliff were adept at teaching and handling the girls. The students loved them. I was extremely happy and look back with fondest memories to the years I spent there.

One of the loveliest girls I ever met was Selma. She was one of the few Jewish girls at Ladycliff, and from the beginning we were drawn to each other and shared each other's confidences. She was deeply religious and would be seen often in the Chapel deep in prayer. She rose each morning to attend Mass and during the day she would make the Stations of the Cross.

One day I questioned Selma about all this.

"Do you really want to know what I say when I visit the Chapel?" she asked.

"Tell me," I said, "for I really should love to know."

"Well," she answered with tremendous simplicity, "I look up at the tabernacle and I say, 'If You are God, I adore You.' "

I was so deeply moved it was impossible for me to express my feeling. How closely her words resembled what I was later to read from the pen of the Greek poet, Euripides, who lived five hundred years before Christ: "I do not know You, I cannot learn of You, but whoever You are, I pray to You." How I prayed that Selma would receive the great grace of faith, so that she would know beyond all doubting, with the certitude of complete faith, that Christ was really before her and that Christ was really the God whom she sought!

Perhaps because I was somewhat older than the others, many of the girls used to speak to me about their little problems. Often they would open their hearts completely and it was possible for me to help them considerably. I thanked Our Lord for using me in this way.

In the elementary school department at Ladycliff there were a number of little boys as well as girls. Often I would be asked to supervise their evening play hour, and I loved to tell them stories and to answer their questions. Whether it was my natural penchant for storytelling or the maternal instinct that every girl has, I don't know; but I do know that these hours with the children were my greatest recreation. They were also the cause of many a silent struggle deep in my heart.

The delight I found in the children and their warm response to my interest in them sent waves of doubt and indecision over my soul concerning my calling to the solitude of Carmel's cloister. Maybe, I thought, my fondness for children was an indication that I should enter an "active" order of nuns so that I might teach children daily in the classroom or go to mission lands and give myself to thousands of orphans. But in the silence of the Chapel where I would take my troubled heart peace and certitude would return, and I would dismiss all doubts as I poured out my love to Jesus. Deep within me, apart from all emotions, came the clear, persistent call of my Beloved to leave the world and to mother only the *souls* of these children—and the souls of all mankind everywhere with my prayers and penance from within the cloister.

How that could be done I did not at that time fully understand, but my years in Carmel's solitude have taught me that one does not have to be visible and physically present to ease the burdens of an anguished world.

My previous experience with the Monticello Dramatic Society proved of some assistance in the student performances we gave at Ladycliff. I was put in charge of the entertainment programs, and I enthusiastically saw to it that our school life did not suffer from scholastic monotony. Innumerable social events and plays en-livened the semester calendar.

Between Ladycliff and the nearby United States Military Acade-my at West Point there was a cordial and friendly relationship. Officers from the Point trained our cadets. We were given passes to football games, which we loved; and the Seniors were privileged to attend the Sunday dress parades and other affairs.

Needless to say, life for us was not all dramatics and social events. The educational program was most exacting; the con-scientious nuns of St. Francis saw to that.

Nor was our spiritual life neglected. They saw to that, too. Once a month a priest from New York came to conduct a day of recol-lection, or retreat. The first month the priest was none other than the good Jesuit Father who had preached my first retreat in the Cenacle in New York. I was not especially pleased at the prospect of being told again that I was too thin to endure the rigors of a Carmelite cloister and that I should know more about the "other side of life" before thinking of any convent.

With the spiritual direction of the nuns and the conferences for and interviews with the girls, the poor man had an appallingly heavy schedule. Although we could not see eye to eye about my vocation to Carmel, I must say his penetrating mind made it pos-sible for him always to give quick, inspired decisions on our prob-lems—even the non-Catholic girls looked forward to the oppor-tunity of talking with him.

"So you have put on some weight!" was the smiling way he greeted me when I reluctantly visited his room for a private talk. This sent a slight ripple of encouragement over me.

As briefly as I could tell it, he heard the story of my life since we had talked at the New York City Cenacle. He heard about my experiences with the "other side of life"—though I confess now I did not stress the pleasure the experience afforded me, despite the fact that Mother Teresa had convinced me that "liking life" was no indication of a lack of vocation to the religious life.

It was a delightful relief when Father finally told me it was quite evident to him that the Holy Spirit was preparing me for my "mission in life." I thought he meant Carmel, but when he went on to say, "Not to a life of contemplation, but to take some part in the 'active apostolate,' " I was crushed.

He had come to this conclusion, he told me, after he had heard from the Sisters and the students of Ladycliff of the influence for good I had on the other girls and the little children.

I still felt that God was calling me to a hidden life. Father Fitz-Gerald was encouraging; Mother Teresa at Carmel seemed certain. But after talking with the Retreat Master I asked myself, "Is it *self* that wants Carmel and God who wants me in the active life?" Obviously my talk with Father left me considerably confused.

I went to the Chapel and poured out my heart to Our Lord. I tried to pray, "Thy will be done, no matter where You wish me to be or what You want me to do." Then, even though the answer would not be clear, peace would return to my soul. Since that time I have learned that in no other way is the soul to be calmed. What a pity that people take so long to discover this fundamental principle of the spiritual life! Even though the answer to our plea and our prayer may be "No," we must learn that God's "No" is always the best for us—at least the best thing for our spiritual and eternal welfare, about which God is primarily concerned. He knows and sees everything and all the ramifications of each thing, and He is our loving Father; we see only a bit about only a few things, and we are but weak children.

During the Easter holidays Father Paul McNally of the Society of Jesus helped out in our parish in Monticello.

I went to confession to the visiting Jesuit, and, as briefly as I could, I unburdened my heart to him. He was paternally patient as he listened to the story of my vocation—my aspirations and fears, my high hopes and paralyzing discouragements.

Father McNally said he knew Carmel and the life in the cloister intimately. A close relative of his, he said, was a Carmelite nun.

"In order not to hold up the other people who wish to confess," he said understandingly, "visit me in the parish parlor after dinner."

(My mother used to scold me about the length of time I spent in the confessional: "What in the name of heaven are you *confessing* all that time?" Obviously Mama was of the school of penitents who liked brevity and who did not take full advantage of the directive aspect of confession. The priest in confession is there taking Our Lord's place not only in judging us but also in helping and advising us.) After our talk in the parlor, Father said, with simple emphasis, "There is no doubt in my mind, Cecelia, about your fitness for Carmel, physically and mentally and spiritually; I think you definitely have a Carmelite vocation."

No one but Mother Teresa had ever said that to me before. As I look back now it seems that the other priests to whom I spoke either did not understand me or wanted me to make my own decision. All priests understand that a vocation to the religious life is a hidden treasure that must be guarded with care and brought to light slowly with tact and prudence. But in the final analysis the one who feels called to be a priest or a nun must accept the judgment of competent authority. All the candidate can do is desire and manifest what he believes God wants him to do; he must then be told by a director or superior that the decision is a correct one or that it is not the life for him—one cannot be called by God to a life for which one is not fitted.

Many excellent directors of souls insist on making a vocation "prospect" wait. They feel that difficulties should be placed in the aspirant's path to determine his persevering qualities, as well as his faith and docility in answering God's call. Often a simple spiritual program is outlined for the candidate to practice while still in the world.

Father McNally took time briefly to explain to me the Ignatian method of particular examen practiced in his Society, and he showed me how to use the string of beads for this purpose. "For example," he said, "suppose the subject of your examination of conscience is 'control of the eyes'; then each time you succeed in refusing yourself the indulgence of idle curiosity, you pull down one of the beads." He gave me a set of beads which I brought back with me to Ladycliff.

After Father's talk I was literally walking on air. Indeed he had "commanded the winds and the waves," after which followed "a great calm."

"Launch out into the deep," were his parting words. He did not have to tell me that the deep he referred to was the calm, pure waters of Carmel. It was there that I was to fish for souls where the Eternal Galilean would fill my nets to overflowing.

One brisk day in the spring of my final year at Ladycliff, while I was playing tennis, I became painfully exhausted—rather an unusual experience for me. I lay on the grass in a state of complete immobility for some time but recovered sufficiently to attend dinner and study hour that evening. However, sleep was impossible that night. The doctor was called in the morning and immediately announced that I had a serious case of diphtheria. A nurse was summoned, and I was quarantined with her during the day and with a Sister all night.

The day nurse was the wife of the school gardener. I was both amused and touched at the romantic way she would drop notes out the window to him several times a day. Just how he got his answers to her I never found out.

During my convalescence I read again Saint Thérèse's *Autobiography* and also Saint Teresa of Avila's *Interior Castle*. These books, together with my solitude, were a great blessing to me, and I rejoined my classes greatly benefited by the graces and experience of my period of quarantine.

Shortly before the end of the school year the Academy produced a morality play. Our relatives and friends came in great numbers for this annual event.

One day the girl who had the part of World Sprite was absent from rehearsal. Since I knew her lines by heart, I roguishly ran out from the wings when her cue came and took over. In a quite fatuous and exaggerated style I proceeded with all the technique at my command (including a few of the wilder steps of the Charleston) to tempt Psyche, who happened to be my former roommate Helen.

My uninhibited antics brought roars of uncontrollable laughter from the girls behind the scenes. But when I observed our dramatic coach, Mrs. Block, move toward Sister Bernice in the rear of the hall, I quieted down and meekly retired to the wings. Sister and Mrs. Block walked down the center aisle and called me before the footlights.

"We are going to make some changes," they said.

Oh, dear, I thought, my foolishness has cost me the opportunity to have a part in the play. They are going to exclude me from the performance entirely.

"Cecelia," Mrs. Block said very seriously, "we have decided that you are much better as the Spirit of the World than you would be as Wisdom. So we wish you to keep this part."

Heaven help me! And I an aspirant to the cloister!

And most distressing of all Cardinal Hayes was to be guest of honor at the performance. Why had I been such a fool? What will he think of me, so soon to enter the convent as a Carmelite nun— doing the Charleston, dressed as a jester and a tempter? Wisdom had slipped through my hands and I was to appear for what I really was.

Some time after the performance, Mother Teresa wrote to me from Carmel and added this P.S.: "Did I tell you the Cardinal told us about meeting you at Ladycliff? He said seeing you on the stage no one would have supposed you were thinking of Carmel."

Cardinal Hayes's niece, Marie Cahill, lived in the room adjoining mine at Ladycliff. One evening after visiting her distinguished uncle she told me how much His Eminence had enjoyed the performance of the Spirit of the World. I felt better. (Incidentally, she also entered the convent and is now Sister Marie Patrice, a Charity nun at Mount Saint Vincent-on-the-Hudson.)

The only other girl at that time, so far as I know, who entered the religious life from Ladycliff was Ruth Whilmann. After graduating Ruth rushed to the novitiate of the Franciscan Missionary Sisters of Mary. The last I heard, she was working among the lepers in India. Ruth, who in those days was far more "contemplative" than I, God called to the active apostolate; I, who was far more active than she, God called to Carmel.

There is no predicting the ways of God. But it is good to know that He never makes a mistake.

As Cardinal Hayes gave me my diploma at Ladycliff's commencement exercises, he whispered, "You will not have to wait long, Cecelia, for your entrance day to Carmel." I was more thrilled with those words than with my certificate of graduation.

Two girls from Colombia, South America, came home with me

to spend the summer with our family in Monticello. They were the only ones in the house who were at all enthusiastic about my vocation.

My mother was adamant. She would not give her consent before I was twenty-one. In fact, the opposition of my whole family became more vociferous as my entrance to Carmel became more certain. It was not that they objected entirely to my becoming a nun. In fact, several members of the family came right out and said they would consider it a blessing on the family if I were to enter a teaching order of Sisters, or even a nursing order. But not a Carmelite cloister—anything but that.

It is quite clear to me now that the absurdly fantastic notions people have about convents in general and cloistered monasteries in particular are the principal causes for most of the objections to our life. Imagine—my fervently Catholic mother telling me that Carmelite nuns sleep in their coffins, never see their families, and dig their own graves and that the cloisters are filled with semi-demented spinsters! Of course, the whole catalogue is so ridiculously absurd that it always affords us a chuckle in the monastery when we hear that such notions are still going the rounds.

Unfortunately, I was not so well prepared in those preconvent days as I feel I am today to answer the questions and correct the persistent misunderstandings concerning our life. While I knew my family's conception of the cloister was absurd, it was only *my* word against theirs. *They* knew.

Like the observant lady who lived across the street from the New York Carmelite convent, when it was located on Gun Hill Road; she actually *"saw* with her own eyes [one usually does] a girl enter the monastery already in her coffin." She told some friends of ours the very day it happened. Really, one could hardly blame the woman for so thinking. How was she to know that the "coffin" was a crate and the "postulant" was a life-sized statue of Saint Thérèse, the Little Flower?

One of my sisters took me aside one day for a heart-to-heart talk about the idea of my entering the monastery of Carmel. She confided, "Celia, you will disgrace the whole family if you enter Carmel. You do not know what you are getting into. Women who go there are women 'with a past.' "

No doubt she was thinking of the dear cloistered Magdalens, those saintly penitents who spend their lives in reparation, and with whom Saint Thérèse said she would have tried to spend her life had she been refused at Carmel.

As I have said, at this time I did not understand fully the tremendous thing the life lived in Carmel really is. But it was clear to me that my sister and the other members of my family, like many people in the world, had a completely warped idea of the whole thing. In my feeble way I did my best to defend the cloistered life of Carmel, because I could not allow such statements to go unchallenged.

I explained to my sister that she could not understand my call to Carmel since she did not experience it. She could not know the love of God that was drawing me to the cloister. Did she not recall what Our Lord said about leaving mother and father and family and everything one had for His sake and how He would give such a one a hundredfold reward, even here on earth? Couldn't she see that I was not running away from life, that I wanted to get even *more* out of life? That was why I was asked to make a bigger sacrifice, just as when a person wishes to get a better car he has to pay a higher price. "Why don't you read the *Autobiography* of the Little Flower or the *Life of Saint Teresa of Avila?*" I pleaded. "They would give you the right angle on life in a cloistered monastery." She would see then that the life led by a Carmelite nun was not a negative one, nor a dull, frustrated one; that it was one of intense, passionate love.

I must have raised my voice in the heat of my explanation, for Mama came to the door and stood watching me.

But I was too worked up to cease, even though my sister seemed in no way convinced. I went on: "I know that you and our other sisters, just like Papa and Mama, were asked to make sacrifices in your married life—daily renunciations—and I know that all of you are more perfect than I, but for some reason, unknown to me, God has called me and I accept His special call and freely elect to give myself to Him. I have been advised by competent directors that my decision is correct. That is why I feel bound to enter Carmel."

Mama had never heard me talk like that before—in fact, I never had spoken like that before.

Neither one of them answered; so I continued. "What is so unreasonable about a person's wanting to get in close contact with God? Don't you admit there is no being to be compared with Him? Then suppose I spend my life thinking about Him and 'doing things' for Him alone and in a place where there will be nothing and no one to distract me—is that so utterly absurd?"

But all this eloquence apparently left my sister and Mama quite unmoved. Mama said, "You have said nothing about the fasts and penances in that place. You could never stand that—your health is too poor. If you did go in, you'd be home in a short time and become a burden to the family for the rest of your life."

I sobbed myself to sleep.

## Chapter 4

# Infinity of Questions

† ECCL. 7:30

To ADD to the perplexity of my heart and to give weight to Mama's concern about my health, a dreadful thing happened to me. It took place shortly after my "defense of monasticism," which had failed to convince my sister or my mother that cloistered nuns were normal human beings and that the call to the cloister was a mark of special favor.

It was Saturday evening. My confession had done little to calm my soul, and my prayers in church had seemed dry and useless. I was down in the depths and discouraged about my vocation. Tired of controversy and weary of waiting. I was complaining to Our Lord on my way home that night. If only He would do something! Like "doubting Thomas" I was wishing for a tangible sign. If only I could be sure that God really wanted me in Carmel!

While in the bathroom before retiring, I felt nauseated and vomited blood—not much, but enough to stagger and scare me. My married sister Catherine was visiting us, and I called her. She promised not to tell Mama until after I had been to the doctor the next day.

There was no pain in my body now, nor, surprisingly, did my

soul seem any longer disturbed. As I knelt before a small picture of a nun in prayer beneath the crucifix, a great calm flooded my whole being. I renewed my act of abandonment to the holy will of God and soon went peacefully into His Omnipotent arms to sleep.

During the night I awoke once, and for the first time in my life I thought seriously of death—my own death. It did not frighten me; instead I was taken up with the beautiful thought of the supreme joy that would be mine to be united forever with my Beloved, Who, I knew, could prepare me in an instant to appear before Him. I thought too of the happiness of being with Papa again. So vivid was the impression that I was to leave this earth and all its contradictions and sorrows that I got up and wrote a note to my mother asking her to forgive all the trouble and anxiety I had caused her and telling her of my love for her. I put the letter under my pillow so that she would have it should I die during the night.

Next morning, Sunday, somewhat disappointed, I discovered that I had not died; but still the possibility seemed imminent, despite the fact that I did not feel weak or in any way ill.

Like a bride preparing for her marriage I dressed in white. "This may be my last Holy Communion," I thought as we drove to church.

After Mass my sister drove me to our family doctor. He discovered that in the roots of both lungs I had tuberculosis. I was stunned.

He said that next day I should have his diagnosis confirmed by X ray. The doctor knew that I was thinking of the convent, and he hesitated before advising me that such a notion should now be put from my mind. "Much better after you are cured," he opined very paternally, "if you were to get married. I shall speak to your mother about a sanatorium. In the meantime, keep away from the children." At these last words my eyes filled up. I felt like an outcast.

The X-ray pictures next morning confirmed our family doctor's diagnosis: lesions at the base of both lungs.

How did I interpret this sword of sorrow which pierced my soul that dreadful day when I was pronounced tubercular? While I was too stunned to think calmly, still I had a deep feeling that my vocation was not thwarted. Had I not, in imitation of the Lamb of God, desired to lay down my life in sacrifice? If the immolation were to be swift, so much the better. I knew that somehow this was God's will, and that was enough for me. I embraced it, as I might embrace God Himself—for even then, in an imperfect way to be sure, I understood that God and His will are the same.

As I look back now, it seems that I had already suffered so much distress because of my vocation and tried so hard to acquire the attitude of holy abandonment in the matter and had shed so many tears of despair over it that by that time, I was prepared to face anything.

It is true that I was then, and still am now, far from the state of mystical union with God about which Saint John of the Cross speaks in his *Dark Night,* the last stanza of which reads:

> *"In oblivion forgotten,*
> *My head resting on my Beloved,*
> *Lost to all things and myself,*
> *There among the lilies*
> *All my cares I cast away."*

Had I known the lines then, I would have sung them in the silence of my heart there in the doctor's office, for they expressed pretty well how I felt—or at least how I wanted to feel.

Mama was wonderful about it all. Maybe she felt that I would recover quickly and would have driven from my mind once and forever the horrible thought of entering the cloister.

It seemed to console her when I assured her that "No convent now would think of accepting me."

After my graduation from Ladycliff and while awaiting my call to enter Carmel I had taken temporary employment in the National Union Bank in Monticello. When I told Mr. Calkins, the president of the bank, the sad news, he could not have been kinder or more Christ-like.

I shall never forget that morning in the bank when each of the employees came to me to console and encourage me. One whispered to me that he had been confined once to a sanatorium and had been completely cured of tuberculosis. I would never have suspected he was once a tubercular patient.

Mama would not hear of a sanatorium for me. She would—bless her heart—take care of me at home. How faithful she was in preparing my medicine and in bringing me frequent glasses of bracing sherry eggnog! From time to time Mama would permit me to sit in the sun on the porch, but most of my hours were spent lying flat on my back in bed.

Among the many precious letters I received from thoughtful friends at this time was one the words of which I committed to memory. Father O'Connor, who had three years before given me the *Autobiography of Saint Thérèse,* wrote: "I know exactly how you feel, Cecelia, but do not think that all is lost. Your vocation is to union with God. Even Carmel is only a means, and it may not have been for you the best means. Increase your trust in God. He will surely lead you to perfection—and over the best and shortest road."

In the silence and solitude of my bedroom, Father had given me much food for meditation.

The trees were adorning themselves in their red and gold evening clothes. It was a beautiful day early in the fall. I was becoming impatient of my inactivity. I was alone in the house and felt unusually strong. "I bet I am as well as I ever was." Though I said those words to myself, there was considerable doubt in my mind that the assurance was deep within me. At any rate, hardly realizing what I was about, I got out of bed, dressed, and hurriedly made for the "playhouse tree" across the fields, then up to the very top of Wintergreen Hill.

I was breathless, but there was no hemorrhage.

Without saying a word to Mama about my afternoon hike, I asked her if an appointment could be made for me to be examined again by the doctor. Mama thought it was too soon to bother the doctor again, but finally yielded.

Doctor Dworetzsky in nearby Liberty, New York, was a noted tuberculosis specialist—and a close friend of Father O'Connor. An appointment was made, and we drove over for the examination. The doctor's voice seemed to be coming from another world. Turning to my mother, he said, "I can find no tubercular symptoms; her lungs seem perfectly normal."

To confirm his opinion, he sent me to the Loomis Sanatorium for X rays. They were negative.

I was ready to burst with joy and gratitude. "According to the multitude of my sorrow, Thy comforts have given joy to my soul." I sang with David.

Mama's happiness over my unexpectedly rapid return to perfect health did not last long. As soon as I started to mention Carmel her heart sank again and the strain on the harmony of the family became so severe that I decided for the time being to say nothing at all about the convent.

But though I was silent at home, this did not mean that God's call was stifled in my heart.

I kept Mother Prioress at Carmel informed of everything by mail. The doctor's report and the X-ray returns I forwarded to her.

Mother Prioress's letters were for me my greatest source of strength at this time.

Let me quote a portion of one of Reverend Mother Teresa's

letters which she so thoughtfully sent to me during those dark days, and you can see why I felt that God was speaking to me through her. I had told Mother Teresa that I was wearing a path —and wearing out my shoes!—going back and forth to the Post Office in my daily search for letters from Carmel, and I had told her how apprehensive I was about being admitted.

In September Mother Teresa wrote:

*"My dear Child:*

*"I was just feeling properly 'compuncted' for giving you so many vain trips to the Post Office when Sister Agnes [our Novice Mistress] happened along and I told her about your two-mile walk three times a day. She considered you very fortunate to be able to take such fine walks—that is one of the things you can't do in Carmel! Whereupon my conscience was salved. And not to put an end to such good exercise, I have, as you see, waited a few days longer to write!*

*"Seriously, I do hope you have completely recovered from the shock given you by the doctors and have forgotten all about it. I do not think you have the slightest reason to think yourself any longer tubercular. And if you were, wouldn't it be silly to fret or worry about it? You go to prayer and tell Our Lord you want nothing but the perfect accomplishment of His holy will in your self and all creatures—and really mean it. But the test of whether you mean it or not lies in the disposition of your will under trial. Note, I say 'of your will'—not your feelings. Let us not deceive ourselves. We can lessen even the feeling of pain, disappointment and many other disagreeable things by cheerful conformity of our will to the will of God. There are so few people willing to let Our dear Lord have His own way! It must be a joy to Him to find one who loves His will just precisely because it is His. Try to be that one, Cecelia. You love to make others happy—make Our Lord happy first of all. You and I are not theologians, so we won't dis-*

*pute about the expression 'make Our Lord happy.' We know He is infinitely happy, but we know, in some mysterious way, we please Him when we do what He wants us to do.*

*"Perhaps you are thinking: 'Mother must think I am tubercular or why should she write like this about union with the will of God?' Well, banish such a thought. I do not for a minute think you are. But I know that 'the devil as a roaring lion goeth about seeking whom he may devour,' and when he cannot 'devour,' he will at least try to disturb, and I want you to laugh at all his suggestions and turn them into profit for your soul.*

*"Our Holy Mother, Saint Teresa, counsels us to offer ourselves to God fifty times a day for Him to do with us whatever He pleases. Whoever does so, and means it, is always happy. To such a one worry is unknown. Besides, I should rather have in the community a tubercular nun who never thought of her health—except insofar as necessary to carry out the observance of the Rule—than a well nun who was always thinking about her miserable old body.*

*"God love you and make you a great saint!*

*Affectionately in Our Lord,*
*Teresa of Jesus, D.C.u."*

I was finally called to the New York Carmel on Thanksgiving Day to make my formal application. Mama half hinted she might give her consent. I was beside myself with excitement. Thanksgiving that year fell on November 24—the feast of the great Carmelite Saint and Mystical Doctor, Saint John of the Cross.

With great trepidation I entered the "speak room," or parlor, to await the arrival of Reverend Mother Teresa on the other side of the iron grille. Imagine the pounding in my heart when I heard not one but several soft-shod nuns enter the enclosure side of the speak room. And then to my utter amazement Mother Teresa opened the black-curtained screen and pulled aside the shutters that ordinarily conceal from view the interior of the adjoining room. Each nun tossed back from in front of her face the black veil which habitually hides her from the world, and for the first time I beheld the gay, delightfully joyous faces of the Carmelite nuns.

These sisters, Reverend Mother informed me, were the "chapter nuns"—professed choir nuns, all of whom had a voice in whether or not the new aspirant was to be admitted into the enclosure as a postulant.

First I was requested to answer a number of questions very briefly: my full name; the date of my birth. Was I a child of a lawful marriage? Had I ever embraced a heretical or schismatic church? Had I ever been married? Had I ever committed a public crime? Or was I burdened with debts which I might be incapable of paying?

So far I was in the clear! But the questions continued.

What schools had I attended? What type of work had I engaged in? Did my parents depend on me for their support? And this, in answering which I had to explain Mama's position: Had my parents consented to my entering the cloister? Had I ever entered another religious community or been refused admittance in another religious order?

Then about my health: Had I any physical deformity? What was the condition of my eyes, teeth, and hearing? Could I bear the burden and labors of the religious life? Was there any hereditary disease in my family—tuberculosis, insanity, epilepsy, etc.?

And finally: Had I the intention of entering the cloister of my own free will, without undue influence on the part of anyone?

These were, for the most part, simple "yes" or "no" answers and did not consume much time. And, with the possible exception of my unfortunate brief bout with tuberculosis, I felt that I had come through rather well.

But this was but the beginning.

Each of the nuns then began in her soft, gentle way to make

inquiries of her own. These questions were interrupted from time to time by some very sage comments from Mother Teresa.

One of the Sisters asked about my family. They were surprised when I told them I was one of thirteen children, eleven of whom were still alive, five already married. The Sister wanted to know if our home life was a happy one and why it was that my family objected to my vocation.

I told her that our family was a very happy one. They objected to my vocation, so far as I could tell, only because they did not understand the life led by a Carmelite religious.

Another nun wanted me to tell her if I "liked people," and if I had many friends, and if I enjoyed parties. These seemed—then— like irrelevant questions, but I confessed frankly that I loved people, and that I had lots of friends, and that I very much enjoyed parties.

"We are happy to hear that you come, not because you have found no pleasure in the world," Mother Teresa said calmly, "and also that you come with at least some vague experience of life outside."

After Mother said that, I was entirely at ease and I loved her for being so wise and understanding.

A very young nun then asked me what talents I had: could I sing? Sew? Play the piano? Paint? Remembering that Saint Teresa had said somewhere that admitting one's talents was in no way incompatible with humility and that to deny that one had been given gifts by God might be sinful, I told about my painting and music and my housework at home under my mother's tutelage.

Then, from a Sister with the face of an angel—Sister Stanislaus —who sat near Mother Teresa: "Cecelia, tell us, have you ever had difficulties with your employers or in your relations with others? How have you handled these problems?"

I could recall offhand only a few minor "run-ins" with people in

Mr. Cooke's law office and one at the bank. I narrated the incidents in detail, simply and directly without exaggeration.

Here Mother Prioress interrupted to explain.

"You see, Cecelia, Sister asked that question because for contemplatives sound judgment, or common sense, is absolutely essential —every bit as important as it is for people in the world. Our Holy Mother Saint Teresa used to say that if a person is lacking in judgment she should not be accepted at any price. She said the 'disease' is incurable—though it is not always immediately perceptible. That is why we try to be very well informed about you, my child, before you are accepted."

I recall how Mother Teresa enlarged most seriously on this theme for several minutes. She spoke of how grace builds on nature and how desirable, as a foundation, are intelligence and unselfishness. A girl, to lead fully the life of a Carmelite nun, must have qualities *above* average, even in the natural order. There is no place in the enclosure for "mediocrity."

"And you will find out," she added, "that the nuns here are not allowed to bury their wits; at recreation we must be of use to others—we must be alive and open-minded."

Another Sister asked me if I could eat anything and everything that was served—even onions? Having been brought up in a big family, I had been cured of whatever tendency I might have had toward fastidiousness at table. We were never allowed to be finical about our food, and I could say, "Yes, Sister, I can eat just about everything—and I like onions."

It seemed now that I could handle almost any question the nuns sent through the grille to me. But I was hardly prepared for the next one.

"Do you ever get moody? And what do you do when you are 'down'?"

I answered that I did occasionally have moods, but that when this happened, I tried to work myself out of the moody spell by taking a walk, or by talking with someone about my problem, or by talking to God in prayer—and I added, "Sometimes I have a cry about it, too."

"Yes," I admitted to another Sister, "I do have a temper, but I try to cool down quickly after I have exploded."

However, most of the interview and most of the questions had to do with my vocation directly. "How long have you wanted to be a nun?" "Oh, a long, long time—since I was about ten." (And here I told them the story of the lamb in the slaughterhouse back in Monticello.) "How long have you been thinking about Carmel?" "About five years ago a priest gave me the *Autobiography* of Saint Thérèse. That was the beginning of my interest in Carmel."

"Do you have a spiritual director?"

"Yes," I answered, "I did have a spiritual director and I did my best to follow his instructions."

"Why do you want to be a Carmelite nun?" asked Mother Teresa, who had been silently taking in my replies to the nuns' questions.

"Well, I think it is what God wants me to be . . . and I am convinced that by a life of prayer and penance I can do the most good for the most people . . . and because I feel somehow that as a Carmelite I can best answer the special call to perfection."

Mother Teresa interrupted. "My child, the call to perfection is not a 'special call.' All Christians are given this counsel. The First Commandment is for everyone. Life in Carmel is the Christian life carried out, as far as we are able to do so, to its logical end. Between your life, should you enter Carmel, and your sisters' lives in the world there will be only a difference of degree, and it is possible for your sisters to attain a higher degree of perfection if they love God more and serve Him better than you do in the cloister."

That was new to me then, but I have since learned that in the early Church there was actually no question of a difference between the two states—every Christian was, in a sense, a religious.

Mother Teresa had more to say on this point, though in the notes I put in my diary following the interview there are only some words about "We are all called to be saints; be ye perfect."

The nun sitting next to Mother Teresa then asked me what I would do should I be tormented by serious doubts about my vocation after I entered.

I told her I thought one of the superiors would help me out.

She softly followed that question with "Would you be able to see the will of God in the decision of your superiors?"

"I should try very hard to do so, Sister," I replied, foolishly assuring myself that there would never be any doubts once I entered.

Another question was "Are you ready to be corrected publicly for your faults?"

Having no idea what this implied in its details, I answered, "It probably will be hard, Sister, but I think it can be done with God's grace."

She nodded unconvinced—as much as to imply "We shall see"; then she looked at me again and asked, "But suppose you are blamed for something you did not do?"

I really did not know what I might do in that case; but I told her that I would try to offer the false accusation up to Our Lord in reparation for all the false accusations He endured.

That pleased her.

Mother Teresa, I recall, was particularly interested in my prayer life. Whether or not I went to daily Mass and Holy Communion. Did I say the rosary faithfully every day and the Stations of the Cross? Did I go into a church during the day for a visit with Our Lord? Had I a special love for the Mother of Jesus? Did I like to make sacrifices? And did I like to pray? Could I meditate, or think, about Our Lord for an hour at a time, and did I like being alone while doing so?

Parenthetically, since it may prove of interest to the reader, I might mention briefly that Mother Teresa, who founded the New York Carmel from the original Baltimore Foundation, is here with me in the Oklahoma City Carmel, which she also founded, and where I am writing this story—although I was until recently Prioress here, I consider myself still, in every respect, Mother Teresa's little daughter.

From my own interview with Mother and the chapter nuns in the New York Carmel that Thanksgiving Day and from interviews with other girls which I subsequently attended as a nun, I must report that above all things Mother Teresa was interested in a girl's love for Our Lord.

She said one must have great love to take up her cross every day and follow in faith her Beloved Jesus. Only such love can make the life possible. Attraction for the religious life is not sufficient. Any girl who comes "to seek peace" is to be carefully and seriously tested, as is one who "loves solitude."

Aptitude also was rated far below the supreme test of love and determination to strive for perfection. Aptitude, or general fitness for the life, is absolutely necessary, but aptitude without a personal love of Our Lord is not sufficient. As to aptitude for the vows, Mother Teresa said, "No one could say she was unsuited to *poverty;* and no normal person would have difficulty with the vow of *chastity;* and even those least disposed to submission can become *obedient*—people in the world must obey their superiors." Nor should there be any difficulty for a normal girl in living a community life. It was, and still is, after many years Mother's opinion that the aptitudes needed for success in the world—the same qualities—are needed in the religious state. And she always added that a person who chooses marriage is not by any means barred from the life of Christian perfection, for there are many saints in the kitchens, factories, and offices of the world. Not all the contemplatives are found in the cloister; among the priests

and nuns engaged in the active apostolate, there are contemplatives, and there are contemplatives in the world. Spared the distractions of the world, we in the cloister should normally be able
to spend more time in contemplation than others.

Mother Teresa summed up the interview in some such way as
this:

"Cecelia, my child, we shall let you know soon what decision
the nuns have come to about your interview. Meanwhile, do not
forget to exercise yourself in all the virtues, especially love and
faith. We in Carmel are supposed to be witnesses before men of
the Great Love that God has for mankind. We are to think constantly of God and rejoice in Him and want to be near Him to
love Him.

"Our cloistered life is one of all or nothing. If you desire to be a
Carmelite, you should want to give yourself completely. You must
have a strong longing for God alone."

As Mother Teresa closed the screen in the grille, she smiled and
said, "God love you, Cecelia."

I thanked her for everything and went into the Chapel, knelt
down, and tried to pray. But I was too excited even to thank Our
Lord for His wonderful gift of my vocation—though I did ask
Our Lady to help me so that Mother Teresa and the nuns would
find no serious obstacle to my entrance.

*Chapter 5*

# Into a Desert Place

†2 MAC. 5:27

O N RETURNING to Monticello I told everyone how surprisingly happy the nuns at Carmel were—positively radiant with joy. I told about Mother Teresa's sparkling brown eyes—later I discovered they were not brown at all, but hazel. Also I spoke of the weak lungs of Sister Agnes, how she was coughing continually into her handkerchief—later she explained to me that her lungs were perfectly normal; she was "coughing" into her handkerchief to keep from choking with suppressed laughter at some of my answers! Her keen sense of humor impressed me from the start. And how I loved Sister Patricia—the one who asked what talents I had, the youngest of the chapter nuns. She was overflowing with enthusiasm.

All along people had been telling me I had "too much life" for the cloister—even some of the nuns in school and also some priests to whom I had spoken tried, on the same grounds, to dissuade me. I recall a priest once pointing to a meek, mousy, pious girl who kept to herself all the time; he said, "Now, take a girl like that; she's the type for the contemplative life, not you."

Well, after a quarter of a century in Carmel I could, with some degree of authority, assure the good Father (long since gone to his reward) that such a girl would (1) in all probability never be admitted or (2) if she were admitted by mistake, she would either leave within a month or be asked to depart within a half year.

How I wished my family and advisers could have been with me in the speak room in Carmel and heard the nuns' voices and *seen* their faces! But alas that could never be, and it seemed useless for me to talk about something they had already made up their minds did not exist.

I was deceived, deluded, and duped. They were trying to "help" me.

The fact that Father FitzGerald had always encouraged me and Father McNally and Mother Teresa had told me they thought my vocation was genuine left my family unconvinced.

I explained in great detail to Mama all that Mother Teresa had told me about the ideal type of girl wanted at Carmel: one who could maintain her high ideals and her enthusiasm day in and day out, one who had good judgment and common sense, one who was generous and possessed of an ardent nature, and, most important of all, one who had a great capacity for love—love for God and love for *everyone* and *everything* that God made and loved.

Mama still felt that the cloister was no place for me. She said something about "wasting my talents and throwing away my life."

I did not then feel up to attempting to show my mother that my talents were not to be wasted nor my life thrown away.

When it comes time to describe what goes on within the enclosure of Carmel, I hope to show you to what exalted use our talents are being put and how, so far from throwing away our lives, we have in very truth found our lives and employ them in serving God and our fellow man to a degree which at that time I never dreamed possible.

The previous summer, before my hopes of entering Carmel had been so suddenly shattered, I had been told that, owing to some building complications, there might be considerable delay before a place could be prepared for me at the New York Carmel. I had been advised by Father McNally to apply to the Carmelite monastery in Philadelphia. In fact, Father wrote to the Prioress there, and the answer came back that a new choir nun could be accepted in that convent. However, I was conscious of an urge to wait, not only for the sake of my mother, but also and chiefly because somehow I thought the New York Carmel was where God wanted me.

In case you are puzzled by this problem of "finding a place" for a new postulant, let me explain briefly that in a Carmelite cloister there may never be more than eighteen choir nuns and three lay Sisters (for an extraordinary reason, however, a fourth lay Sister may be admitted). The community may never exceed that number. Often, for one reason or another, the number is purposely kept smaller. Saint Teresa, the founder of the Reform within Carmel, gave some very sound reasons for this: reasons which are just as good today as they were when she gave them four centuries ago. Chief among these reasons, of course, was the fear that too many people—just like too much of anything—might tend to distract the nuns from the one thing necessary.

Well—to return to the question of which Carmel I was destined to enter.

The old nuns in Carmel say there is a vocation to a particular monastery as well as to the life itself. I believe this is true. Several nuns in the Oklahoma cloister have told me that they visited other Carmels but never felt quite the same until they called at the Carmel they eventually entered. And there are nuns in other monasteries who feel the same way about their special call to the particular convent where they are now.

You see, much of the soul's purification and sanctification in a convent (as well as in the world) is brought about by association with the persons with whom one lives. And, in His Providence, God has this in mind when He directs a girl to a particular monastery. He knows what is best for her perfection as well as what is best for the entire community. That is why so much thought and prayer and prudent counsel are necessary before a girl can be sure that what she "feels" is a divine call is not a whim or a mere attraction.

When Our Lord directed me to the New York Carmel, He knew that I needed everything that was there waiting for me: the deep, tender understanding and motherly patience of the New York Prioress; the wit and wisdom, as well as the love and example of the Novice Mistress; the heroic lives of mortification, humility, and charity of the other novices and nuns. And perhaps most of all I needed the particular dispositions of certain religious who, by God's grace, were to file away many of my rough edges and open my eyes to glaring defects of character which no one had heretofore dared hint that I possessed.

It is possible, of course, that my presence in Carmel has had some purifying effect on others.

God works similarly in all walks of life. He calls every soul to intimate union with Himself and is constantly offering us graces and helps, often in the form of occasions to overcome temptations or for the practice of some virtue. After all, our perfection is His work, although we can interfere with it and refuse to let Him work in us. Without our consent His hands are tied. As Saint Augustine has put it: "He who made you without your co-operation will not save you without it."

Saint John of the Cross says that "God exercises more power in sanctifying a single soul than He did in creating the world, for in creating the world He met with no opposition." There is food for many a meditation in those few lines—try it some evening when you are alone and when you can look up at the star-studded heavens and feel your soul awed by the vast majesty of the material universe.

Because of the unsympathetic attitude of my family I went personally each day to the post office for the letter I was expecting from Mother Teresa. Often I would be standing dejectedly under our box in the office looking up pleadingly at the glass window. It never occurred to me that my anxiety was being observed. One day the understanding clerk leaned over the counter and said to me, "What's the matter with that guy of yours—doesn't he *ever* write to you?"

I had all the depressing symptoms of a neglected sweetheart.

But at long last the interminable waiting came to an end. The letter from Carmel arrived. Mother Prioress and the chapter nuns had accepted me for the cloister. I was to enter on the Feast of Saint Agnes, the following January 21.

My heart was racing madly with joy.

It was the week before Christmas, and as I walked back from the post office in high exhilaration, I was deeply grateful to my Beloved Jesus for ordaining everything so generously. And I told Him so, as I poured out my overflowing heart to Him in the church before returning home.

Should I tell Mama immediately the good—I mean, sad—news? Or should I rather not disturb the family joy of the pre-Christmas preparations?

I decided to wait for at least a few days.

But it was impossible for me to restrain my full heart any longer. The day before Christmas I broke the news to my mother.

Without uttering one word or expressing in any way the anguish that filled her heart, Mama walked out of the room and left me in tears alone.

A heavy pall of gloom settled over the house, as when a member of the family, long expected to die, finally breathes his last.

Let me hasten again to record that I loved my parents dearly. My mother was in every way generous and self-sacrificing. She was constantly aiding our neighbors when they were in trouble. God had blessed her with vigorous health and a large family and enough of this world's goods; but she wanted nothing for herself; she wished only to rear her family well and, if God willed it, in relative comfort. My mother was faithful always to her prayers (even the rosary she would always say kneeling upright), and, of course, she would never miss Mass—and she made certain that her children followed her example. With watchful diligence she kept us from all harmful influences; she instilled in all of us respect for authority and a consciousness of the Presence of God.

Then why did she object so strenuously to my answering the Call I felt certain God offered to me? I do not know.

It is true my mother feared for my health; she thought by entering a contemplative convent I would be ruining my life. But she also feared, perhaps, to lose me.

As I look back now, I can say—and I'm sure my dear mother would now say the same—no daughter is nearer her mother than the one she has given to God. All vocations are, we know, a pure gift from Our Lord. It is possible, in some mysterious way, that my vocation was passed on to me from my father, who at one time wanted seriously to become a priest. But it is still more likely that I owe my vocation to my mother. Somehow I'm sure it had to pass through the heart of my mother before it could reach to me. Unknown to herself, she prepared the ground in which the seed of my vocation was to germinate, she provided the atmosphere in which it was to grow. May God reward her for all eternity.

You will forgive me if I make one final digression before we pass through the cloister door at Carmel.

I should like to say a few words about the wonderful parents of our American homes.

It is my sincere opinion that many of our wonderful American mothers and fathers are real saints. I hope to live to see at least one native-born American, preferably a married person, raised to the honor of sainthood. Much of the holiness in America is still in the hidden stages, as it was in the Holy Family of Nazareth. But solid piety does exist in our American homes, and also a deep spirit of sacrifice.

It is no doubt too much to expect that all parents have the magnanimous spirit of Saint Thérèse's mother and father, who thought it would be a wonderful honor to have *"all* their daughters Carmelites!" Of course, they desired it only "if it be God's will"—and, you may recall, God's will it was, for all their daughters became religious—four of them Carmelite nuns!

Monsieur and Madame Martin encouraged these vocations. Whenever little Thérèse was taken to the Carmelite monastery chapel for a visit, her father would point to the hidden choir and whisper in her ear, "See, little Queen, behind that big grille there are holy nuns who are always praying to God."

While I am aware that the divine choice of vocation is not influenced always by the play of heredity and environment, still no one can deny the importance it has in this vital matter.

I am quite aware also that a nun in the convent looks upon a religious vocation in a very different light from the mother or father of an aspirant to the cloister. For me it is hard to understand how many good Catholic parents, outstanding for their charity toward everyone, can fail to be just as magnanimous toward God. Gladly will they give any number of their children to creatures in marriage. Why do they object so strenuously to giving even one to God, the Creator?

It takes great faith—the faith of Abraham at times—to make the sacrifice of one's dearest treasure to God. It takes the faith of Saint Thérèse's father to know that life is fleeting; that it is, as he puts it, like a flower—"One evening it looks splendid, and in the morning an hour's frost will wither and beat it down."

Not that the parents of Saint Thérèse did not feel a pang at the thought of separation from their children. They did. Faced with the prospect, it is only natural that even the best-controlled natures would fail and tremble. "Do not think," M. Martin said to each of his daughters as she left him, "there is no sacrifice on my part, for I love you so much . . . God alone could require such a sacrifice."

Yet amid his tears his heart was overflowing with joy. And therein lies the paradox.

In his famous *Monks of the West,* Montalembert says the last word on this subject. "But who is then this invisible Lover who died upon a gibbet nineteen centuries ago, and who thus draws to Himself youth, beauty and love? Who appears to souls with a splendor and fascination which they cannot resist? Who swoops down upon them all at once and makes of them His prey? Who takes, all living, the flesh of our flesh, and slakes His thirst with the purest of our blood? Is it a man? No, it is God. There lies the great secret, the key to the sublime and sorrowful mystery."

Now we shall return to my final Christmas with my family.

Deep, dead silence seemed to enshroud the whole house. It was unbearable to think that I was the cause of the gloom.

There were about a dozen at the house on Christmas Eve. We went off to Midnight Mass in three different cars. On entering the church, I went to join the choir in the balcony. After the services, there was considerable confusion outside the church; friends were greeting one another, and it was a gay gathering.

When I finally went to the spot where our cars had been parked, my heart sank to find that all three cars had already sped home— each driver thinking, like Joseph and Mary, that the child was with somebody else.

There was nothing else to do but face the long, cold walk home.

Feeling utterly abandoned, I took the path over the hill and through the fields as a short cut.

The house was still brightly lighted, and the sound of many excited voices came from within. But I could not steel myself to enter. Instead I went sadly to the door of our barn and stood there in the cold, clear moonlight and cried, as I thought of Bethlehem.

Finally I crept up to the house and entered by the back door.

When I was discovered in the kitchen, everyone came noisily out to greet me. Having dashed back to the church to find me gone, they had imagined the worst possible misfortunes befalling me.

But the spell was broken. Everyone laughed, and I relaxed completely. And for the rest of the night and next day there was no talk of CONVENT.

At this juncture, you may recall, we are abreast of the New Year's Day predawn adventure in New York City with which we opened this story.

You may have been wondering what happened to the young man who escorted me to and from church that morning. It would make an exciting climax to the narrative if I could report that my strange companion later turned his back on his worldly ways and entered a Trappist monastery. Such a happy ending is not beyond the realm of possibility, but it is beyond my knowledge, for I never heard of the young man again.

After completing my business in New York I returned to Monticello to make last-minute preparations and bid farewell to my family and friends.

And though I was thrilled at the thought that my entrance day had finally arrived, I did not feel any the less the sharp pain of those last hours when I was leaving everything forever behind me. Just when I wanted most to be forgotten, everyone was most touchingly kind and thoughtful, which made me feel even more the sacrifice of the separation.

Of all the objects that filled my eyes, what I remember most was Grandma's picture—Mama's wonderfully devout Lutheran mother. She looked with a satisfied smile at me from her picture on the parlor wall. I can still see in her eyes the heroism of her life. And I wanted to be a strong soul like her. Mama had told me often how patiently and silently she had suffered throughout her life.

To leave home is, to some extent, to die. What emotion there was in that last look around at the familiar rooms and the things in them—never to see them again; it was as though those inanimate creatures had sprung to life and had the power to cling to me and love me.

It was snowing heavily the day I left home—large, gently falling flakes which seemed to add to the quiet that suddenly enveloped everything and everyone. Though I had thought of some consoling, grateful words for my mother and sisters, I could say nothing.

During Mass that morning I tried to tell Our Lord how much I loved Him for His goodness to me, and I begged Him to make my dear mother understand. I was just about to ask Him to forgive every offense I had committed in my life up to that moment, when I thought of something I had done as a schoolgirl to hurt the feelings of one of our neighbors. True, I had already asked her to forgive me several years ago, but somehow I felt that she never had.

I promised Our Lord that before I left Monticello I would visit her, throw my arms around her, and ask her again to forgive me. I did visit her.

Climbing the stairs that led to her door was one of the most difficult tasks I had ever, up to that moment, undertaken. But I had promised Our Lord that I would ask her again to forgive me. In answer to my knock she opened the door about five inches and peeked out. I was about to explain the reason for my call but got only to the point that I was leaving town. . . .

She slammed the door in my face.

Perhaps my pride was hurting as much as my heart. I was sick. I had not yet learned that "the disciple is not above the Master"—it is enough if he be *like* the Master. Enough? My Beloved, is it not infinitely more than enough for any one of us to be like Thee in any way at all?

Father FitzGerald came with Mama and me to New York. That, as you may well imagine, was a great relief to me—and a consolation to my mother.

We had dinner together in New York, and Father teased me about my last meat meal: "There are 365 fish days on the Carmelite calendar, Cecelia!" He offered me a raw oyster. But I hadn't yet learned to consume one of those delicacies which replace turkey on the cloister menu.

I expressed a desire to see for the last time the white lights of Broadway. Our Lord apparently did not object to this last worldly wish; the taxi strangely stalled for at least five minutes at the corner of Broadway and 42d Street!

Mama and I stayed that night—my final night in the world—at my sister Anna's. They begged me to dress in my postulant's habit. To please them I did. And just for fun—and for the last time—I did the Charleston.

At the completion of my dance Anna said, "Cecelia, you'll last about three weeks in that monastery."

"If I can hold out for one week, Anna," I assured her, "I'll be there for life." May God's grace be with me always so that those bold words may indeed be true.

Father FitzGerald offered the conventual Mass at Carmel next morning, the feast day of Saint Agnes.

During Mass, Mama and Anna, who knelt beside me, wept continually. How I begged Our Lord to strengthen us during the next hour, which I knew would be life's most trying for me.

As the moment came for the enclosure door to swing open and I embraced my dear mother for the last time, I tried to think of something funny to say to keep her from breaking completely under the strain. I recall what it was I whispered to her, but I haven't the humility to repeat it.

It worked. The spell was broken; Mama laughed.

My heart was beating so violently I wondered if it would break; I went toward the enclosure door and stepped inside.

# Chapter 6

# A Garden Enclosed

† CANT. 4:12

The moment the enclosure door was shut and bolted, I found myself kneeling in the midst of three veiled nuns, one of whom handed me a crucifix which I pressed to my quivering lips. "Passio Christi, conforta me." These were the first words I heard on leaving the world's tumult and its pleasure. Passion of Christ, comfort me!

It did indeed comfort me. In the older sense of the word comfort, the Passion of Christ gave me strength.

Is it not indisputably so that it is from Our Lord's Passion that strength comes to us in every crisis of life? For the early Christians the Cross of Christ was the attraction that appealed most to their burdened hearts. "I preach Christ and Christ crucified," said Saint Paul. Our Blessed Lord's message—"take up your cross daily"—made its most favorable impression upon and held its keenest fascination for those who were suffering. Jesus died for us on Calvary. We do not face our life, with its difficulties and problems, alone.

Nothing could be more fitting than that the Carmelite postulant

70

on the threshold of her life of penance and solitude should be reminded of this. I was not facing my cloistered life alone. "Behold
I am with you all days." Though it was true I was to be "hid in
the top of Carmel," it was *not* true that I was to "dwell alone in
the forest, in the midst of Carmel." My Beloved would be always
at my side.

When the three nuns who received me at the door threw back
their veils, I saw that it was Mother Teresa who had given me the
crucifix. She and the other two nuns then embraced me affectionately. My bags were carried off, and Mother Teresa escorted
me through the silent corridor to the room adjoining the sanctuary of the Chapel. This was the choir, the Sisters' part of the
Chapel, where they assist at the Mass offered on the altar, chant
the Divine Office, and make their meditation. It was a simple
room, without adornment, but not without beauty.

It was all like a dream. I was in a world completely different
from anything I had ever imagined. My every quick breath seemed
to be nourishing my soul rather than my body. The whole monastery, not the choir alone, had the atmosphere of the interior of a
church. Everything seemed tinged with God, in Whose presence
everyone was living. This is where I had longed to dwell, to adore,
praise, and love God all the days of my life.

In the choir I knelt in silent adoration for several minutes before the Blessed Sacrament. While I knelt there, Reverend Mother whispered in my ear, "My child, offer yourself completely to
Our Dear Lord, and ask Him to make you a perfect Carmelite."

What better gift did I have to offer Him? I gave myself and all
I was and had to my Beloved. Then she led me to the lovely shrine
of Our Lady in the rear of the choir. The statue was directly above
the Prioress's choir stall.

Pointing to the image of Mary, Mother Teresa said, "There is
the real superior of the monastery. Put yourself into her maternal

hands. She will always be your mother, and she will mold you into a perfect spouse of her divine Son."

When we returned to the broad, bright corridor, Mother pointed out to me the spiritual quotations inscribed on the walls. There was, for instance, a verse from the prophet Isaias: "Holy, holy, holy, Lord God of hosts: the heavens and earth are full of Thy glory."

An adaptation of a famous line of Cardinal Newman's: "Every soul that perfects herself elevates the world."

A half verse from the First Epistle of Saint John: "My little children, love one another."

We then proceeded to the recreation room. Mother smilingly whispered to me that I was to be presented to the entire community of nuns. Standing like a guard of honor in two rows, the smiling nuns were waiting for me. The Mistress of Novices led me up and down the lines introducing me to the owners of those tranquil, cheerful faces.

Each of the Sisters embraced me and gave me a warm welcome into the Carmelite family: "Welcome to Carmel! I wish you much joy!" To each word of welcome I gave the Carmelite response: "God reward you, Sister." Because I was so intensely happy and excited, I threw myself enthusiastically into each welcoming embrace. When I found out later that the nuns are somewhat wary of a cold, stiff postulant, I was glad I had made no attempt to restrain my enthusiasm. Too much gazing at the ground can prevent one from seeing Heaven.

In the excitement no one had suggested that I remove my winter coat and "stay a while." But when the final introduction was completed, the Novice Mistress helped me remove it. There were a few muffled giggles from the other nuns. They were surprised and amused at the style of the 1928 skirt line. In the commotion of the last-minute rush before leaving the house that morning, I had forgotten to employ a trick I had of letting the skirt down a bit—as I had judiciously done when I bade farewell to His Eminence, Cardinal Hayes.

The nuns then sat down on their straight-backed wooden chairs and indicated me to do the same. For about ten minutes we chatted about my departure from home and my first impressions of Carmel. It was too soon to form an impression of anything in detail; but all in all I felt that I was already in Heaven. I was as happy as Christmas morning. God was so good to bring me "into the land of Carmel to eat the fruit thereof and the best things thereof. . . ." I prayed that I would never defile the holy spot or "make His inheritance an abomination." Already I could dimly understand why "Carmel is the Lord's living Garden, the Mountain friendly and agreeable in which it pleases God to dwell."

Sister Marie, a delightfully cheerful nun (and one full of common sense, I later learned) was appointed to be my "Little Mother." It was Sister's duty to take me in hand and render me every possible service during my first three days in Carmel. Sister inspired complete confidence, and I was not afraid to confess my ignorance of the strange customs or to ask her to clear up the mysteries and problems that confronted me.

Judging by the sound of Sister Marie's extra broad A's, I thought for a moment I was being accompanied by one of the Goulds or Astors. But Sister soon put me straight when she told me that she had lived in South Boston before entering the cloister.

Naturally I was curious to see everything on the inside of the enclosure—the choir, the community room, the corridors—but I was most curious to see the room I would henceforth call "our cell." Let me explain that a Carmelite nun is never permitted to refer to anything, except her faults, as "mine." She owns nothing, not even her clothing, her bed, her tableware; all are referred to as "our." On entering our cell, an ocean of peace inundated my soul. The individual cells of the nuns are in the section of the monastery called the Dormitory. Hanging near the clock in the middle of the corridor is a large wooden clapper. This is sounded by one of the Sisters to awaken the nuns each morning. It is used also to sound the end of the day. Just before retiring, the Sister who has the office of Reader in the Refectory for the week says three times in a loud and distinct voice the "retiring sentence." This sentence is a quotation from the Bible or some other spiritual book, and it usually bears on the subject matter of the following morning's meditation. My first night in Carmel, after the clapper sounded the end of day, Sister gave this sentence from the office of Saint Agnes's Feast: "My Lord Jesus Christ has espoused me with His ring, and as a bride hath He adorned me with a crown." I can hear the words yet; I hope that I shall hear them to my dying day.

A Carmelite nun's cell is a small room, not more than 10 feet by 10 feet—often smaller—on the walls of which there are no adornments except a large cross at the head of the bed. Our bed is constructed of two wooden planks placed across two wooden trestles. We do not, as one postulant naïvely suspected, sleep on a bundle of hay piled in a corner of the cell. On our bed boards there is a canvas sack neatly stuffed with straw. The bed is covered with a brown spread.

The cell was simply furnished with a straight-backed wooden chair, a pitcher and basin, and a small table on which was a miniature plaster skull. There was no mirror. The windows had shades, but no curtains. I looked about me and noticed there was no clothes closet or wardrobe in the cell. Sister Marie explained that there would be no need for a wardrobe because when one needs a clean habit or clean clothes she procures them from the Vestier, who has charge of the community clothes.

From the moment I stepped inside our cell I fell in love with its austere simplicity. Its unadorned walls and crude furnishings seemed in perfect harmony with the spirit of the monastery; a place stripped of everything that might suggest comfort or luxury was, after all, exactly what I had longed for. As Saint Teresa said, in her usual practical way, "Beautiful walls and furnishings are not necessary; it is not our business to look at walls."

The plain wooden cross, Sister Marie told me, had no corpus because in spirit I was to take Our Lord's place there; as a Carmelite I was to perpetuate on earth the suffering life of Our Lord. "With Christ I am nailed to the Cross." The small skull on the table was to be a constant reminder that life on earth is fleeting; it would make me conscious always that one day I was to die and that consequently the inconveniences and penances I endure now are insignificant and temporary.

From my suitcase I took out my brown postulant's dress. I then removed my secular clothes for the last time. When next I appeared before the nuns, I proudly wore the Carmelite postulant's graceful, neatly pleated, full-length skirt and the wide circular cape, under which I was supposed always to keep my hands modestly folded when not using them. The change of costume seemed to please the nuns very much—and it pleased me very much too.

Before entering the enclosure that morning I had taken breakfast with Mama, Anna, and Father FitzGerald; so my first visit to the Refectory was after the examination of conscience and the prayers in the choir which immediately precede dinner. Eleven o'clock seemed a rather unusual hour to take one's principal meal; but when I discovered next day that breakfast (after three hours of prayer, including Mass) consisted only of bread and coffee, I saw clearly that it was none too early.

The Carmelite Refectory is, like everything else in the monastery, immaculately clean and, also like every other room, austerely unadorned.

Mother Prioress and the Subprioress sit under a large wooden cross at the far end of the Refectory at a somewhat longer table. On their table in full view of all the nuns is a normal-sized human skull. You may wonder what my reactions were when I saw the skull looking out at me from its place of honor on the Prioress's table. Frankly, I didn't give it much thought. It looked rather "monastic" to me and seemed to fit into Carmel's penitential atmosphere.

Since my own "first day" in Carmel, I have learned through the years that reactions caused by the presence of the skull vary greatly—the same is true of many other Carmelite customs. Some are a bit startled, to put it mildly, at their first sight of the skull. One new girl was noticeably disturbed. Finally she steeled herself to walk up to it at the end of the meal and gently pat its bald pate. After that, it caused her no more concern. A recent postulant here in our Oklahoma monastery confessed to me that for the first three days she "gagged every time" she tried to eat; she just couldn't seem to swallow any food because she thought the skull kept staring right at her during the meals.

Of course, once the purpose of the skull's presence is understood, there is never any problem. We find it a good reminder that we are not to pamper the body—part of which is to end up in some such shape as the skull. It helps us to be uncomplaining about a meal that does not satisfy and to eat food that is distasteful to our appetites.

In the Refectory the nuns sit in pairs on benches behind small rectangular tables arranged along two sides of the Refectory. The nuns face the center of the room. A lector's rostrum stands at the end of the Refectory opposite the Prioress's table. And, of course, throughout each meal a nun, clearly and distinctly, reads a passage from the Scriptures and then continues for the rest of the time reading another spiritual book. There is no reading while we take the coffee and bread in the morning; our breakfast is taken standing.

It was not easy to acquire perfect monastery table manners. Refectory rubrics in Carmel, as in the dining rooms of all religious communities, are rigorously carried out. We file into the Refectory in silence; at the center of the room each nun bows to the cross, then proceeds to her place, where she stands until after grace has been said. At the signal from the Prioress, we sit down and unfold our napkins and fasten them biblike to our habits. The reading begins, and the meal is served by the nuns appointed for that duty.

In Carmel our forks and spoons are made of wood. The Trappist monks make and supply us with the articles—they charge us less than five cents a piece for each fork and spoon. (Obviously this is not an advertisement, for the poor monks would have to abandon their hours of prayer in order to fulfill the deluge of orders that might come to them were their wooden implements put on the open market at five cents apiece!)

A nun is never allowed to speak in the Refectory. This I found difficult in the beginning. Like one of our younger nuns, I thought the silence would be broken on Sundays, but Sunday came, and there was no talking. Then I thought talking would be allowed on great feast days like Easter, but Easter came, and still there was no conversation. It's just outlawed! Actually, we are permitted to talk in the Refectory on the silver and golden anniversaries of the nuns of the Community.

In Carmel we do, however, make use of a sign language to draw the Sister waitress's attention. I should mention that a nun may never request anything for herself in the Refectory, except bread and water. It is each nun's duty to make sure that the Sister with whom she is sitting has everything needful. If one's table partner has need of something, one may request it, by sign, of the Sister server.

At a signal from Reverend Mother Prioress the meal comes to an end. The crumbs which might be on one's napkin are gathered up and consumed. This is a reminder of Our Blessed Lord's admonition: "Gather up the fragments that remain lest they be lost."

Occasionally a friend writes to Carmel to ask about the type of diet followed in our monastery.

Let me preface whatever I may say about our food with this apparent paradox: we are told that we must "eat well in order to fast well." That is why the superiors in the monastery are somewhat concerned about the perseverance of a postulant who does not eat well at mealtime.

Our menu consists of wholesome food—nothing fancy. Our friends, thank God, make it possible for us to obtain sufficient bread, butter, fish, eggs, milk, vegetables, and fruit to maintain a diet which allows us to follow our long, arduous day.

A Carmelite nun may never eat meat except in case of illness. We do not eat meat, not because we think it is a bad thing, but because we think it is a good thing—otherwise there would be no point in our "giving it up." While this deficiency may add somewhat to our fatigue and while it may affect the blood pressure of some of the nuns, it does not, judging by traditional above-average Carmelite longevity, impair our health in any way. After all, we are reminded that there are many of the world's poor who can afford meat but rarely, and we are aware also of the large number of vegetarians who voluntarily abstain from meat. So our meatless menu is not a problem to cause concern.

During the major part of the year we observe what we call the "Fast of the (Carmelite) Order." This fast begins on September 14—the Feast of the Exaltation of the Holy Cross—and lasts until Easter. During this time we partake of a cup of coffee and some dry bread for breakfast, a full meal at eleven each morning, and a collation of vegetables or fruit, dry bread, and tea in the evening. On Fridays, and on the days of Lent, as well as on all special fast days of the Church, we keep the Black Fast. On these days we may not have eggs, butter, or milk or anything made from them.

It is to be expected in our life of penance that often we do not get what we want and often we get what we do not want. We would become very worldly if we had always what we wanted; our cloistered life is supposed to be one that cannot be led in the world —that is why we are here.

Already, on my first day in Carmel, I had seen the nuns in the choir devoutly at prayer, kneeling upright without support on the plain floor. I was with them as they silently ate their frugal dinner. Now I was to be in their midst during the brief period of recreation following the meal.

In Carmel each day we are permitted two recreation hours. One is held after dinner and the other after the evening collation. By recreation we do not mean that we engage in any competitive games; in fact we don't engage in games at all. Our recreation period is work accompanied by conversation. We may talk, and that's amusement enough.

I noticed that the nuns during recreation were quite jovial. They seemed to me, in contrast with the world I had just left, to be divinely human. There was no bickering or arguments, no gossip. It was a completely relaxed, happy, keen group of women, eager to enjoy a humorous story or a pun, but just as eager to swing the conversation back to God and spiritual things—and this seemed so natural for them to do! Every fifteen minutes the Monitress of the week sounded a small wooden clapper as a reminder of the presence of God. I was the only one in the room who was not doing something during the conversation period— all the other nuns brought their sewing or embroidery work with them. And this, I learned, is the normal procedure each day at "recreation."

The hour for relaxation is brought to an abrupt end by the ringing of the cloister bell. I must confess, nothing I had ever seen before was that abrupt. The bell caught one nun in the middle of a story and another with an incomplete sentence. Both stopped as though they were shot. The story would be continued next day

—"now as I was saying yesterday. . . ." A nun may not speak after the bell unless given permission by Mother Prioress.

Sister Marie then escorted me about the monastery to observe the nuns carrying out their manual-work assignments. Each nun works alone in absolute silence. There is no common workroom. Saint Teresa thought that in this way there would be less occasion to break silence; so the chore is done either in one's cell or at the spot called for by the particular duty.

It was startling to me to discover the wide variety of practical work undertaken and the skill and dexterity of the silent nuns performing the tasks. One nun was finishing an exquisite embroidery pattern on a set of red Mass vestments. Another was making dozens of little silver reliquaries for the precious bones of the recently canonized Jesuit martyrs of North America. Some were busy baking, cutting, and packing thousands of altar breads, which are used in the parish churches for Holy Communion. Another was making altar linens; two Sisters were cutting cloth for some new habits; one was absorbed in translating a Spanish spiritual book into English.

Here in our Oklahoma Carmel the nuns are, on occasion, farmers too. Our large property makes it possible for us to grow many of our own vegetables. We also have an orchard, chickens, and a cow. The Sisters here learn to milk the cow, feed the chickens— and, when necessary for a sick nun's diet, kill a chicken. Many a big-city girl learns for the first time how to plant, cultivate, and harvest vegetables. There is never an idle moment in Carmel. No Carmelite nun is without a job.

Sister Marie explained that our manual work is a psychologically essential diversion from our many hours of silent and vocal prayer—"a form of recreation," she added, "and a form of silent prayer also."

Appreciating the value of work, dignified by Our Blessed Lord

Himself, each of us must perform some manual task—"He who does not work, neither let him eat."

It is true a Carmelite monastery is not a factory, but we are able to accomplish a great deal during our short periods of manual work, and this helps appreciably to support ourselves in the enclosure. Sister Marie pointed out to me a few lines in the Rule relative to manual work: "You shall do some kind of work, that the devil may always find you occupied. . . ." We are to live among the people like Saint Paul, who said, "We are among you in toil and labor working day and night lest we should be a burden to any of you. . . ."

Our holy Rule further mentions that we are not to engage in any elaborate work; our sewing, painting, and similar occupations do not ordinarily absorb the mind excessively or hinder the spirit of recollection.

I noticed as the silent nuns passed each other in the corridor they bowed graciously, the younger saying, "Praised be Jesus Christ!" to which the older answered, "May He be forever praised!" I thought, "What a beautiful way to honor Christ in one another!" When the Prioress passed, they gave the same salutation but instead of bowing they knelt and kissed her scapular in token of their reverence for authority. By this simple act of homage they were also making up for their own former lack of submission and for the insubordination of all who, through obstinacy or neglect, refuse to submit to legitimate authority.

As I went about the cloister, it was obvious to me that life in Carmel, while simple and quiet, would never become monotonous or boring. There was a harmonious combination of the active and the exterior with the passive and the interior. But even the active duties were performed "interiorly," pleading for souls all the while in union with Christ. This was Carmel burning with zeal for souls, quietly carrying out small duties, patiently enduring the difficulties of everyday life.

The manual-work period is interrupted at two o'clock for the chanting of Vespers. This seemed a rather unusual hour for the prayers which I had always associated with the evening. . . .

The time between 2:30 and 3 is spent in spiritual reading, after which the nuns return to their manual-labor assignments and work until 4:45, at which time we prepare for the presupper hour of mental prayer in the choir.

There was no minute of the long day when the nuns were idle. It was a vastly different type of life from that which my family and friends thought I would lead. Whether at work, at prayer, or at recreation there was an atmosphere of complete self-mastery, and nothing of the spineless helplessness which many erroneously associate with cloistered life.

It was the businesslike thoroughness with which each assignment was carried out that impressed me. Each nun had the cheerful assurance of knowing the life's inestimable value. This, too, was a far cry from the type of existence we were supposed to lead.

I was exhausted when finally I climbed into bed that night. There was no question about it: the bed seemed hard and the straw seemed rough and the woolen "sheets" and pillowcase were warm and stuffy. I wanted to cover the woolen pillowcase with something softer and smoother, but I overcame the temptation. The sheets, I found out later, often have the effect for the first few nights of making postulants dream the monastery is on fire—especially should they enter during warm weather.

I can readily understand this because even now I can recall my first summer nights in Carmel, when I felt that unless I got air on my feet, at least, I would be unable to sleep. So I used to leave one foot exposed. I got a scruple about this and mentioned it to the Confessor. He said nothing at the time, but when later I asked him —in a moment of excessive fervor—for permission to do some extra penance (one may never perform extra penance without the consent of the Confessor and the Superior), Father said, "What about that foot getting back under the covers?" Father thought that would be a penance more pleasing to God than the one for which I had asked.

Since then I have never aired my foot at night. And the woolen sheets have never interfered with my sleep.

It was not the hard bed or its coarse covering that kept sleep from overtaking my fatigued body that first night in Carmel. I was overstimulated from the strain of all the last farewells, and then, too, the beauty of Carmel's spirit had so overwhelmed me I did not want to lose any of the present delight by falling asleep.

I thought back over the long, weary wait I had endured to reach my goal; I thought of the sad, strange struggle of my departure from home, which somehow was necessary for me to endure before I could be brought to this way of peace. A sacred silence seemed to envelop the entire monastery. Even here in the midst of the world's largest, busiest, and noisiest city no sound seemed able to penetrate the austere walls.

Since the enclosure door had shut out the world, I had all day heard nothing that might offend my heart or ear. In my joy I told myself that this peaceful quiet was the reward of my many tears.

These nuns, overflowing with sober happiness, had come from many different cities and from very different backgrounds. Each one, I knew, had understood the vanity of earthly things. It seemed as though I looked back into a dim, distant past as I recalled on that first night in Carmel the toys of which I had previously made my joys, and I recalled how weakly I had understood my Beloved's great and gracious invitation to be with Him in this cloistered solitude. How little I had left behind. It is true I knew that I should always miss my mother, and I wept again when I recalled our final embrace—but even that was not too great a price to pay for this, the sweetest service of my Beloved.

Still no sleep was strong enough to overtake me.

As I lay there on the straw in the darkness, every step I had taken through the cloister came back vividly to my mind. The austere furnishings of the monastery, the sweet voices of the nuns at prayer, and, most vividly of all, their faces, their smiles! They were at peace in the certainty that they were walking with God, Who had given them the wisdom to see life as He sees it. "The world is passing away with its eager desires, but he who does the will of God abides for ever." They seemed to know what I was soon to learn: that there can be no comparison between the wisdom from below, "earthly, sensual, demoniacal," and the wisdom from above, "pure, peaceable, gentle, docile, full of mercy and good fruits, without partiality, without pretense."

"You are a lucky girl, Cecelia," I whispered in the emptiness of the cell, "to be allowed to enter here, to live with Christ in this place of His dwelling."

I was to be a part of this chosen group, dedicated to a life of solitude and silence, united in the bond of charity, invited to meditate and pray and sacrifice and die to self. Yes, the skull upon our simple cell table will help me die to the comfort-loving, pleasure-loving girl I have been.

Will I be able to endure? Will my treacherous tongue submit to the strict silence of our Rule? Will I be able to control the impulses of my heart and mind? Will I be able to see, to remember, that my dying to self will bring life to the world? Will I be able to choose suffering and thereby ease the Saviour's sorrow and lift a bit of the world's cross of sin? Will I be able to make mine the ideal of the great Saint Teresa, that dauntless Virgin of Avila, whose virile faith and ardent love for Christ Crucified enabled her to triumph over all obstacles?

Help me, my Beloved, to be true to the call You have given me; help me to ease the sorrow of Your Sacred Heart; help me to pray for the heedlessness of a world rebelling against You; help me to prevail even if the world and all that is in it should fall in ruins at my feet. . . .

# Chapter 7

# The Path of Life

†PROV. 15:24

I AWOKE with a start. The clapper sounding the dawn of a new day was like a martial call to battle stations. It took several seconds in the pitch blackness before I could recollect myself sufficiently to know where I was and what the excitement was all about.

I jumped out of bed, fell to my knees, and made my morning offering. Turning on the light, I drowsily stared at one wall, then the other, in a futile attempt to locate the mirror. Then the truth dawned on my dreamy mind: there was no mirror. Spared the necessity of applying cosmetics and of prettying myself in any way, I was dressed and ready for the day's business faster than ever before in my whole life.

For the three days following my entrance, while I participated in the monastery schedule as closely as I could, I was, in a sense, a guest under the personal care of my Little Mother, Sister Marie. My recreations were spent in the company of the professed nuns, of whom I had grown so fond that it was almost like leaving home again when I was told at the end of the third day that I would

85

henceforth spend my hours with the novices and postulants.

During this time I copied a small book of prayers and a notebook of instructions on our customs. During these first three days I had the thrilling honor of leading the procession into the choir for the Saturday night chanting of the Salve Regina, the beautiful hymn to Our Lady which is solemnly sung in her honor every Saturday and on the eve of her feast days.

Parades always fascinated me, and to this day the solemn processions in the monastery give me a real thrill. So when Sister Marie took me aside before the prayer bell that first Saturday evening in Carmel and told me that not only had I permission to participate in the Solemn Salve procession but, as the youngest, I was to lead the community of nuns into the choir, I trembled with excitement.

My Little Mother gave me my instructions, and with a large lighted candle in my hand I took my place at the head of the community. Over the brown habit each of the nuns was wearing the long, graceful white mantle which is used only for Mass and other solemn occasions. They entered the choir slowly and reverently and in perfect order made their way to their places. The Salve seemed to be chanted by angels, and it left me with no doubt about the high place given to Mary in Carmel. Surely she would not fail to turn her "eyes of mercy" upon us and upon the whole world.

At the time of my entrance, there were three novices and one postulant in the New York City Carmel. Even though they had been in the monastery only a relatively short time before my arrival, they seemed years ahead of me in the religious life. I felt my own imperfections and ignorance keenly, and I wondered whether I could ever attain to the degree of perfection they had already reached. Their eyes modestly cast down, their voices properly modulated, their posture always erect—everything so precise and perfect, it seemed impossible that I could learn.

I had to be taught how to genuflect properly, how to bless myself, how to hold my hands folded under the cape—and later under the scapular, when I received the habit. I was constantly forgetting this, and I would walk jauntily along the corridor with my hands swinging freely at my sides. That is, until an observant nun would gently remind me where my hands should be. I used to think how much better I'd feel if only I could see one of the other nuns forget about her hands. Then one day I saw one of the novices caught with her hands uncovered, and I felt somewhat relieved.

The Novice Mistress spent considerable time teaching me how to walk. My country stride had to be measurably shortened and my pace slowed in half. A nun must never run or even rush; she must always strive to keep in mind Our Blessed Lady, whose recollected modesty she tries to imitate at all times.

My eyes, so I was told, were altogether too inquisitive. Curious by nature, I was in the habit of taking in everything about me. The strangeness of the enclosure made me want to gaze and gawk continually at everything and everyone. The Mistress of Novices put it something like this: "Cecelia, keep closed those outer gates which are the senses—particularly your eyes—then your soul can go nowhere else but to its goal, God within you."

After several weeks I was tempted to congratulate myself. It seemed to me that I had become quite nunlike, at least in my exterior deportment. However, whenever custom or ceremonial violations were mentioned during the evening Chapter of Faults in the Refectory, it was apparent even to me that there was still much to be desired in my demeanor.

There is no question about it, public correction is a very effective way to bring home our faults to us. Some postulants are not able immediately to accept as they should the public declaration of their faults—and I was one of these. Others seem to realize from the beginning the great value this has in accelerating their spiritual progress.

Just the other day one of our newest postulants—who incidentally told us she had been a cheer leader in college!—was seen sliding along one of the well-waxed corridors. She was admonished publicly for the breach of proper conduct. Afterward she said to me, "I just can't understand, Reverend Mother, how I am able to accept, without any feeling of rebellion, the corrections given me in the Refectory. I used to feel humiliated and embarrassed whenever anyone corrected me even in private." She added very humbly, "Please, Reverend Mother, never allow anything that is not perfect in me to pass uncorrected."

My own reactions, I must confess, were, in the beginning, not so lofty or so humble. One evening in the Refectory I was admonished by the Zelatrix, whose duty it was to observe and report the defects committed during the day. She said, "In charity I admonish Cecelia for standing with her feet about sixteen inches apart." Even though I knew it was reported "in charity," instinctively I thought to myself, "She didn't have to give the measurement, did she?"

It was dawning on me slowly why, in the interview prior to my admission, one of the nuns had asked me if I thought I could stand being corrected in public. Even though I honestly felt that "everyone in the monastery but myself could be canonized," still I felt humiliated each time I was corrected. It was not easy in those days to prostrate myself meekly on the floor in response to each admonition—to "turn the other cheek" and pray, as we must, for our admonisher.

There was much of the world and my old self that persisted in clinging to me; and I was wondering if ever there would come a day when I could be as perfectly mortified and recollected as the nuns seemed to be who moved in such an otherworldly way all about me.

I recall one evening being more than usually tired when I finally reached our cell after Matins. I was sorely tempted to omit the prescribed prayer which we say each night at the bedside before retiring. In fact, I yielded to the temptation. I said to myself, "Just this minute I finished talking to Our Lord for two straight hours down in the choir." Then to Our Lord I said, "You know me, dear God," kissed the floor, and jumped into bed.

When I mentioned this to my confessor some time later, the priest said simply, "You have beautiful confidence, my child."

Those who have had the perseverance to follow my story this far will not be surprised to learn that a talkative person like myself experienced some difficulty with the strict rule of monastic silence. I know now that my experience was not uncommon. Almost all postulants at first find this rule trying, although in varying degrees.

One evening during Strict Silence, which begins after Compline and ends after Prime the following day, I was in our cell putting the finishing touches to a small painting. I was rather pleased with the work, and in my thoughtless vanity I imagined that some of the nuns might like it also. So, without giving a second thought to the rule of silence, I softly walked to the cell door of my neighbor, knocked, and on opening the door whispered that I had come to give her a look at a little painting I had just completed. Sister smiled blandly, looked at the picture, and, without registering any expression, in silence closed the door. I tried the next door. The same "no comment" treatment greeted me here also. After the third cell had been disturbed, it began to dawn on me that perhaps one does not make comments on paintings during the Strict Silence. And at the Chapter of Faults the next day I was convinced. As I look back now, it is clear to me that during my postulancy Mother Teresa and the nuns were very patient with me. The gentle manner of introducing me to my new life and their thoughtfulness in correcting my worldly ways has become more apparent to me as time goes on.

It had always been my way to rush at any task given to me. I always was impatient to be through with work, to have it over and done. This habit did not leave me when I passed through the door of Carmel.

One of the first duties which followed immediately our coffee and bread was to make our beds, straighten up our cells, and read a short passage from the *Imitation of Christ*. I found that by hurrying I could do my private chores, then dash for a dustpan and brush and start on my assigned duty of cleaning the stairway and get it almost finished before the next bell rang. It felt good to be ahead of schedule.

But my efficiency was silently ended when one day a senior novice stopped me, slowly tied an apron around me, turned up my sleeves, and with great deliberation pinned up the apron bib. By the time she had completed the rather mysterious task of getting me fixed up, the bell rang. I had not started my sweeping duty. However, the deliberate delaying action had its proper effect, though I confess it annoyed me considerably at the moment. In fact, this was the first annoyance I experienced in Carmel.

When I spoke of this to the Novice Mistress, she told me how to conduct myself in such situations. She said, "At such a time you have a wonderful opportunity to make 'an act.' " This means that you are to endure with meekness and love, in imitation of Our Lord, something you do not like. It was like the sacrifice game I used to play with my roommate, Helen, at Ladycliff; if there was a difference, it was that here in Carmel I tried to have a purer motive. The Novice Mistress told me to say this little prayer at such times: "My God, I love You, and I do this simply for the love of You." She added, "Never forget, Cecelia, if you but dry a dish and do it for the love of God, it could be worth more than a martyrdom endured through self-love."

The bitterness of the little "dusting" annoyance began to melt away, and in a very imperfect way I began to think of Mother's explanation of the value our *motives* have in the acts we perform.

It is clear enough to me now that life anywhere on earth is filled with opportunities of silently accepting contradictions, humiliations, and misunderstandings. For the most part they are small annoyances; yet they can be potent factors in ridding ourselves of our selfishness and pride and in preparing ourselves for real recollection and loving union with God. These disturbing situations are hard to accept in the beginning. But we need not be saints to realize that we ought to try to do more than put up with them. If we embrace them wholeheartedly, they become desirable; they cannot be embraced wholeheartedly unless we turn to God and ask for His help, and it is precisely this recognition of our need of God's help and our asking for it which immediately brings Him to our aid and leaves us with a consciousness of His nearness and His love, so much so, in fact, that many would not want to be without trials which bring such peace to the soul.

Everyone is bothered at times with interruptions while in the midst of an absorbing task or interesting book. Here is how Saint Thérèse advised one of her novices about this problem: "When someone knocks at your door, or when you are called, you must practice mortification and refrain from doing even one additional stitch before answering. I have practiced this myself and I assure you that it is a source of much peace." The Saint advised the novice to imagine the knock came from Our Lord, Himself.

The novice followed the advice, and one day the Saint observed her putting it into practice in a trying situation. She called her aside and said, "At the hour of your death you will be very happy to find this to your account. You have just done something more glorious than if, through clever diplomacy, you had procured the good will of the government for all religious communities and had yourself proclaimed throughout France as a second Judith."

The new arrival at Carmel soon learns to value not only the annoying and trying incidents in the day but *every* act of the day; for the most insignificant action, when performed through a motive of pure love, is important. Saint John of the Cross, speaking of souls acting in union with God, says, "A very little pure love is more precious in the sight of God and of greater profit to the Church than are all [exterior] works together."

One of the chief reasons we are not all saints is that we so often fail to have a pure intention in the good we perform.

As a postulant (and I confess still now as a professed nun) I have often begun something purely for God. Then somewhere along the line I became absorbed in it for its own sake, or for the pleasure I found in doing it, to the extent of finishing it through self-love. Not that finding pleasure in what we are doing for God, or for our neighbor for the love of God, makes the act any the less meritorious, as I erroneously thought during the days of my postulancy. On the contrary, the Lord loves the cheerful giver, and the more we love God, the more joy we shall find in serving Him. If our assignment is agreeable, how can we do otherwise than find pleasure in it? Finding pleasure is very different from seeking pleasure. It is in God's power to give us pleasure, and He gives it as we need it; unless He gave it we could hardly persevere for long in the life of grace. Saint Teresa reminds us, "Our nature is weak and requires some indulgence." I dare say there are some souls who raise their hearts and mind to God more quickly from the pleasure of a cup of coffee than some would-be ascetics do from the pain of their penances.

Postulants are new brides; and like other new brides, for the most part, they are blissfully ignorant of the trials that lie ahead. They walk on clouds in the early weeks and months. It seems that

I was more than usually buoyant by nature, and my cup of happiness during these first months was flowing over. My Beloved stayed near me to give me continual joy and consolation. He made of me, His bride, a veritable princess, and I imagined myself at times reigning in His court. These were the days, so to speak, of my honeymoon: no sacrifice seemed too hard, no difficulty too great; I could endure a thousand deaths for my Spouse, who sheltered and protected me. At that time I never dared think it possible that my Beloved might leave me for a time, that His strength might be withdrawn, and that I would be alone and have my faith and trust put sorely to the test.

For the moment all was bliss.

When I whispered one evening to Mother Teresa that I felt like a princess, she said, "My child, you *are* a princess. You are a bride of the Son of the King of Heaven."

One day Mother Prioress sent me to the supply closet to bring her a large box, on the side of which I could see clearly written the word PENANCES. Mother said that a priest had come to the turn* to purchase an instrument of penance, and she wished to show him some samples.

I was beside myself with curiosity. I had heard about hair shirts, disciplines, and other penitential articles, but I had never seen any. Reverend Mother opened the box, and I furtively looked in with a gasp of amazement.

To let you see how far I was removed at that time from the spirit that accompanies the wearing of a hair shirt or the inflicting upon one's body of the stinging discipline, I shall tell you of the mischievous scheme that came to my mind just as Mother handed me the box to replace in the closet.

I impishly removed from the box a hair shirt, and with a smile I asked Reverend Mother if I might have it long enough to play

* On page 130 will be found a description of the turn for those not familiar with Carmelite monasteries.

a joke on the professed nuns, with whom we were allowed to recreate on the feast next day.

I explained the joke, and Mother (reluctantly I'm sure, but in order to allow me a bit of indulgence) agreed to let me have the shirt.

After dinner next day with prudently downcast eyes I entered the recreation room a bit late, having been delayed by my dish-washing duties. I took my place between the Mistress of Novices and another postulant. There was an interesting spiritual discussion going on. I made a serious effort to appear interested. After a time, in a rather loud voice, I made some irrelevant remark about the matter of grace, which turned nineteen pairs of raised eyebrows in my direction. The newest postulant thinks she is a theologian!

At that moment I casually tossed back a part of my cape and stared innocently around at the amazed nuns. None of their eyes met mine; all eyes were fixed on the hair shirt, which I had roguishly put on *over* my postulant's dress. Convinced that they had seen the "penance" and had been duly horrified to have so stupid a girl in their midst, I flipped the cape back down and modestly folded my hands underneath. For several minutes, pitying me because they thought I knew no better, no one dared mention my hair shirt for fear of embarrassing me. Finally Reverend Mother broke the spell and smilingly asked me what it was I was wearing under my cape.

For a moment I feigned embarrassment, but the nuns caught on, and we laughed over the joke until tears trickled down our cheeks.

While in the world I had acquired many slang expressions which occasionally slipped into my convent conversation. "Gee," "golly," and "gosh" had been pretty well eliminated after Mother Teresa's gentle preentrance admonition. My talk, however, was still peppered with phrases and words not encouraged within cloister walls!

I was recreating with the novices and our other postulant one rainy day in the temporary, ill-furnished, overcrowded recreation room on the top floor—the week's wash hanging above our heads. Another slip was chalked up against me.

We were talking about divine love and comparing it with human love. Having done a bit of philosophizing on the matter during some recent spiritual reading, I offered some of the fruits of my research. "You know," I said sagely, "don't you think it's wonderful how the love of God makes us so indifferent to temporal things? I was thinking just today that if a young man in the world brought his bride into a dump like this and made her wear shoes like the ones we wear, and eat the way we eat, she'd think she was the most miserable girl in the world, wouldn't she?"

Instead of ready acceptance of and agreement with my conclusion, there was an embarrassing—and to me inexplicable—silence. I could not imagine what it was that displeased them. Finally one of the novices said, "So you think this is a dump, do you? Well, of all things!"

I recalled immediately that I had used the word without noticing it, and I flushed red with discomfiture. The Novice Mistress, seeing how upset I was, eased the tension; smiling, she said, "And after all the hard work we did beautifying the place before Cecelia's arrival."

Despite my many falls and lapses, I continued to make daily—yes, hourly—resolutions to improve. I wanted with all the desire in my heart to be a good Carmelite, even a saintly Carmelite if it pleased God.

The minute details of the holy Rule and Constitutions of Carmel were extremely difficult for me to remember and follow perfectly. Everything was new, and only gradually do the external customs and regulations become familiar and instinctive. It's something like learning to drive a car. At first the traffic laws and the mechanics of handling the car distract you and make you feel ill at ease; but when you have learned the traffic regulations thoroughly, and deliberately and carefully practiced proper traffic maneuvers with an expert, then follows gradually a feeling of confidence and ease.

The days of my probation were nearing an end. It was seven months since my entrance into Carmel. There was so much for which I should be grateful. My dear mother was becoming more and more resigned—even pleased—with my vocation to the cloister. On her monthly visits to the monastery and in her weekly letters the change in her was apparent.

The high tide of my initial enthusiasm had washed away many of my worldly ways. But in the depths of my soul I knew there was still much of self left. In my exterior demeanor there were vain reminders of the world, and in my heart there were memories impeding my abandonment to God.

*Chapter 8*

# The Bride, the Wife of
# the Lamb

† APOC. 21:9

IN CARMEL the postulancy, or period of preliminary testing, lasts from six to twelve months. There is no fixed date on which the postulant receives the religious habit of our holy Order.

My reception ceremony was set for the day on which we commemorate Our Lady's birth, September 8, and I received the habit alone.

Before entering upon my solitary eight-day retreat, which immediately precedes the ceremony, I had to take care of a number of preparatory details. High in importance in my mind was the traditional bridal gown. Since my sisters were still not completely reconciled to my cloistered life, I hesitated to ask any of them for her wedding dress. Nor did I wish Mama to incur the expense of buying me a new one. So I wrote to Mama and asked her to send me the dress in which I was graduated from Ladycliff; it was white georgette crepe, accordion-pleated.

Of still more importance for the novice-to-be is the choice of name. You have noticed that during the postulancy the new Carmelite is called by her baptismal name.

97

For some time the novices, realizing that no decision had yet been made about my religious name, good-naturedly made many humorous and fantastic suggestions—and, of course, some quite serious and reasonable ones also. Many of the names mentioned had to do with the Saints and holy founders of our Order, and since I was deplorably ignorant of much of this history, it was difficult for me to determine which were the serious suggestions and which were offered merely in fun.

About a month before my reception, I told Reverend Mother that during prayer the previous evening a name came to me. It is a wonder Mother didn't tell me to dismiss such distracting thoughts during prayer time. Instead she thought the "inspiration" rather good. She and the Mistress of Novices gave me permission to announce it to the novices during the evening recreation.

Bubbling over with excitement, I could hardly restrain myself until the prayer opening recreation had been said: "O Lord, Our God, we are about to spend some time in recreation . . . may it be for Thy honor and pleasure, and grant that this exercise may enable us to perform the works of Thy service with greater fervor. The same grace we ask of thee, most gracious Queen of Heaven."

"Guess what," I cried, "my religious name is going to be Cecelia of the Trinity. Do you like it?"

There was no enthusiastic acclaim; it was obvious that I was the only one really impressed with my "inspiration." There were a few polite "Isn't that nice" and "That is a rather good name," but no eager response.

Actually, before entering Carmel I had always wanted the name Agnes, after the virgin Saint who was martyred for Our Lord. I wanted her name because it meant "chaste" and "pure" and also because it resembled the Latin word for "lamb," the animal I had watched being led to slaughter in Monticello. But the New York Carmel already had a Sister Agnes whose good health made it obvious that she would not go to her reward before my clothing day.

I chose "Cecelia," not because it was my baptismal name, but because I loved my patron Saint dearly and admired the way tradition tells us she lived: her joyous reaction to suffering; her confidence in God's providence; her loyalty in martyrdom; and her deep devotion to the Holy Trinity, which she continued to proclaim during her last agony, raising three fingers of one hand and one finger of the other to testify to her belief in the mystery of three Persons in one God.

As soon as the matter of my name had been settled, I wrote joyously to Mama to announce the good news.

By return mail Mama sent a hastily written note in which she said, "While I like the name Cecelia, I had been hoping that you might choose Catherine, since, I understand, nuns often take their mother's name."

It never had dawned on me that Mama would have any sentimental preference one way or the other. Even though it meant more teasing from the novices, I was happy to think that my vocation and my cloistered life meant that much to my mother. Indeed I would ask Reverend Mother to permit me to make the change. But I added to myself, "If I take Mama's name, why not take Papa's too? It will be Sister Catherine Thomas, if Reverend Mother agrees."

Mother Prioress was pleased to give her consent, and even the novices seemed to approve of the change. It was a relief to have it settled.

I might explain that all Carmelite nuns add a title to their name. Since Divine Providence had arranged everything so favorably for me, and since I liked to think of Our Heavenly Father watching over His children constantly, I decided to place myself under the shadow of His wings. So for the remainder of my life, please God, I would no longer be Cecelia Walsh, but Sister Catherine Thomas of Divine Providence.

The reception ceremony fell on a Saturday, and I was happy about that. Our Lady seemed very close to me.

Dressed in my "bridal gown" and beautiful veil, I was permitted to spend an hour with my family and friends outside the enclosure, immediately before the ceremony. (This permission to go out of the cloister is no longer granted.)

As the enclosure door opened and I was about to emerge again into full view of those outside the cloister, I felt strange and uncomfortable. Eight months within the enclosure had convinced me that my life was meant to be a hidden one; and I was not at all certain that my family had become fully reconciled to my life of solitude.

It seems unnecessary to repeat that I loved and admired my mother and sisters; apart from the one problem of my call to the cloister, we had never had a serious disagreement within the family. However, I was never very demonstrative in expressing my feelings. Mother Teresa had noticed from the tone of my letters home that I did not express as I should the love I felt toward my mother. Reverend Mother suggested that I change my ordinary simple "Dear Mama" salutation to "My Dearest Mama"—which I knew, as soon as I wrote it, was what my heart had been saying all along. To Mother Teresa and my New York Carmel superiors, I owe a great deal for their understanding help in this weakness of mine. One of the older nuns, observing my shyness, said to me, "Don't hide your warm Irish heart under your cool German exterior."

There was no need for uneasiness when I met my family the morning of my reception. It was at once apparent that a great change had come over not only Mama, but my sisters also. They seemed more than pleased; they were proud of my vocation, and their sweet attitude removed all my strangeness and added greatly to the happiness of the occasion.

At the ringing of the tower bell, our family visit was interrupted, and, together with my sister Ruth, my bridesmaid, I took my place near the altar for the Mass.

The Gregorian chant of the Solemn High Mass was beautifully sung, and the graceful dignity of the three priests at the altar was most impressive. Father FitzGerald, who was Deacon of the Mass, preached an inspiring sermon on the meaning of Carmel. And to add still more pleasure to my heart already overflowing with delight, my brother Tommy assisted the priests during the Mass as Master of Ceremonies.

As the Sacred Host was elevated at the Consecration of the Mass, I felt an urge to offer myself to the Divine Lamb as a victim. I was fully aware of what I was whispering, though I was quite ignorant of the permission ordinarily required to make such a solemn offering: I said, "Jesus, my Beloved, make of me a lamb for sacrifice. I offer myself to You as a victim."

Following the Mass, a procession formed to the enclosure door, which was now closed upon me for the last time. I was led to the nuns' choir for the remainder of the ceremony. There, through the choir grille, the priest turned to me and asked, "What do you request?"

In a surprisingly clear voice and with unambiguous words I answered before the Church and the world that I wished to remain until death behind the walls of the monastery enclosure to serve God and my fellow human beings.

The priest then asked, "Is it of your own free will and inclination that you desire to take the habit of religion?"

I answered, "Yes."

After that, I laid aside my worldly attire and put on the longed-for brown habit of Carmel.

For the family the saddest part of the beautiful ceremony is the "prostration." The new novice, covered completely with her pure white mantle, her arms outstretched in the form of a cross, lies prone on the floor in the middle of the choir. This is the sign of the mystical death whereby the novice promises to die to the world and to self.

During the prostration, while the choir chants the hymn Veni Creator Spiritus, the novice prays for all the desires nearest her heart: she prays for herself, that the Holy Spirit may strengthen, guide and protect her; she prays for her monastery and for its benefactors, and for the salvation of all mankind. She prays for all the written intentions which the nuns have slipped under the carpet on which she lies. The nuns feel that the new bride of Christ is very close to His Sacred Heart at that solemn moment in the ceremony and her requests are certain to be heard.

My own "intention slip" was pinned over my heart. I included on it everyone I knew—even "my enemy."

Every moment of the deeply moving ceremony was for me filled with the highest spiritual delight—despite my excitement. The pleasure my dear mother derived from the experience was a source of deepest gratitude for me. Still, there was an even more convincing sign of love given to me by my Beloved that morning.

You will perhaps recall the sadness that was added to my already heavy heart the day of my departure from Monticello by my unforgiving friend's hasty shutting of her door in my face. Not only because I felt she would not be interested did I not send her an invitation, but also because only a very few intimate friends were allowed to attend the ceremony. But to my utter and eternal amazement she came.

I could not keep back the tears of deep joy that overwhelmed me when I saw her approach the grille in the guest room after the ceremony.

"Am I forgiven?" I whispered, between cupped hands, so that

those around would not hear. She winked and smiled. I knew she had forgiven me. God love her forever.

What a priceless gift to give His bride! Uniting me with that woman, Jesus showed me so clearly that in Carmel He wished me to be henceforth one with all those whom He loved.

In the Refectory at dinner I was privileged to sit at the head of the table between Mother Prioress and the Subprioress. This was my day, and in my new habit I was bursting with happiness. The dinner was an especially good one—Mama had made the bridal cake—and I was feeling like a princess, and more than a princess!

For three days after the ceremony of reception, the novice has permission to receive visits from her family and friends. Many of my friends from Monticello and my classmates from Ladycliff came to see me, and it was good indeed to visit with them.

On the afternoon of the third day, I was called to the speak room to see a young woman whose name was unfamiliar. A sweet, youthful face smiled at me when I drew back the screen. A conspicuous deformity in her spine forced her to stand and sit in a pitiable posture, leaning toward her right side. Her disfigurement helped to explain her sad, suffering eyes.

She had heard there had been a clothing ceremony at Carmel, and she came hoping to be allowed to see the "new bride." She told me that when she was a small girl she had dreamed that one day she might be a cloistered nun, but now that vocation obviously was closed to her. Having lost her parents five years before, she had been forced to seek employment as a scrub girl in a downtown New York office.

As she talked to me, it was obvious that with all her infirmity and despite her sad eyes, she had a burning love of Our Lord. She spent several hours each day, she said, in prayer in the Franciscan Church on 31st Street. Our Lord's invitation, "Come to Me all you who are weary and heavily burdened and I will refresh you," had been accepted, and her Master always gave her the strength of body and peace of soul she so ardently prayed for.

This crippled, humble scrub-girl contemplative, whose cloister was the canyons of Wall Street and whose choir was the nearest parish church and whose cell was a cheap rented room in the slums—this Carmelite without vow or habit—taught me many things about suffering and about prayer. She taught me also how to be grateful for all that God had done for me.

While I was naturally happy to see and speak with all those who were kind enough to visit me, still I was impatient to return to the absolute solitude for which my soul longed.

What a joy on the night of my reception to enter our cell finally and close the door behind me. My Little Mother, who had resumed her duties for the three days following the ceremony, had most thoughtfully placed a small statue of Our Lady on the cell table, and before it flickered the flame of a blue light which played on the Virgin's face. A single red rose looked up at her.

I was kneeling beside the bed, tired, but with a heart overflowing with peace, when I heard a piece of paper being slipped under the door. It was a note from Mother Prioress: "At the Elevation of the Host this morning during Mass, I was strangely impelled to offer you as a victim—in soul and body—and I did, for the glory of your Beloved and for the salvation of souls."

This mysterious message started my heart pounding like a piston within me. I felt certain that it was more than a coincidence that the two of us should have had the same thought at the same moment. Some scientists, I know, propose a reason for such an occurrence—something about mental telepathy. But I had a reason for it, too; it was a reason beyond the realm of science.

Somehow I knew that God was speaking to me; but since I was such a young religious, not yet one day in the holy habit, I thought He would not yet exact the price of my offering. He would not ask me to suffer until I was spiritually stronger and more generous. The days of my novitiate, thank God, were hidden from my eyes that night, and I did not know that far sooner than I feared God would put my offer to the test.

"Grace comes with the habit," we say at Carmel, and add, "and so do trials."

As I entered upon the intense novitiate schedule, the glamour of the earlier months began to wear off. In its general outline the day followed the schedule of the professed nuns. We rose at 4:40, except during the period of the Fast of the Order, when our daily routine began an hour later. At 5 we were in the Chapel for an hour's mental prayer, which was followed by the chanting of Prime, Terce, Sext, and None of the Divine Office; then Mass.

After our coffee and bread we went immediately to our manual work until the bell for examination of conscience in the Chapel. Dinner was at 11, followed by an hour's recreation in common. Then the novices had a study period. The chanting of Vespers at 2 was followed by spiritual reading, novitiate exercises, and manual work. Another hour's mental prayer preceded supper or collation, and after supper there was another hour's recreation. From 7:45 to 8 we were in Chapel for Compline, after which we had a free hour in our cells for private devotions, spiritual reading, writing, or the like. The final exercise of the day was the chanting of Matins and Lauds of the Divine Office at 9, which took about an hour and fifteen minutes. After a fifteen-minute examination of conscience we were back in our cells and retired around 11. During the summer we were allowed an hour's siesta in the middle of the day.

The spiritual joy I had been experiencing in my prayer during the first months in Carmel had suddenly left me, and a period of great dryness set in. It seemed that I was hanging between Heaven and earth, with no support from either. Prayer was a torture. I had not yet learned that true prayer does not consist in thinking much, but in loving much; that God listens most to the voice of silent love. Up to this time I had been attached to the consolations of God rather than to the God of consolation. It was now being daily impressed upon me that true love consists not in feelings or consolations but in the union of our will with the will of God.

The Novice Mistress patiently guided me during those difficult times. I recall how she explained the system of meditation used in the Society of Jesus, the famous Ignatian method. She told me to steep myself in the Gospels, as Saint Ignatius and Saint John of the Cross and, in fact, all the Saints so strongly advise us to do, paying particular attention to our Lord's reactions in order to impress His principles deeply upon my mind and imagination.

I tried this, but as often happens in the case of beginners in the spiritual life, I felt that all this system was hampering my freedom. Nevertheless, my directress insisted that I at least memorize the method and try as best I could to put it into practice. It seemed of no use.

Some time later I was asked how I would go about making a meditation on the Gospel story of Jesus and Mary Magdalen.

In my crude fashion I haltingly reconstructed the scene and spoke of Our Lord's compassion and the Magdalen's great sorrow and love, of the corresponding sentiments that welled up in my own soul; and I drew a conclusion or resolution applicable to my own life.

When I was finished, the Novice Mistress fitted the whole of my meditation over the framework of St. Ignatius' method for mental prayer and tactfully showed me that the Saint's system is nothing more than a scholarly outline of the way our minds normally work. I was convinced.

When a girl leaves the world and enters Carmel, she expects a hard life. Strangely, the things she expected to be difficult—like separation from her family and friends, lack of worldly amusements, change of diet, sleeping on a hard bed—these she finds

relatively easy. The things she never expected would be difficult
—like prayer, fatigue, silence and obedience, and the endless ac-
cumulation of little exactions throughout the long day—these
pile up to overwhelm her.

She soon understands how exacting love can be.

Entrance into a cloister marks a critical stage in a girl's life.
Even though most applicants are previously prepared and trained
by their spiritual guides for a considerable time, nevertheless they
usually experience difficulties of one kind or another in the adjustment from an active life in the world, with all its sense impressions, to the quiet, solitary life of Carmel.

In my own case, the difficulty of adjustment was not experienced until after the reception of the habit. It began with aridity
in prayer. Then a false idea of perfection subdued me considerably
—especially at recreation—but as soon as Mother Prioress noticed
the strain, she called me to her office and lovingly counseled me
and corrected my errors.

I vividly recall her words of wisdom: how she stressed liberty of
spirit as one of the first effects of true prayer; how she spoke of
the danger of extremes and pointed out that virtue lies always in
the middle course, that common sense is the highest form of in-
tellectuality. I recall how clearly she explained what dying to the
world and to self really means and how beautifully she analyzed
meekness and humility of heart in connection with all this.

Repeatedly she would insist, in her casual talks with the novices
in those days, that we were not expected to lose our individuality
or to be fashioned after a stereotyped pattern but that we were
always to be ourselves—our better selves. Far removed herself
from complicated ways and methods and gifted with a single-
minded spiritual vision, she was ever leading us toward that utter
simplicity of the pure of heart who, forgetful of self, see God everywhere—in everything and in everyone.

Fortunately Sister Agnes, the Novice Mistress from whom I received my religious education, was patiently prudent and gentle. She introduced me to the strange customs of the cloister and the sacred truths of Carmel with understanding thoroughness, and I admired everything I heard. She welcomed from me every question my curious mind might offer. With maternal instinct she helped and guided my every step.

That, of course, is the duty of everyone who has the tremendous responsibility of leading a young soul into the way of perfection. Because she was exact in her fidelity to the Rule and generous with us in the countless demands we made upon her time, she instilled the spirit of generosity in me just as a mother would instinctively do in her child. Submission was easier where love commanded. Anxieties faded where confidence of success was so evidenced in her example.

In the beginning of my noviceship I had for the most part the disposition of a child, secure in the confidence I had in my Mistress, and completely dependent upon her. In Carmel we speak of the postulant as a "baby"—well into my year as a novice I was still a baby.

Slowly I began to mature. As I observed myself—my exterior deportment, that is—I was surprised all at once to see that my movements, my gestures, my speech and demeanor were becoming more and more like those of a nun. The conventions had been acquired by observing the others. Living the Carmelite life and imitating the Carmelite manners, I became in my outward appearance a Carmelite. My normal, natural intelligence made that adaptation relatively easy.

But to acquire the habitual attitude and the inner spirit which really make a cloistered nun—well, that was something else again.

Today as I look back, I realize that subconsciously I had turned to Mother Prioress, my Novice Mistress, and my Sisters to find many of the things I had left behind in the world: my mother's love and the affection of my friends.

Sometimes Our Lord—ever divinely tender in His dealings with souls—only gradually takes the place of creatures and, for a time, permits natural supports, but He does not want our dependence upon others to last too long. Nor does He want us to be mere imitators of those around us. The Novice Mistress, on the watch for this, is quick to explain that everyone has limitations; that creatures are poor models at best; that a religious should model herself solely upon her Bridegroom Christ—"Splendor of the Father"— as He is so clearly and attractively depicted in the Gospels.

# Chapter 9

# In the Obedience of
# Charity † 1 PETER 1:22

A MILD cyclone is whirling around the barn loft where I have come to write a few pages this afternoon. I wonder how I am going to get back to the monastery. There is no letup to the gale, and the rafters sound as if they might tumble down on me at any moment. The sand is blowing in through the louver boards at a great rate, and although I dusted the chair opposite me only a few minutes ago, I can again trace my name in the dust. But I had better get on with my story.

The previous chapter left me struggling in the canonical year of novitiate, which begins with the reception of the habit and has for its object the forming of the novice by a study of the Rule and Constitutions, by learning the meaning and obligation of the vows, by meditations and assiduous prayer, and by exercises regulated for rooting out faults, controlling the emotions, and acquiring the virtues.

"You will have to go through all three volumes of Rodriguez's *Practice of Perfection and Christian Virtues* before you take your vows," one of the novices whispered to me. Volume One had given

110

me such an acute attack of spiritual indigestion that I instinctively gasped to think of consuming two additional volumes of the same concentrated food.

But after thinking the thing over, I characteristically decided to make quick work of Rodriguez and finish him off in short order so that I might be free for an intense study of the writings of Saint Teresa and Saint John of the Cross and some of my other favorites. So for the next month or more I devoured Rodriguez, not only during lecture time, but every Sunday and holiday and whenever I had any free time. Finally I came to the end of Volume Three, heaved a sigh of relief, and left it—together with a little note—at the cell of our Novice Mistress and patiently waited for her to give me a new book. I had not long to wait. It was no time before I heard something gently placed at the door. I hurried to pick it up. It was Volume One of Rodriguez! And I had to go through all three volumes again—this time not so quickly!

One of the most difficult problems for me during my early years as a nun was the matter of submission—*complete* submission with the proper motive.

At the end of my first year as a novice I would make my temporary vows of poverty, chastity, and obedience; and even then I knew that the most difficult of these, for me at least, would be obedience. It was necessary, therefore, that I understand it thoroughly.

Of course it had been explained to me, even before my entrance, that in Carmel—as in every religious order—obedience is never given to the person who issues the command, but to God, Whom she represents. To keep this principle in mind is the crux of the entire matter, for we would refuse God nothing if He spoke to us directly. The difficulty we experience—or most of the difficulty—comes from the fact that sometimes we hear only the human voice in a superior and fail to remind ourselves that God is speaking to us through her.

When I answered God's call to enter the cloister, I was obedient, in the same way as Peter and Andrew and James and John were obedient, in the same way as every religious is obedient: "If any man has a mind (a will) to come My way let him renounce self, take up his cross and follow Me." To follow Him, of course, is obedience: "At the head of the book it is written, behold I come to do Thy will." I was to follow Him who became "obedient unto death, even the death of the cross." When I accepted the call to Carmel, I accepted automatically everything that went with the call. That was my intention as I stepped inside the enclosure.

Very soon, however, I began to see, as many another novice has seen, that to renounce one's possessions is far easier than to renounce oneself. My religious obedience asked me to surrender both.

This may seem to some a hard saying; yet in it lies the secret of true peace in religious life. This renouncing of self does not mean that we lose our personality or that we cease to make decisions. It means simply that we freely and intelligently renounce the independent use of our will and that we submit to the all-holy and adorable Will of God as manifested to us through His Commandments, through our Rules, and through the orders of superiors.

Whenever I receive letters hinting about the liberty of which I have been deprived by my religious obedience, I smile to find in the same letters mention made of events in the writers' own ordinary daily life in which they are constrained often to do things that they did not want or like to do or that were against their preference. In the world there is a constant call to obedience, constant because we are in an order willed by God. There is a natural hierarchy of irrational and inanimate creatures which constitutes the order of the world, and there is a hierarchy among rational creatures which constitutes the social order.

I never cease marveling at the beauty and harmony of the order of the universe. So unerringly do the heavenly bodies follow God's will, which is stamped on them and from which they cannot deviate, that scientists, so we've been told, can foretell 10,000 years ahead of time, even to the precise quarter of a minute, when there will be an eclipse.

Whenever at the Divine Office we recite the *Benedicite*, wherein we call upon all created things—"sun and moon, mountains and hills, beasts and cattle . . ." to praise their Maker; or whenever I look at the stars or at the birds and flowers around me, I am enraptured in contemplating the perfection and fidelity with which they follow the laws of nature.

For the religious it is her pleasure no longer to do her own will. It is her pleasure and joy to do the will of her Beloved. It is, or can be, that simple.

Now, that shouldn't sound strange to any person in the world who has been in love. The more intense the love, the more does the lover enjoy complying with the will of the beloved. "Whatever you wish, my dear" are words uttered sincerely only when there is an ardent love.

That's exactly what a religious says in effect to Our Lord: "Whatever You wish, my Master. I have renounced my own will and have promised to follow You in Your passion, even if it means for me crucifixion also."

I can hear you object that authority in the hands of human beings might be abused. That, of course, is true, and Saint Teresa warned against it; she insisted that there are virtues, too, for those who rule and that they are never to usurp what belongs to God. If the superior is steeped in humility, prudence, wisdom, charity, and justice, there will never be any problem.

Were I a learned theologian, it would be difficult for me to resist the urge to speak much about obedience. Still, while I am unable to speak as a scholar about anything, I nevertheless know the value of this virtue, not only for us in the monastery but for everyone everywhere. No person in the religious life could possibly object to the supreme importance of obedience, for if she did not intend to submit, she was in the first place very illogical in placing herself under a superior whose duty it is to guide her.

This does not mean that obedience is easy, but it does mean that it is reasonable.

As far as I have observed, Carmel is never accepted by a timid soul, any more than the desert was populated by timid Christians in the fourth century. They sought the desert not because they feared the world and its temptations; the era of the Roman martyrs had come to an end, and they sought slow, voluntary martyrdom in the desert, where they waged daily battle against the insidious tyrant SELF. They were spiritual athletes who displayed a systematic effort to purify, control, and unify the forces of human nature and so bring back to it some of the harmony and glory that it had before the Fall. But in one sense it was easier for the anchorite living alone and regulating his own life than it is for a religious living in community. Saint Basil seems to imply that our way is therefore more perfect, or at least more difficult. He says, "How can you exercise patience if there is no one to run counter to your own will?" The bodily mortifications of the desert dwellers could and, unfortunately in some cases did, produce puerile rivalry in penance, which begets pride. Community life helps us to know ourselves better, and because humility is truth we are in a better position to become humble.

The difficulty I had been having in adjusting myself to a life of submission was due not so much to the rigorous demands of the Rule itself as it was to the fact that in my obedience I was paying too much attention to creatures and too little to God, Whom they represented.

There is no doubt about it, during my early months in the monastery and well into my novitiate year, I was, to a great extent, obeying my superior because I liked her and admired her as a person and because I wanted to please her and feared to displease her, even in small matters. I wanted earnestly to receive her nod of approval and her motherly smile of affection. Obviously, much of the moral value of my conformity was lost.

This "natural" attitude also accounted for the difficulty I was experiencing in renouncing my own inclination with regard to some of the orders given me by different officials in the monastery, even though I would, of course, carry out the order promptly.

One way of helping the young religious to control the emotions of their souls—especially their likes and dislikes—so that in all things they may be guided by principle instead of by feelings, is to give them work to do under someone toward whom they are not particularly attracted or toward whom they may even feel a natural antipathy.

One day I confided to our Novice Mistress the struggle I was having with my feelings in regard to this. Mother gave me much encouragement merely by saying, "I understand." How important those two words are in the vocabulary of anyone who has the direction of souls or the direction of others in any way—whether as a superior in a monastery, or a parent in a family, or an employer in business. "I understand."

After those two words I was docile and ready for the help Mother so patiently offered me.

She said that I would never become a spiritual person so long as I allowed myself to be influenced in my obedience by the characteristics—pleasant or otherwise—of those in charge. In fact, she suggested that I go down to Our Lord in the Blessed Sacrament that very day and tell Him that, in so far as my own personal feelings were concerned, I would endeavor, for the rest of my life, not to prefer one superior to another.

To help me to see only God in superiors and in those under whom I was working, she told me to consider a person at the telephone: how he pays no attention to the instrument before him, but only to the voice coming over the wires. I found that advice extremely helpful.

When I was confused about the rather complicated subject of obedience of judgment, or "blind" obedience as it is sometimes called, Mother encouraged me to continue striving for it with all my might. She straightened me out by explaining that we practice it when we do not rely on our own understanding, but on the understanding of the superior.

There was a feeling at times that the multiplicity of assignments could not be taken care of in the time allowed. I was always impatient of results and wanted to finish one thing quickly and completely so as to be ready to start another. Even though I knew that neither God nor superiors ever expect the impossible, sometimes I would be tempted to become upset in these situations and I would recall an incident that happened to me one day in Mr. Cooke's law office.

Mr. Cooke had given me an hour's dictation the first thing one morning. He was leaving town and wanted the letters done as quickly as possible. Halfway through the transcribing, one of the other lawyers in the office rushed up with some dictation he had to have typed by noon. The third lawyer in the firm, at this juncture, finished interviewing a client for whom he wanted, immediately, the details of the case typed out.

The result of all this rush was that Mr. Cooke's letters did not make the mail, and I was completely upset and troubled. In my own mind, I was accusing each of the men of being quite inconsiderate, and I was obviously annoyed all day.

I told the whole story to Father FitzGerald when I called at the rectory that evening for direction (and for the sympathy I really wanted—even more than the direction). I was completely taken aback by Father's answer.

"*You* are the inconsiderate one, Cecelia," he said. "What you felt was heroic patience on your part was actually imprudence

and poor judgment, and as a result you lost your mental poise."
I was silent.

Father went on. "How can you expect anyone to be cognizant of
a preexisting obligation unless you make it known? . . . If you had
politely and calmly told the second gentleman what Mr. Cooke
had already told you to do and left the decision and responsibility
entirely up to him, you would not have lost your peace of mind—
likewise with the third gentleman. . . . In trying to oblige, you
neglected to use your common sense. No one will ever expect the
impossible of you. Next time you are in a situation like that keep
your balance; take it for granted that others will listen to reason,
if you state the case calmly."

Later on in the law office and after I entered the cloister, I found
that Father was right. People are ready to listen to reason when
we are calm ourselves.

With the slow and painful but steady progress in the submission
of myself I began to feel a corresponding liberation. I saw more
clearly now that everything done through obedience and love
had great value regardless of how the act turned out. If I were unable to do the task as perfectly as I desired, it was perfect in God's
eyes if I could truthfully say I had done my best. Obedience was
conquering gradually much of self-love, pride, and my innate
longing for honor and attention—all of which had been militating
against the love of God and my growth in the spiritual life.

I resolved that once the vow of obedience had been made, it
would cover every act of my life, and I would not rebel, even in a
small detail, against the authority to which I bound myself or
against the perfection I professed to pursue. I would take nothing
back. I would abandon myself completely to Divine Providence.

Love makes obedience a joy. I wanted the kind of love that
Jesus bore His Heavenly Father, the type that would spontane-
ously take the form of total surrender to grace in the most minute

acts of the day: "Since thou hast been faithful over little things. . . ."

I wanted, like Saint Thérèse, to be able to say on my deathbed that God would do my will in Heaven since I had not done my own will on earth.

We are often asked if this type of obedience can be learned by the modern girl (about whom, I understand, it is a commonplace to say she is independent and self-indulgent). People wonder how she can submit herself to the rule and discipline of a monastery such as Carmel.

It may be that other societies have observed some noticeable differences between the present-day postulant and the one of twenty-five years ago. Frankly, I do not think the modern girl is any different from the girl I was. Mother Teresa, who has been observing girls entering Carmel for the past forty-five years, feels the same.

From my experience as Novice Mistress in our New York Carmel and here in Oklahoma, I do not think that the girl who applies for admission into the cloister today resembles in any way the worldly type of girl about whom we hear so much in our letters and from visitors to the speak room. We do find, I think, that the modern girl on entering Carmel is more apt to ask questions and reason out the purposes for acts. All of this, of course, we try to encourage, realizing that reason is not to be stifled, nor judgment discarded. The young people we have seen in Carmel seem to have more urgency, it is true, to do the act, a swifter pace; but, despite the rumors we have heard, we find them docile, and extremely generous with God, and mature.

We have a young professed nun here in our Oklahoma City Carmel who exemplifies the so-called modern girl and her approach to, and adaptation in, Carmel.

Perhaps it would be better to use Sister's own words and follow her steps as she advanced toward God and His Church and finally into the cloister. Shortly after her conversion to Catholicism a newspaper story appeared in her own words. Here is a part of that story:

*"I am a convert. I am more grateful for the gift of Faith than for anything that ever happened to me.*

*"I suppose I was a typical example of modern youth, who thought that religion was for a few pious old souls, but unnecessary for me.*

*"In high school, after hearing that man evolved from monkey, I decided that the Bible was wrong and my biology teacher right and I ceased to believe in much of anything. I could never completely deny the existence of a Supreme Being, for the magnificence of the heavens forced me to admit that Someone had to be responsible for their grandeur, but that is as far as I would go. I denied the existence of hell because the idea was displeasing to me. My code of ethics could be summed up in the words: 'Be fair to your fellow man.'*

*"I had been baptized an Episcopalian, but since I grew up in a small town where there was no Episcopal Church, I went to the Sunday School that most of my friends attended. Fifteen minutes' instruction on the Bible once a week really left me rather ignorant about my religion, but I was content in my ignorance.*

*"After high school and evolution came college and atheism. Two English professors in whose classes I enrolled were professed atheists and informed their students of the fact. I remember one instructor gave us a list of what he considered the ten best books that had been written in the last twenty-five years. I do not remember all of the titles, but I do remember that those I read were full of filth. He said this was 'life' and we must face it. He said the period of romanticism had passed. Life was bad and we must realize it, or we were just dreamers and idealists. Knowing no*

*better, I naturally accepted his words. He was the teacher, after all.*

"*The Episcopal rector lived across the street from where I was staying, and each Sunday evening many students met at his house. I told him one evening that I had come to doubt much of the Bible, and to my utter surprise he said that I did not have to believe it, if I found it too difficult. Certain parts, he said, had been disproved by science and we need believe only what was reasonable to us.*

"*Another time I asked him why, in the Apostles' Creed, we said: 'I believe in the Holy Catholic Church,' when we were Protestants? He told me that Catholic meant universal, and 'ours was a universal Church.' . . .*

"*I attended church on Sundays rather regularly, but I did not know why, except that the beauty of the services and a certain reverence was there that I did not experience in other Protestant churches—but still something was lacking.*

"*After college I found a job in the city and religion was practically forgotten. I went to church when I was in the mood, but I was seldom in the mood.*

"*One day at the office a discussion on religion came up. Two of the girls in the group were Baptists, one was a Catholic and myself. I aired my views and felt very broad-minded and superior. . . . When we resumed work the Catholic girl told me she had a book she would like me to read. I knew little about Catholicism and was curious . . . all I had ever heard about that Church was bad and I wanted to see if it could be quite that black. She gave me Arnold Lunn's* Now I See.

"*Lunn deflated my ego in a hurry . . . he destroyed my belief in evolution and once again gave me respect for the Bible. He appealed to my reason instead of my emotions. Though his logic was convincing, I was not quite sure. I kept on reading under the direction of my Catholic friend: Newman's* Apologia, *the lives of several saints, books on the history and doctrine of the Catholic religion. I read every book she gave me and any others I could find that had to do with the Catholic Church.*

*". . . Christ became a real person. My life began to have a purpose. . . . I had long ago forgotten how to pray. Again it was my Catholic friend that came to my rescue. She gave me a rosary and taught me how to pray it. I had not been able to find courage to pray to God after I had been such a cynic, but it was not as hard to take my prayers to the Virgin Mary. She had been a human being and I could approach her better. My own mother had died when I was three years old, but now I discovered that God had given me a Mother in Mary. . . . I just talked to my Mother Mary, and I soon found that I could talk to God. Being able to pray again helped, but the battle was not yet over.*

*"Like Francis Thompson in 'The Hound of Heaven,' I was afraid 'lest, having Him, I must have naught beside.' Could I accept God and His Church and be true to it? It meant giving up my old life and taking a new life about which I knew very little. It meant facing the ridicule of Godless friends. It meant explaining to relatives who, I knew, hated the Catholic Church. It meant accepting the Church and God for life.*

*"Did I have the courage to become a Catholic? Would I ever be ashamed, as Peter was, and deny Christ? . . . I wavered for some time, but finally my Catholic friend took me to Mass and to meet a priest and I began to take instructions. I also attended the evening devotions that preceded the doctrine class.*

*"One evening at the Benediction of the Blessed Sacrament, I was suddenly sure. That White Disc that looked like bread was God. I had found God's Church. I was certain. Tears of gratitude filled my eyes. . . . How could I ever have doubted? What a fool I had been. From that moment I knew I must become a Catholic. What difference did it make what friends and relatives said? I had found God! A great calm came over my troubled soul. . . . I was ready to accept the 'Faith of My Forefathers!'*

"*It took several more months to complete my instructions . . . in church I had still to watch others receiving the Sacraments . . . and I longed for the day when I might be permitted this privilege; meanwhile I attended Sunday Mass and kept the Friday abstinence.*

"*I went ahead with my reading for I knew there would be much explaining to do and I wanted to be able to answer the questions of my non-Catholic friends intelligently.*

"*As a Catholic I have found certainty and peace. I thank God every day and pray for strength to be worthy of this greatest of gifts. Soon after my Baptism, I was received into the Legion of Mary, which gave me a better chance to work for my Mother Mary, for the true Church and for God.*

"*One day soon after my reception into the Catholic Church, one of my relatives came to see me and tell me how I had disgraced the family by becoming a Catholic. He suggested that I give up the Church. Could I possibly give up what had changed my life and given me the peace and certainty I found nowhere else? The answer was emphatically no! I had only now found the pearl of great price, for no man would I cast it away.*

"*I had lost so much time, I want to make amends. I know what a Godless existence is and I want no more of it. I have found a Mother, where I never knew a Mother's love. . . . I now know my Saviour, whom I had thoughtlessly crucified in the past. When I think of the agony He suffered for me, the crucifixion with its three long hours on the cross, could I crucify Him again? No! Never!*"

The young agnostic college student who found peace of soul in the Church followed the graces that came to her. Because it is an interesting example of how a modern girl finds her way to the cloister, you will not, I trust, object if I interrupt my own story for a moment longer to have her tell you in her own words how Carmel came to her and how she came to Carmel.

*"At first [she says] I thought God, through His Church, was asking a lot to request me to attend Mass every Sunday and Holy-day. But when I began to understand more deeply the things of God, Sunday Mass was not enough. Soon I found myself getting up every morning and hurrying out to early Mass.*

*"The closest place for me to hear Mass was a nearby hospital conducted by the Franciscan Sisters. As I slipped into the back pew a few minutes before six each morning I found myself staring at the backs of about forty nursing Sisters. The sameness and monotony of those forty religious habits was the very antithesis of the rugged individualism I once so deeply cherished. Here were nuns who had freely given up the one thing I had thought most sacred. It started me thinking still more seriously to try to discover what God really wished me to do. After many months of prayer and prudent counsel it seemed certain that God was calling me to the religious life.*

*"When I was baptized I had taken Saint Thérèse as my patron saint, principally because there seemed to be a number of popular books written about her and I wanted a patron whom I could get to know. At that time I had no special love for her nor did I have any thought about the Carmelite Order to which she belonged.*

*"My Catholic friend introduced me to a Carmelite Father who enrolled me in the brown scapular. I was now in a special way under Mary's protection. My friend also told me the importance of spiritual direction. The Discalced Carmelite Father who had enrolled me in the scapular became my director. He told me of the monthly recollection day for women conducted by the Carmelite Sisters of Saint Thérèse (non-cloistered). My friend, Catherine, explained the Catholic idea of a retreat, so I decided to try it.*

*"Saint John of the Cross would have called it spiritual glut-
tony. There was so much that was new and I wanted it all at once!*

*"There are no accidents with God. Could all of this be another
instance of Saint Thérèse keeping her promise: 'I will spend my
heaven doing good upon earth'? My next step was to visit the
Discalced Carmelite nuns . . . speaking to the nuns began to
awaken in me the desire of giving up my theory of 'rugged individualism' to Our Blessed Mother in Carmel. This was not easy.*

*"It seemed there was still too much of the world clinging to me.
I had been keeping steady company with a wonderful boy and we
had made tentative plans to marry. This, of course, had to be
broken. I wanted somehow to show to God my gratitude for His
great goodness and mercy toward me. The solitude of Carmel was
the only way I could see of giving God all in return for the All He
had given me.*

*"After a wait that seemed to me interminable I was at last ad-
mitted to Carmel and since then I have never ceased to realize
how good God has been to lead me through such dangerous paths
into the peace and solitude, the joy and certitude of the cloister."*

It is readily understood why Carmel with its life of solitude
presents a mystery to many who have not approached our monasteries. Even for many of our friends it is difficult to understand
fully the purpose of our life. It is indeed "a trackless desert, a water-
less land which only slowly surrenders its secrets." There were,
even after a year in the cloister, many things I could not understand. No doubt it was because of my impetuous nature that the
"secrets" for me seemed to surrender themselves with tortuous
slowness.

Carmel is a rigid discipline, and constantly—until our dying
breath—shall we be obliged to overcome our natural inclinations
to indulge self. Even today I had to overcome my inclination to

delay answering a bell. But oh the "tranquillity of order" and the sense of the presence of God that follow restraint!

Cadets at West Point used to tell us, when I was at Ladycliff, that the exactitude with which their discipline and training are enforced often exasperates the young plebe. No carelessness is ever tolerated. That, of course, is the reason for the matchless discipline of our young military and naval officers.

It is the same here in Carmel. We must go one step further, however. A nun is obliged by her profession to keep also her interior life well disciplined; our Rule tells us that we must so regulate our exterior as to give evidence of the spiritual order within.

That is why the days of one's novitiate cannot be otherwise than difficult and trying. A great and exacting work is going on. I knew too much of the world and its distractions, too little of my Crucified Christ and His love for me. It takes time to appreciate the pivotal point of the Gospel teaching: "Take up my yoke upon you and learn of me because I am meek and humble of heart: and you shall find rest to your souls. For my yoke is sweet and my burden light." His yoke is indeed sweet and His burden light, and these words will forever remain true for all of us, inside or outside the cloister.

Before I could find God dwelling deep in my soul, I had to discipline it and empty it of all that did not pertain to Him. . . . "O thou soul," says Saint John of the Cross, "most beautiful of creatures, who longest to know where thy Beloved is, thou art thyself that very tabernacle where He dwells."

What progress I was able to make in the way of perfection was due, I acknowledge, next to the grace of God, to Mother Prioress, to my Novice Mistress, and to the direction of my confessor. They patiently taught me to overcome my selfish, natural inclinations, to want to do things which I found hardest to do, and they helped me to still the silly murmurings of the world's wise sanity, so that I might listen to the stillness of God within me.

At the end of my novitiate I could, in all truth, repeat the words of Carmel's poet nun: "There is nothing in the valley, or house, or street worth turning back for—Nothing!"

*Chapter 10*

# Sorrowful, Yet Always
# Rejoicing     †2 COR. 6:10

Wᴴᴇɴ a nun goes blissfully along for months on end without any trials or problems we suspect that there is something wrong somewhere.

The interior struggles I experienced during my novitiate assured me somewhat that there was nothing wrong with me, at least on that score. But in addition to the trials of aridity in prayer, and the breaking of my will and molding it in obedience, I suffered a great deal physically as well. "O my Lord, how true it is that he who shall render Thee a service is often rewarded by a great cross! If only we knew it at the time."

Early one morning long before dawn, I awoke with a severe pain in my side and became violently nauseated. Realizing it was the time of the Great Silence, I foolishly thought it would be wrong to leave the cell to summon aid. So I resigned myself to wait until the rising signal sounded. Unable to lie down, I huddled in a corner of the cell in pain, the like of which I had never before experienced. I thought it was the end, so I tried to remain in God's presence and to offer my suffering to Him in union with the Passion of My Beloved for the souls of the world. This calmed me somewhat, and the pain became less unbearable. "Suffering borne by two is almost joy."

It was a long night, and I was able to offer each hour of it for some vital intention: for those who were dying that night, so many without the aid of priest or Sacraments; for all the priests in the world; in reparation for all the offenses committed against the Divine Majesty; and in reparation for my own offenses against the Divine Majesty.

The Infirmarian came to our cell shortly after the rising signal and relieved the pain with some medicine and hot applications. I felt much better.

But the next morning I suffered the same intense pain, and the illness continued with me for a long time. Physical exercise was one of the remedies prescribed; so a very energetic novice of the athletic type was assigned to give me daily setting-up exercises. She entered upon her assignment with all the enthusiasm of a swimming instructor getting his protégé ready for a Channel swim. And all this was done outdoors in silence on practically an empty stomach. What benefit it did my physical ailment I'll never know; I do know it worked havoc with my interior peace, that is, until I learned to accept it with complete submission; then it did become of some value to me—spiritually at least.

What bothered me more than anything else during these months was the thought that this sickness would be interpreted as a sign I had no vocation. Any novice who frequently becomes ill and must be excused from the community prayers and penances is naturally suspected of not having the physical stamina needed for our life. That I understood clearly. Also I understood clearly that I would do wrong to feign perfect health when a serious malady afflicted me.

Mother Prioress reassured me somewhat when she said that in her opinion the trouble was in large part due to fatigue and the strangeness of the life—adjustment was hard for me. "Do not think too much about your body, dear; try to forget yourself." I tried, but the body, in no uncertain terms, kept reminding me that there was something wrong with it.

It was an upsetting dilemma—to speak and (as I feared) be sent home, or to be silent and deceive the Community on the threshold of my Profession.

Chanting Matins on the evening before the day we commemorate Saint Aloysius, I pleaded with the youthful Jesuit Saint to cure me before my Profession or obtain for me the grace to die before I had to leave Carmel.

During the discipline which followed Matins, the pain returned with excruciating intensity. That night I passed a kidney stone, the cause of all the trouble! The doctor came and assured the Prioress that my health was perfect. I could not contain the joy that overflowed my heart.

Right here let me clear up a possible misunderstanding. When I say "the doctor came," this did not mean that the "cloister was broken." There are in each Carmel designated people who may, for certain obvious reasons, enter the enclosure.

Here is how it works: For anyone, priest or layman, to enter the enclosure of Carmel, very special permission from the Bishop of the diocese must be obtained. At the beginning of each year the Prioress records the names of those whose presence she thinks might, on occasion, be necessary in the cloister. For example, the names of a doctor, carpenter, plumber, and electrician are submitted to the local Bishop for his approval. In an emergency the approval may be presumed.

When the doctor, for instance, is called to visit a sick nun, he is met at the enclosure door by two nuns with faces veiled. The door is opened, and after he enters, it is shut and bolted again. One nun, ringing a small bell, leads the way to the infirmary. The bell warns the other nuns of the presence of an outsider within the enclosure, and each nun must then keep her face veiled or remain in her cell. The same procedure is followed, of course, whenever essential workmen are called into the enclosure. Two nuns ordinarily remain with the person wherever he goes within the cloister.

Occasionally a workman may be left alone at his task, as happened one day when a husky painter was engaged on our side of the turn near the front door. Always there is a nun assigned to answer the doorbell. From inside the enclosure she pushes an electric buzzer which automatically releases the door, permitting the visitor to enter the monastery.

(For the benefit of those who have never visited a Carmelite monastery where there are no extern sisters to attend the door, or for those who have never been to a Carmelite monastery at all, the turn is a revolving cylinder four feet high, two or three feet in diameter, set in an aperture in the wall. Half the cylinder is cut away; when the turn is closed, the solid half faces the outside; to open it, the nun releases the latch and spins it around so that the visitor may put on it his message or whatever he may be bringing to the monastery.)

Well, this particular day when the front doorbell rang and before the Turn Sister arrived, the helpful painter, from inside the enclosure, released the door and admitted a very good friend of ours to the turn. She expected, of course, to hear the gentle "Deo gratias" of the Turn Sister. The woman told us later that it took her ten minutes to get over the shock she received when the invisible workman's deep, bass voice came booming through the turn: "What can I do for you?"

Most workmen who enter the enclosure accept our silence and our veiled faces, even though they may not understand it; they feel that there must be a reason for it, since it is one of our customs. Occasionally a man will enter who we know is upset by the atmosphere because he gives the impression that he can't get out fast enough. In fact, we heard of one such workman who had to take the rest of the day off "to recover" after his first experience in the cloister!

Before we were distracted by my attempt to explain the mystery of the turn, we were talking about an illness I had and about my fear that it might be a reason for refusing to permit me to make my fast-approaching Profession.

However, I am happy to report that at the conclusion of my year's novitiate I was permitted to take my temporary vows of obedience, chastity, and poverty for three years. In Carmel, we remain in the novitiate under the direction of the Mistress for at least two of these years. With us the Profession is a family ceremony in the sense that no one, Bishop, priest or relative, is invited to attend. The simple, but deeply impressive ceremony was conducted in the Chapter Room. Kneeling before the Prioress and solemnly placing my folded hands in hers, I made my promise to God to obey and to remain chaste and to remain poor.

At any time during the postulancy and novitiate and also at the expiration of my temporary vows, I was quite free to leave the convent and return to the world. That is why in each ceremony the presiding priest or prelate or prioress asks the question, "Do you do this freely?"

These are years of "testing" one's vocation. Formerly the "perpetual" vows were taken after only one year of novitiate, but now the process is somewhat more complicated, and as many as six or seven years may be necessary before a nun is allowed to make her Profession of Solemn Vows by which she dedicates herself completely and irrevocably to God.

Let me remind the reader that during the postulancy no promise or vow is taken at any time. A postulant is for all practical purposes still a "secular," and she may leave quite freely at any time, or she might be asked to leave by her superiors at any time should they consider her unsuitable for the life.

During our canonical year of novitiate the nun is considered a "religious." The Rule is no longer mitigated for her as it is for postulants; it must be observed in all its rigor. And because it is important to discover early the disposition of the novice and her qualifications for the life, she is considered still "on trial," and often put to the test so that those in authority may judge rightly concerning her.

I had come through the first two periods of my training fairly well and had taken my temporary vows.

During the three following years I had ample opportunity to prove to myself that the cloister was what I wished and also to prove to my superiors that I was fitted for the life.

At the end of that period, my vows expired and I was free to leave the convent and return to the world, a thought which came to me seriously only once, as I shall presently explain.

My wish, of course, was to persevere in Carmel, and in due time I made my final vows alone at the ceremony of Perpetual Profession in the Chapter Room before the members of the Community. A few days later at a public ceremony, I received the black veil and had the privilege of seeing my friends again, as I had when I received the holy habit. The black veil is a sign of complete renunciation and self-effacement; it signified for me the fidelity that I was to show my Beloved Bridegroom. My face, eyes, and whole being were to be now for Him alone.

Now I was bound for life. (If, for some extraordinary reason, and the cases are very exceptional, it should become impossible for a nun to continue in the convent, she can apply to the proper ecclesiastical authorities for a dispensation from her vows.)

I have taken the time to run through quickly the steps a nun takes prior to her perpetual, voluntary offering of herself in religion, because I want to make it abundantly clear that we are free to enter or not to enter, and once within we are free, after tasting and testing the life, to leave should we find it not compatible with our disposition or if we feel after consultation and prayer that we do not, for any reason whatsoever, belong.

Serious and continual illness, for obvious reasons, would be normally an indication that a person was not physically strong enough to follow Carmel's exacting schedule of prayer, penance, and fasting. So naturally I was anxious about my vocation when suddenly I became ill again six months after my first vows.

There was a recurrence of renal colic, and other abdominal disorders, all of which were aggravated by severe migraine headaches which forced me to bed again and required exemptions from the Rule of the Order. How easy it is to wish for suffering when one has none, but how hard to bear with it joyfully when it comes.

Fortunately, at this time, a Baltimore-trained nurse applied to our New York Carmel for entrance. Although we had not our full quota, we were nevertheless overcrowded; still, Mother Prioress accepted her. She was, as her name Dorothy signified, a "gift of God."

With unselfish devotion she watched over me day and night. Very efficiently she made out her daily charts for the attending physician. She had me complaining of everything: "Patient complains of pain in the back. . . . Patient complains of headaches. . . ." I thought I was suffering in heroic silence, but no one who took literally the nurse's report would think so!

One day Dorothy explained to me how it was so easy for her to be patient toward the sick: "All sick," she said, "are the suffering Christ, and I try to be for them the compassionate Mother of Sorrows."

It was she who reminded me to unite my sufferings with those of Our Lord. Perhaps the Heavenly Father looking at me in pain might recognize His Beloved Son in me "made conformable to His death."

When I thought of what my Beloved had done for me I could not logically shrink from attempting to suffer something for Him —to spend myself, wear myself out, to return in some measure His gift.

Every woman is capable of withstanding deep suffering. That is part of her vocation. Most psychologists, I believe, admit the superiority of the "weaker" sex in this regard.

But if God asks silent patience of all women in bearing their crosses, He has a right to expect a religious to be ready for a literal daily carrying of the cross of suffering. That, after all, is not surprising: "If anyone will come after Me, let him deny himself, take up his cross daily and follow Me." "The servant is not greater than the Master." And I believe, on the whole, doctors who have treated nuns agree that they have some extra source of strength in their suffering that enables them to endure with more than ordinary patience and in many cases with sincere joy.

I know that this is true in Carmel. For the most part the nuns must be cautioned about hiding pain because of the possibility of endangering their health permanently. Our willingness to endure proves the sincerity of our immolation. As Saint Teresa reminds us, Force yourselves to suffer whatever God wishes. Any other way of yielding Him our will is like offering someone a jewel, begging him to accept it, and holding it fast when he puts out his hand to take it. The Saint, in her practical manner, puts it this way, too: Remember how many poor people are ill and have no one to whom they may complain—poverty and ease do not go together. Many married women do not tell their husbands all their trials and problems so as not to distress them. We are free from many worldly problems: we should suffer more, and suffer silently.

We are reminded often of the crucifix we put to our lips as the enclosure door shuts out the world: "Passio Christi, conforta me!" A nun is told to prepare for suffering when she enters Carmel as Mary did when she accepted her honor as Christ's Mother. She knew her future and her Son's: "Be it done unto me according to Thy will."

I began to understand what the plain, wooden cross meant in our cell. I was to offer myself to be crucified on that cross: "If we suffer with Him, we shall also reign with Him."

Somehow it became clear to me that Our Lord could make use of even my sufferings, the splitting headaches, the nauseating pain in the side, the constant fatigue, if only I could get strength to endure in patience. After all, I reminded myself, I had asked for suffering, not realizing at the time the presumption of my request. I wanted my Beloved to feel free to ask anything He wished of me, to feel that I was completely at His disposal.

I had been warned that in Carmel God has something more than peace and joy in store for us: "For each He has a special cross."

It began to look as though my cross was to be bodily suffering.

A nun here in our Oklahoma City Carmel who has suffered far more than I perhaps shall ever suffer receives the great grace to be overwhelmed with happiness in her excruciating pain. She has become a mystery and an inspiration to every doctor and nurse who have seen her.

I wanted that grace too.

My faith told me that what Mother Teresa said was true: if I would but have confidence, I would understand that God is my Father—He will not let us suffer more than we can bear, physically or spiritually—that "He fits the back to the burden" and "tempers the wind to the shorn lamb."

But at that time I could not appreciate fully that the deeper I drank of the chalice the sweeter the cup would become.

If my attitude toward suffering during the early years of my cloistered life was imperfect, I could not lay the blame at the door of my Novice Mistress or Mother Prioress.

"The aim of our desire must be not rest, but suffering."

The theory had been explained to me in all its lofty and practical detail. As I lay in the infirmary bed, I could recall the words of Mother Prioress: Sickness can be a great blessing; it has aided many Saints to reach a high degree of sanctity. It is one of the best means of purification. In the ransom of souls it has a purchasing power beyond human calculation.

But she had taught me also that health is a great treasure, too, and that each nun in Carmel is to safeguard it carefully. With the precious gift of health, one is ordinarily better able to serve the Master. So every reasonable means, including medical help, is used to preserve one's health and life, even in the cloister.

Often the torment came to my mind that possibly I was coddling my body. I thought of fathers of families in the world who forced themselves in illness to carry on their work to support their families. Or mothers of families, too poor to call in assistance in time of illness, obliged to care for their homes and children. Saint Teresa knew that our poor weak human nature tempts us to pity and indulge the body should the spirit lag at all; and she spoke out with some humorous exaggeration against the nun who seeks dispensations from the Rule and who stays away from choir "one day because her head aches, another because it has ached, and three more days so that it will not any longer ache!"

Would the Community think that I was overconcerned about my body? I recalled Saint Teresa's words: it is a great imperfection to be always complaining of trifling ailments. "This body has one fault, that the more people pamper it, the more its wants are made known." The Saint of Avila had this final word for her Sisters on the subject of illness: "You who are free from the great troubles of the world, learn to suffer a little for the love of God without everyone's knowing it."

These words kept haunting me, and I wished to force myself to get up and join the nuns at the Divine Office and other Community exercises. But now I was under obedience to remain flat on my back. Perhaps my outward sign of patience and resignation and joy would be a small contribution that I could make to Carmel and to souls at this time.

I prayed to my Beloved to give me the grace to be cheerful. In time of health it was easy for me to be gay—now I was put to the test.

I wanted to do His will alone. I wanted to endure in patience like the martyrs of the past and of the present. "Not my will but Thine be done." If You wish me to serve You in this way, it is all right with me: those are the words I spoke; nevertheless in my heart I was yearning for just enough strength to follow the observance. My soul had not reached the heroic attitude of Saint Gertrude, who (in answer to our Lord's words, "Do you wish for health?") replied, "I wish only for this: I desire nothing but Thy holy will."

One day I read this story about Saint Francis of Assisi, and I realized how far I was removed from the dispositions of the Saints.

Saint Francis had been suffering agonizing pains for a long period, and a Brother said to him, "Father, ask God to treat you with a little more tenderness, for His hand appears to be heavy upon you." Saint Francis answered, "Brother, listen to me. Did I not know that what you have said comes from thoughtlessness, I would never see you again, for you wish to censure what God does." After these words the Saint threw himself down and kissed the floor. He said, "My God, I thank Thee for these pains, and I beseech Thee to increase them, if it be pleasing to Thee; for I desire nothing else than to do Thy will."

What impressed me most during my first serious illness in Carmel, as it has many times since then, was the great charity practiced by the Sisters toward the sick. Literally they vie with one another to be of service, to console, and to be kind. For me it was a source of considerable embarrassment even though I realized it was Our Lord they saw and served in me; they would not leave Him neglected. "I was sick . . . and you visited Me."

But somehow the consoling visits of the Sisters, the special care given me by the postulant nurse, the soft bed and linen sheets of the infirmary seemed to disquiet rather than comfort me. Despite the clarity of the doctrine of suffering and my attempt to look upon it as the Saints and Our Lord did, still I could not find real peace and complete resignation. I was concerned about my vocation. Temptation came frequently to disturb me, to make me feel that my ill-health was a sign that I did not belong in Carmel. I was even thinking about leaving at the expiration of my vows. . . . Perhaps I had withheld some pertinent facts about my poor health before entering. . . . Returning to the world would be an even greater suffering, you should do that for your Lord. . . . Don't you see you are a burden to the other nuns? . . . You are unable to follow the observance of the Rule.

Just when I needed God's presence most, He seemed to abandon me. I weighed the matter as best I could and prayed as well as I knew how and then clearly manifested my disposition to Mother Prioress, to the Regular Confessor, and to our Higher Superior when he came for his Canonical Visitation. I had determined before I spoke that I would accept, in perfect faith, their reply as the will of God. They patiently listened to me and then unhesitatingly answered that I should put all such thoughts out of my mind once and for all; that without a doubt I was where God wanted me to be. That was the end of that.

Since then I have learned that such abandonment is not unusual in the spiritual life—whether in the monastery or in the world. A longing loneliness set in, and I know now that such is the price all must pay who wish to do the Master's will. Did He not experience it Himself? "My God, My God, why hast Thou forsaken Me?" And He was innocent of all imperfection.

In the *Spiritual Canticle* Saint John of the Cross teaches us what this abandonment is. He himself had experienced it. People in the world can appreciate it—parents tragically separated from their children, lovers who are parted for a time, those who give themselves completely to God and who know the anguish of desolation. "Whither hast Thou hidden Thyself, and hast left me, O Beloved, to my sighing? Thou didst flee like the hart having wounded me. I went out after Thee calling and Thou wast gone. Quench Thou my griefs, since none suffices to remove them, and let mine eyes behold Thee, since Thou art their light and for Thee alone I wish to have them."

"A Carmelite's life is supposed to be a real martyrdom," Mother Teresa said. "Your harvest of crucifying pain can equal the merit of a martyrdom by blood—if you are able to accept it in the spirit of the martyrs."

How clear this has become to me since then—not only in my own life, but in the lives of other nuns whom I have watched. They could walk their road to Golgotha without detour or false turn—a drop-by-drop giving of their blood. One nun in particular comes to my mind at this moment; she could bear life's trials with a charming patience and meet each suffering with a smile. And when that goes on day after day, year after year, all, I think, agree it takes more courage than facing a firing squad.

After making me feel how far my feeble efforts to endure were from the patient joy and silent suffering of the Saints, as was her custom Mother told me not to be discouraged if I found it hard to refrain from complaining. "Even the greatest Saints at times expressed to God and complained to Him about the feelings in their troubled souls." That consoled me very much.

Then she pointed out the prudence and balance that we see in Saint Thérèse and that is so much to be desired. The Little Flower, wasted with tuberculosis, bore the damp cold of the long Normandy winters—as indeed she bore every pain and inconvenience —with heroic silence. But when, under obedience, in her *Autobiography* she wrote about those winters, she said with human frankness, "I felt like dying in them." Then she added this very wise and practical suggestion for her superiors: "It would be prudent to take note of the difference of climate and temperature when applying the Rule." Saint Thérèse sounded to me like a very sturdy Little Flower when I heard those words—and a very human one, too.

At another time one of the nuns recounted for me a rather amusing story about Saint Teresa of Avila, which illustrated again the human side of the Saints and was intended to show me that my tears were not to discourage me.

Toward the end of her life the Saint was making a long, hard journey from Avila to Burgos to establish the seventeenth monastery of the Reform. She was crippled with arthritis and fever. It rained continuously for three days, and the roads were muddy and flooded. At one critical moment Teresa jumped from the falling oxcart and landed sprawled in the mud. She had reached the end of her endurance. Looking up toward the weeping skies, she in tears complained to her Master: "Lord, amidst so many ills this comes on top of all the rest!" The Voice answered her: "Teresa, this is how I treat My friends."

In her practical way the Saint replied, "Alas, Lord, that is why You have so few!"

Our Lord treats His friends with suffering because He wants us to be like Himself.

Yes, I am aware of the fact that I speak of a mystery—great doctors and philosophers have filled volumes with the theme. Had I not drunk a little of the chalice of pain, I would not so much as mention here the eternal problem. I did not intend to attempt to solve the mystery philosophically for you but merely to show you how one's attitude toward it is changed and perfected in Carmel.

Now, it is different. Though I retain some of my physical ills, I see more clearly why it must be so. Are there not two great mysteries, both revolving about the subject of suffering? These mysteries move toward each other from opposite directions—nonsuffering Divinity must be united with pain in order to become like unto us who suffer; the suffering creatures must be united with pain in order to become like unto God.

It is that simple.

When this is understood, the rest is easy; when it is not understood, agony unbearable results. And the greatest mystery is how a person without faith can endure at all. How can such a one suffer? What a tragedy, their hopeless wait for death! Their heartbeat hammering the nails into the coffin of their despair.

Many times since coming to Carmel I have waited for death, too —much as I waited for the letter of acceptance from Mother Prioress before coming into the cloister. For me, as for everyone who loves Our Lord, it was a joyous longing. I was assured of an eternal perfection, as my glaring imperfections were being burned away in the crucible of pain. "Life is to live in such a way as not to be afraid of death."

All who are in despair should put their uncertain feet upon this road. Its goal is the goal of all the world: joy.

## Chapter 11

# Having Nothing, Yet
# Possessing All Things

† 2 COR. 6:10

Oᴜʀ little New York convent on Gun Hill Road had reached its quota of twenty-one. A new property had been purchased on University Avenue. Tentative plans had been drawn up by Maginnis & Walsh for the construction of a permanent monastery—the magnificent gift of an unknown benefactor in the city.

Then it was that Bishop Kelley of Oklahoma City expressed a desire to have a Carmel in his diocese. The Bishop had been reading, with delight and edification, the *Autobiography* of the great Saint Teresa when the inspiration came to him.

The Reverend Vincent Martinez, O.C.D., Provincial of the Discalced Carmelite Fathers of Oklahoma and an intimate friend of Bishop Kelley, visited our New York monastery shortly after the triennial elections had left Mother Teresa free, and he said to her, "Mother, now you must come to Oklahoma!" The Bishop lost no time sending us a formal invitation in writing.

Bishop Kelley had asked that Mother Teresa be the foundress of the new Carmel. So Mother, in spite of poor health, was to start out again to make another foundation just when her long-cher-

142

ished plans for the permanent monastery in New York were about to mature. But that made no difference to Our Mother. The work of God had to go on. Willingly she left to the newly elected Prioress, Mother Marie, the responsibility of carrying out the plans for the construction of the new building. The joy of seeing fulfilled the dream of so many years—she would leave that too.

The chapter nuns (that is, all the choir nuns with Final Vows) were asked to pray for the foundation and to weigh the matter before God. As is customary, the proposition was put to a vote. It was enthusiastically approved. Then volunteers were called for. Weeks later, when the names of the nuns chosen to make the foundation were read out in the solemn Chapter assembly, I do not know which was greater—the joy of the five who were going with Mother or the sorrow of those who were being left behind.

We are sometimes asked how we move from one monastery to another without being seen. Some have even thought we go by moving van! No, we travel from place to place in a quite normal fashion; and we do not have to veil our faces on these rare occasions.

A small group of relatives and close friends gathered in Grand Central Station that never-to-be-forgotten day of departure in 1939. I was confined to bed in the French Hospital at the time and was happy to be spared the heart-rending farewells.

The Carmelite Fathers were at the Oklahoma station to meet the nuns when they arrived and were as anxious as the Bishop to have their Sisters join them in spreading the Kingdom of God in the Southwest and, by their presence and prayers, aid and encourage them in their difficult and often discouraging work in this mission territory.

In 1939, Oklahoma City had only seven parishes, only two of which had permanent churches. The Bishop was in the midst of an extensive building program, and the small number of Catholics—only 2 per cent of the total population—was already under a heavy financial burden. Yet, in spite of this, Carmel was welcomed with open arms, and as soon as the people realized that we live almost entirely on alms, they proved themselves very charitable and generous.

It was good Father Vincent, the Carmelite Provincial, who purchased a residence for the Nuns on 18th Street, with the understanding that they would reimburse the province when and as they could. The erection of the wall and the work of renovation were not completed as promised when the nuns arrived at the appointed time; so until the house was ready for occupancy they remained at Villa Teresa, the mother house of the active Carmelite Sisters in the city, to whom we can never be sufficiently grateful for their warmhearted and sisterly hospitality.

Much as they enjoyed the welcome of their Sisters at the Villa, the nuns were, of course, eager to be again in their enclosure and to be able to follow every point of monastic observance.

The day for the opening and First Mass was finally fixed. There was no rest for anyone the night before. The carpenters having been late in leaving the premises, everyone else's work was consequently held up; it was way after dark before the artist was free to finish gold-leafing the chapel altar; and Mother Teresa is still talking about the patience and graciousness of a non-Catholic businessman in the city—Jim Longmire of Harbour-Longmire's —who, after having waited for the others to finish, worked with his crew on the drapes behind the altar until midnight—and then sent no bill!

After the last workman left, half the Community, with brooms and dusters and assisted by several kind and generous ladies, made everything spick-and-span; the other nuns were busy decorating the sanctuary and doing the hundred and one things that have to be left until the last minute. When they were finally finished, the Chapel was indeed a fitting place for His Majesty who within a few hours was to take up His sacramental abode there.

Whenever Saint Teresa made a foundation and had provided in a new place a tabernacle for Our Lord, she felt she had achieved a tremendous victory over the forces of evil. And so she had. Only in Heaven shall we appreciate what it means to a particular vicinity to have Christ, our Victim in the Holy Eucharist, offering Himself to the Father every minute of the day and night and making intercession for us without ceasing. Our age has seen great destruction, and greater destruction threatens, even total annihilation of the world; yet we are able to face this without fear—yes, even with confidence and serenity; Our Blessed Lord is with us and will be "even to the consummation of the world." As long as there is a priest to say Mass, Our Lord will be present among us, "Jesus Christ yesterday, today and the same forever," wielding the same power over the hearts of men that He wielded when He trod this earth in His mortal body. Countless are the souls who are drawn to God through the presence of Jesus in the Blessed Sacrament. At His feet, for some reason which they are unable to explain, they are able to pour their hearts out in prayer, and they go away comforted and strengthened and with new energy to face the burdens of life. They somehow understand that in this great Gift of God we have a unique power not to be found anywhere outside the Church. How well Saint Augustine described this great Gift when he wrote, "God, all-wise though He be, knows nothing better; all-powerful though He be, He can do nothing more excellent; infinitely rich though He be, He has nothing more precious to give, than the Eucharist."

For three days before the First Mass and the Canonical Sealing of the Enclosure, the monastery was open to the public. Visitors of all denominations came by the thousands. Since ours was the only cloister in the state and since our manner of life was entirely new to the people, they had numerous—frequently amusing—questions to ask as they were accompanied from room to room by several of the nuns appointed for this. Catholics and non-Catholics alike showed genuine pleasure at having Carmel in their midst. Only one man voiced any objection. He lived in the vicinity and said he was going to bring "the case" to court!

A beautiful article from the gifted pen of Bishop Kelley appeared in the paper encouraging the people of the state to write to his "praying nuns" whenever they felt the need of special prayer. Many letters of petition came to the monastery, and many were the expressions of gratitude for favors received.

The nuns were not in their monastery a month when their first postulant—a girl from New York—entered. She was soon followed by several Oklahoma girls, and as time went on the cells were all occupied. Unfortunately the house on 18th Street was not large enough to hold more than thirteen. It was hard for Mother to tell so many promising applicants, "We have no room."

The size of the property did not allow for expansion; so after about ten years Mother Teresa was ordered to leave the enclosure with two nuns to look for a new site. A large solitary tract of land on the corner of Meridian and 42d Street, just at the edge of the city limits, appealed very much to her. It was already fenced and almost completely surrounded by tall trees, mostly pines and cedars. There was a four-room bungalow on the premises, and a barn several hundred feet away.

The Community went ahead and bought the property. With what? They had, thank God, paid off the debt with which they began life in Oklahoma; so they took out a mortgage on the 18th Street house and another on the new property. Within a year they were able to sell the former to advantage, pay off the mortgage there, and still have enough cash to add, in a modest way to be sure, to the bungalow on Meridian.

It was at this time that another nun and I were transferred from our New York Carmel to help out here—exactly ten years after the arrival of the original group.

There were government barracks for sale at McAlester, 150 miles away. A 30-foot piece, containing two half baths besides what could be converted into a laundry and five cells, was offered and purchased for two thousand dollars, transported to Oklahoma City, and attached to the bungalow. We ourselves were architect, contractor, and foreman all in one, and from day to day we depended upon God to give us all the needed materials and to provide the wages for the workmen. Jimmy Ranallo, a relative of one of the nuns, became, in the providence of God, a veritable Saint Joseph to us. Almost singlehanded he added room after room to the barracks as Our Lord provided the funds.

Every day Mother and several nuns would visit the site of the new monastery to direct and help with the work. Mr. Charles H. Makins, owner of a paving plant in the city, and whose pasture land adjoins our property, generously offered to give us all the concrete we needed for foundations and walks.

To let you know the extent of my knowledge of building: One day Mother said to me, "Sister Catherine, call Mr. Makins and tell him we need three *yards* of concrete this afternoon." I thought Mother was distracted, or my hearing had failed; so I asked, "Is it three tons you want, Mother?"

Finding it imperative to have more hands helping with the increasing work, Mother decided to transfer the entire community from 18th Street and not wait until everything was completed, as was originally planned.

I shall never forget that last procession with Our Lord in the Blessed Sacrament. It reminded me of the Corpus Christi processions in Catholic countries. There were three cars waiting for us outside the enclosure on 18th Street that afternoon. One of the priests, clothed with cope and humeral veil, took the ciborium from the tabernacle, got inside the first car with four other priests carrying processional torches, and led the way. The nuns, in their white mantles, followed after in the two other cars. Slowly we rode through the streets of Oklahoma, silently making the five-mile journey with His Majesty, the Lord of the Eucharist. The thought that we were privileged to be carrying in procession Him who sustains and rules the universe was breath-taking. A group of friends were at the new convent to meet us when we arrived. The Carmelite Fathers, also in white mantles, led the procession into the "chapel," where Father Evarist, O.C.D., gave Benediction before placing Our Lord in the tabernacle. The *Te Deum* was then solemnly chanted, after which Father addressed a few words to the nuns and people.

The "chapel" which Our Dear Lord entered that afternoon—a poor bare room with unpainted walls and unfinished floor—was very different from the little gem on 18th Street. But then, He was the only One who could do anything about it. We tried to make up by preparing for Him an extra-attractive dwelling within our hearts. He really is most at home in a lonely and loving heart.

"God helps those who help themselves." As the building progressed, the nuns doing all they possibly could to keep down expenses, more and more people became interested in us and eventually we were able to complete the monastery—even the Chapel.

The nuns, in the spirit of the pioneer woman, valiantly puddled the concrete, taped and plastered the sheet rock, finished the woodwork and floors, and painted the inside rooms and a good part of the outside of the monastery as well.

It looked like rain one evening; so several of us got permission to climb the ladders and prime the unpainted rafters. After a while, Mother, fearing lest we be seen from the street, called out, "Come in now, Sisters, the moon is too bright."

Everyone was amazed to see how soon the Chapel was ready for dedication. As promised years before, Jessica Dragonette, a devoted friend and benefactor, flew from New York to sing at Benediction that memorable day.

When we were in a position to receive more subjects, I, who had been told by our New York doctor that I would never be able to be up more than five hours a day, was well enough to be made Novice Mistress. Then when election time came, to give Mother Teresa a much-needed rest, the Community elected me Prioress for three years. My term of office is now happily over, and I am once again back in the ranks, my natural element.

One of the many advantages afforded by this large property on Meridian is that we now have ground enough for the hermitages which, according to Rule, are to be erected within the confines of the enclosure. To these individual hermitages the nuns may withdraw from time to time for greater solitude.

I am spending my work time this afternoon in the one farthest from the monastery. Besides being the most solitary, it happens to be the coolest. It is 103 degrees in the shade at present—almost too hot to think.

This particular hermitage was here when we bought the place. You see, this property formerly belonged to the WKY Radio Corporation, and this little 7-by-7-by-7 concrete hut was used to house the transmitter underneath one of the radio towers. It is very austere-looking. There is a small window near the ceiling, and except for the crucifix on the brick wall and the chair I am on it is utterly bare and reminds me of the caves of the ancient hermits on Mount Carmel or the prison cell of Saint John of the Cross in Toledo. Volunteer Chinese elms have sprung up on three sides and are already twice my height. They seem to be the favorite haunt of the mockingbirds.

Some fortunate souls take to poverty with the joy and confidence of a bird taking to the air. Mother Teresa is such a person. Like her patroness, the great Saint Teresa, she seems to reason somewhat like this: I have entered the service of the Master. My Master is bound—as is a master in the world—to maintain the servant while employing him, unless He Himself be reduced to poverty. But the riches of my Master can never be exhausted; therefore He is able always to take care of me in accord with His divine Justice and His paternal Providence.

Mother Teresa won't mind, I hope, if I give you one of the many examples we might use of how this theory works for her in practice.

The normal beginnings of any enterprise are as challenging as the call to battle posts, and as uncertain as the wind. Mother Teresa, who has had the experience of founding two Carmelite monasteries without material resources of any kind to begin with, knows the thrill and the challenge as well as the problems that accompany all new ventures.

As in private homes and places of business, bills arrive in monasteries too. Transforming a dwelling into a convent, needless to say, entails much work and a great deal of expense. Mother tells this story about the early days in New York City when she was transforming the original house there into a convent.

The nun whose duty it was to handle the monastery funds reported several times to Mother Teresa that she had a number of bills but no money with which to pay them. Calmly, as the deadline drew near, Mother asked for the statements; confidently she knelt down before a small statue of Saint Joseph on her office desk.

"Saint Joseph, remember we put this monastery under your protection, and you are the head of the House. You are called a 'Just Man'; now just men pay their debts!" Without further pleading, Mother carefully put the little packet of bills at the feet of Saint Joseph and went to her cell.

Next morning a total stranger, on her way to the hospital to undergo a serious operation, stopped at Carmel and left a substantial check on the turn. Besides her plea for prayers, the good woman had only one further request: since she wanted her affairs

"Speed Graphic" being passed through the turn to Mother Catherine. *Ginter Photo, Oklahoma City, Oklahoma.*

A reporter interviewing Mother Catherine. *Ginter Photo, Oklahoma City, Oklahoma.*

Mother Teresa scraping up some plaster from the new chapel floor on the day of the transfer to the new barrack monastery. *Staff Photo by A. Y. Owen, Oklahoma Publishing Company.*

A nun arranging one of the original barrack cells the day of the move. *Staff Photo by A. Y. Owen, Oklahoma Publishing Company.*

Mother Catherine writing
in barn loft.

Mother Catherine typing in
Saint Elias's Hermitage.

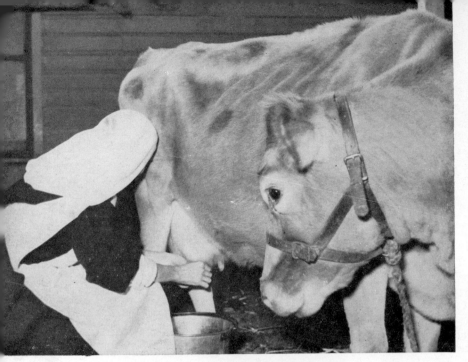

Nun milking the monastery cow.

Nuns at work in the monastery tailor shop.

Sister Cook dishing out the collation.

Nun painting in cell.

Nuns in procession outdoors.

Nuns in procession, starting from the choir.

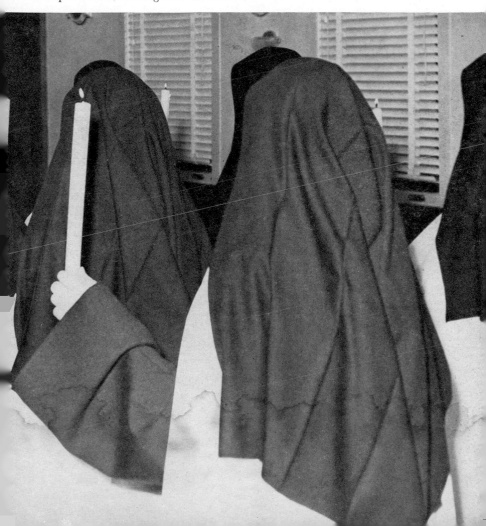

Mother Prioress presenting statue of the Infant Jesus to nun on her Day of Recollection preceding Christmas.

Nuns in procession ending at "Bethlehem" in the recreation room. A Trappist made the stable.

settled as soon as possible, would the Mother Prioress cash the
check that day. Mother Teresa readily obliged!

The holy Rule of Carmel states explicitly that the sick are to be
treated with great charity and tenderness and with every indulgence in accordance with our poverty. If, however, they lack anything during their illness, they are not to be distressed, because
they ought to be prepared for this when entering the Order. And
we are reminded that to be truly poor is to want necessaries in
time of greatest need.

To be hungry and without the means to buy food, to be sick and
unable to get medical relief, this is misery indeed; but it is a greater
affliction still to be poor and cold and ill and at the same time to
have lost even one's spiritual appetite; to be without faith in Him
who had no place whereon to lay His head. In Carmel we are often
told of those in the world who, although they may not understand the meaning of the vow of poverty, understand from bitter,
daily experience what it means to be poor. And our hearts go out
to them.

Like all religious, Carmelite nuns freely accept poverty, and we
make a solemn promise, or vow, to God that we will remain poor
in reality as well as in spirit. Like other religious, some Carmelite
nuns may have done something in renouncing worldly things—
even though many, like myself, had "nothing but nets" to leave
behind. Yet even the one who gives up the most does nothing when
we consider what Our Master renounced for us. Actually, as I hope
these few reflections on our vow of poverty will show, we who are
religious give up nothing—we merely make an exchange. In exchange for the poverty we profess and practice, we enjoy the special Providence of God and receive the infinite riches of His love.

We exchange the voice of a human suitor for the heavenly call
of Christ, the Eternal Bridegroom; the earth, the here and the
now, we exchange for the timelessness of the cloister; the tinsel

treasures and the passing pleasures of the world we exchange for the priceless spiritual riches and the incomparable joy of living for others with Christ in poverty and penance. In exchange for running after shadows, we receive the privilege of touching reality. In exchange for the possibility of success in the world, we receive the certainty of the failure of Calvary; in exchange for social position and prestige, we accept the humility and hiddenness of Carmel. In exchange for the variable affections of the world, we receive the steadfast charity of Carmel; in exchange for radios and newspapers, we have the silence of Carmel; in exchange for mad jazz and concert music, we have the Gregorian chant whose only audience is God; in exchange for cigarettes and cocktails, we have fresh, pure air to breathe and "living water" to drink. We have exchanged the rush and rumble, the headaches and heartaches, the problems and frustrations of the world for the silent solitude of the enclosure's peace; so please do not feel sorry for us—please do not pity us.

In Carmel we try to follow the example of the saintly reformer of Carmel's Rule. Teresa of Avila had no desire to tour the enchanting countries of the world; she could take far more thrilling trips around the world of the spirit. She saw, in her day, greedy conquistadors return from the New World with their ships laden with gold and silver; she returned to earth from visions of the Kingdom of Heaven laden with graces which the hull of no ship could hold. To an age that wanted to conquer new worlds by force of arms, she presented a far more grueling feat of conquest: subject your own body; conquer the impulses of your flesh; vanquish your pride and vanity.

The Saint has said that whoever despises earthly goods holds dominion over them. It is equally true that when we possess least, we are most free—free from anxieties, free from envy, free of honors. In Carmel we are free of all things that might hinder us in approaching the Poor Carpenter of Nazareth, Who we know will never fail those who have no other desire but that of pleasing Him.

Our monasteries are strict enclosures; we may not receive visitors within the cloister, nor may we visit with them except through the parlor grille. We are able therefore to keep everything within the monastery the simplest and the poorest. With the exception of the Church, there is nothing ornamental throughout the entire monastery. The straight-backed wooden chair and the small table are the only furnishing needed in our cell, outside of our bed. We need no bookshelf because the book we are reading may be placed on our table and when finished returned to the library. We need no wardrobe or closet because our change of clothing and our habit are received from the Sister whose duty it is to take charge of the common wardrobe and to distribute the garments to the nuns as they need them.

A Carmelite nun does not wear shoes; that is why we are called the unshod, or discalced, Carmelites. (Actually we do wear a soft hemp sandal.) You would be amused to see how the word "discalced" confuses people. On our mail we are called "Discarded Carmelites," "Disgraced Carmelites," "Discharged," and even "Disabled Carmelites"! Saint Teresa wanted her nuns to discard shoes because to her mind shoes represented the spirit of worldliness. To Teresa the shoe was a symbol. It was to her a sign of noise, relaxation, wandering, modernity. Bare feet meant silence, penance, humility, a return to the original austerity of the Primitive Rule.

Our separation from creatures, the coarseness of our habit, the lack of comfort in our furniture, and the absence of daintiness in our diet, all these help us to remain poor—at least externally. We pray that by this exterior poverty we may be able to enrich a world which so inordinately craves social prestige and physical comforts.

The modern world has gone mad in its persistent effort to devise "timesaving" devices. The trouble is that few seem to know exactly what to do with all the time that is saved. In the cloister we eliminate a great deal of work, too. We don't have to spend time laundering tablecloths, curtains, doilies, and drapes for the simple reason that we have no such articles. We don't have to use part of every twenty-four hours to set, curl, and beautify our hair; the close-cropped hair we have requires very little treatment. Our schedule, to say nothing of our income, would not permit us to spend time adorning our faces and polishing our nails; not that we have any objection to these things, but you will admit they would hardly be considered compatible with the vow of poverty and the desire to be unnoticed.

The spirit of poverty is very different from the spirit of the world. The spirit of poverty seems always to have something to spare, seems always able to do without, to cut down on personal needs; the spirit of the world can spare nothing because it is always seeking and demanding more. One who has the spirit of poverty can exclaim with the Poor Man of Assisi, "O Poverty, how beautiful you are!" One who has the spirit of the world looks on poverty and sees a curse, a running sore in a land where mammon reigns in so many hearts.

However, the vow of poverty and the entire problem of voluntarily choosing to be poor go much deeper than merely not having things. We are taught that there is much more to it than external appearances.

It is said that some people in the world are so dependent on things outside themselves that unhappiness and poverty seem to them to be the same. "The fear of the poor is their poverty."

We know that gold can be a stumbling block in one's approach to union with God. The danger is that man may put in wealth the trust he should put in God. The New Testament tells us that the rich find it pretty hard to enter the Kingdom of Heaven. No one would deny that the desire for wealth is a dangerous distraction from the things of faith and of the spirit. That is why, no doubt,

Our Blessed Lord's followers came, for the most part, from the poor, who found it less difficult to attach themselves to the Saviour and to understand and follow His teaching.

When Our Lord began to preach, He reminded His listeners that "This day the scriptures are fulfilled in your ears." The poor were having the Gospel preached to them. Looking out with loving sympathy at the poor, the crippled, the miserable of all kinds who came to hear Him, Jesus said, "Blessed are ye poor. . . ." In those words we feel the deep, tender meaning of His message. He seems to say: How fortunate you are to know at last that the good news of redemption is brought to you, you who have so little of this world's comfort! More important than My curing the sick and raising the dead, "Tell John the poor have the Gospel preached to them."

Jesus understood the poor; He was one of them; He knew what it was like to be in need and to have no means, humanly speaking, to satisfy that need.

Born in a stable in utter poverty, He lived unknown in an obscure town, the Child of a simple workman.

Later, during His public life, He had no place whereon to lay His head. His apostles were for the most part poor men. He encouraged them to depend on His Heavenly Father rather than on money and human ingenuity to spread His Kingdom. They were to be as sheep among wolves. They were advised to "take nothing for their journey, but a staff only; no wallet, no bread, no money in their girdle. . . ." And those who followed the early apostles, with few exceptions, were the poor. Those few people of means who came to Our Lord and were faithful to Him were loved by Him because of their beautiful poverty of spirit. They did not find it embarrassing to be one with their Divine Model, Who lost everything and Who, at the end, was stripped even of His clothes, which is the utter extreme of poverty.

Finally He lost His friends—or most of them—and for one

agonizing moment He appeared to lose even the comfort of His Heavenly Father. So, when we consider Our Blessed Lord, we realize that, in comparison, we are living in luxury. Mother Teresa once asked us, "Can we live in comfort when Our Lord was so poor?" She always says that we should want our Carmel to be the poorest in the world.

During our novitiate days, before we take our temporary vows, the meaning and the beauty of poverty are made the subject of special study and meditation. With the Gospels before us, we outline and follow Our Lord's life of poverty from His birth in the stable of Bethlehem to His death on the Cross, and it is repeatedly pointed out to us that it is not the possession of material things which makes a man great or virtuous or learned or noble or happy. Of course, man as a human being must use some material things. He must have food and clothing and shelter; and the normal person must have books in order to learn; he must have some means to satisfy his need for recreation; but only a moderate amount of all these things is necessary.

In imitation of the athlete of whom Saint Paul speaks, who, in order to run more freely, disencumbers himself before the race, we who are "striving for the mastery" are encouraged to strip ourselves of everything that would retard us in our ascent to the summit of the Mountain of Love.

Lest we yield to the temptation to be "proud of our poverty," we are told that riches and poverty have no value in themselves. It is our reaction toward them that counts.

How often I heard Mother Prioress in the early days of my religious life say: We are not to despise the material world; it is not, in itself, evil. Everything God made is good. The things that are in this world are here to be used by man to help him fulfill his destiny. But although these things are good in themselves, experience proves that they very often divide the heart, and so the Carmelite must reduce her use of creatures to a minimum, and she must never become attached to anything. That is why we may never call a thing "mine"—we own nothing but our faults and imperfections. It is "our" cell, "our" habit, "our" breviary, even though at the moment it may be given to us to use. With Saint John of the Cross, Mother would say, hold all personal possessions in abhorrence as if they were the plague.

Just as the vow of obedience had made clearer for me my proper relationship toward God my Creator, so the vow of poverty made clearer my proper attitude toward His creatures.

In explaining the right use of creatures, our Novice Mistress suggested that we imagine the words "for God alone" stamped on everything that had been given us—whether it was our friends, our cell, or just a book.

The first time I heard in the Refectory this passage from the Rule, "The religious shall possess absolutely nothing as their own, nor may they have the use of anything without permission from the Prioress," I felt as lighthearted as a bird. I had come to Carmel because I wanted God alone. It was obvious that everything about the life was going to help me attain this goal.

How I wish it were possible for me to express what I feel about this most valuable virtue of poverty; how I should like to send warm words of comfort into the hovels of the poor and calm words of caution into the mansions of the wealthy! If only the people of the nations and the rulers of the world could understand how true it is that the things we in Carmel have given up are at the root of all misery and all evil! How often are the members of a family divided over the desire for money! And is it not true that avarice and greed are at the bottom of most of the world's wars and distrust and hatred?

Unfortunately, it is merely for the sake of possessing that many people want to possess—that is why they believe they can hoard or destroy or misuse as they please. It is true that man has been given power over material things and if he has earned them honestly they are his; but it is equally true that absolute dominion belongs to God alone. We are God's creatures; we have for our use in this world certain goods given to us by Him, but we must use them according to His will for the *common good*. That, it seems to me, applies just as truly to the man in the world as it does to a Carmelite nun. The difference is that in the world the thing a man uses he may call his own; in Carmel we may not because, actually, by our solemn vow of poverty we give up all right to ownership.

It is always a source of much edification to hear about the great charity of so many toward those who are naked and hungry; and to know that there are so many wealthy people fully aware of their "stewardship" and conscientiously managing the Master's goods. Because America has been blessed so abundantly with the goods of this world, and because our people are so generous, the charity of Americans has become a byword among the poor of the world—despite the fact that there are those in many devastated areas who, through malice, give a perverse motive to our aid. Yet it seems a pity to me that much merit is lost because in many cases our giving remains on the natural plane. How much greater would be the gift if Christ were seen in the poor—a chance of salvation is missed: "Come ye blessed of My Father; as long as you did it to one of these, My least brethren, you did it to Me."

At least in one external feature, religious and all the poor resemble Christ—we have poverty in common. When we lack what we need, we take on the marks of Christ; when we possess all we desire or more than we need, the poverty of Christ is not in us.

There is still another advantage to poverty. It can be a driving force in a person's life. Not only does it impel a man to work for the support of his family—poverty has forced men and women throughout the ages to produce great things to develop and beautify the world. Christ, the great Landowner, dignified the state of the workingman by belonging to a poor working family and by Himself engaging in manual tasks.

In Carmel we also engage each day in manual work, and at times we are forced even to beg. And since we are mendicants, it would not do for us to live luxuriously with the alms we receive from the needy. As Saint Teresa says, "All buildings will tumble at the last day. It would not look well if the house of poor women made much noise when it fell, for the real poor make no commotion."

It seems needless to remind you that the poverty which is implied in a religious vow has to do with something besides the idea of merely not having things. Absence is not detachment if the desire remains, says Saint John of the Cross. Saint Augustine puts the same thought this way: "Those who do not have things, but *wish* they had are not poor in spirit; God considers not what we possess but what we COVET."

So the young novice in Carmel is taught to become detached from everything and everyone; to lay at the feet of her Spouse all that she has and is. Desiring no earthly treasures, she is to be attached to God alone. Infinitely more dear to Him than the birds of the air and the lilies of the field which, in His Providence, He feeds and clothes with such fatherly solicitude, she casts far from her all concern for the morrow, all anxiety about the future. He is Our Father, and He will not leave us in want. He has promised, and He always keeps His word, "Seek ye *first* the kingdom of God and His justice and all these things will be added unto you." If we do our best, no more is expected. We are to live prudently and providently; and above all we are not to be careless with what He gives us. God has always sent us what is needful; if we are what we are supposed to be, He will continue to do so.

We do not need many things to be happy or to be pleasing to God. What we *are,* not what we have, is the important thing in His sight. Our Lord would deprive us of all that would hold us captive to this world, in order to draw us to Himself.

A good proof that we are truly poor in spirit is this: if, while desiring for ourselves nothing except God's love and His grace, we can at the same time sincerely rejoice over His gifts to others as if they were our own. Saint Gertrude formed the habit of thanking God for His gifts to others, and one day Our Lord revealed to her that whenever she did this He gave her spiritual gifts equal to the blessings she had praised Him for giving others.

Perhaps we should repeat: It is not riches that we wish abolished —lack of goods is not in itself good—it is the inordinate love of wealth, so common in the world, that must be combated. Saint Paul says, "The *desire* for money is the root of all evil" and he adds, "Some in their eagerness to acquire riches have strayed from the faith and have involved themselves in many troubles."

The Scriptures warn those who have wealth that they should not be proud, nor should they foolishly trust in the uncertainty of riches; rather they should put their trust in the living God. It is not easy for a rich person to be detached from his money, nor is it easy for the poor man to refrain from thinking of accumulating more money than he needs. Both are equally blameworthy. One of the most terrible sentences in the Gospel is the one in which Saint Luke, after reporting Our Lord's words, "You cannot serve God and mammon," goes on to say that "the Pharisees, who were fond of money, were listening to these things, and they began to sneer at Him." Money and worldly possessions tend to make us blind to the things of God and to make us forget the true condition of our existence here. "We brought nothing into the world, and certainly we can take nothing out."

To introduce luxuries into Carmel would be fatal to its spirit. Comforts would interfere with our prayer and destroy the meaning of our work. We would be bound by golden chains, not to the feet of God but to this earth. Our vow of poverty liberates us, frees us from the world's fuss and bother, from "slavish captivity to things," and from anxious solicitude. It sets us free for divine thoughts. We know that attachment to worldly goods would certainly hamper our love for God and make it impossible to follow His will. In the final analysis the vow of poverty is an adjunct to our vow of obedience. We follow the Rule, which tells us in every detail how we are to be poor. We are poor in common with each member of the community.

That there are advantages to such a life I am quite aware. But if we in Carmel felt only the advantages of our common life, it would not be enough. We must feel some privation, some real need also, so that we may be forced to throw ourselves entirely upon God's bounty. Where there is no need, there is no poverty. Our vow to remain poor is not an end in itself—it is merely a means to the proper attainment of our contemplative life. "Blessed are the poor in spirit for theirs is the Kingdom of Heaven."

It is not difficult for a nun who accepts completely her vow of poverty to be detached from all earthly comforts and all human praise. We have chosen freely the Rule we lead; whatever "results" we may achieve are due to Our Blessed Lord, since we have vowed to empty ourselves of everything else so that He can fill us with His love. After all, it is not easy for Our Lord to find even a small corner in a heart that is filled with plans for earthly wealth and with desires for earthly pleasures. "Where your treasure is, there is your heart also."

Our Lord stands at the door of our hearts and knocks; He enters when we open and make room for Him. And once the Divine Guest has taken possession of our hearts, we begin to realize how utterly worthless are those things which formerly we made our treasure. A burning desire takes hold of us to detach ourselves from everything and everyone that might prevent us from going to God.

Saint John of the Cross had this in mind when in his *Spiritual Maxims* he wrote, "Whether it be a strong cable or a slender, delicate thread that holds the bird, it matters not, if it really detains it; for until the cord be broken the bird cannot fly. So the soul, held in the bonds of human attachments, however slight they may be, cannot, while they last, fly upwards to God."

# Chapter 12

# The Value of the Fruits

† LEV. 25:27

To THOSE unfamiliar with Carmel and our hidden life of silent solitude, the mystery of the cloister prompts them to ask, What is the value of such a life? What do they accomplish shutting themselves off from their fellow beings? And why does the Church, so aware of the need for apostles, teachers, and nurses encourage young women to enter the enclosure?

One might answer simply by telling the story of Martha and Mary. . . . Jesus entered a certain village, and a woman named Martha welcomed Him to her house. And she had a sister called Mary, who also seated herself at the Lord's feet and listened to His word. But Martha was busy about much serving. And she came up and said, "Lord, is it no concern of Thine that my sister has left me to serve alone? Tell her therefore to help me." But the Lord answered and said to her, "Martha, Martha, thou art anxious and troubled about many things, and yet only one thing is needful. Mary has chosen the best part, and it will not be taken away from her."

Or one might quote a passage from the Pope of Catholic Action, Pius XI, who says, in his letter *Umbratilem:*

163

*"From the earliest times this mode of life (contemplation), most perfect, and most useful and more fruitful for the whole of Christendom than anyone can conceive, took root in the Church and spread on all sides. Since the whole object of this institution lay in this—that the monks, unoccupied with any exterior ministry and having nothing to do with it, should fix their thoughts exclusively on the things of heaven—wonderful was the benefit that accrued from it to Christian society. . . . In the course of time this pre-eminent institution that is called the contemplative life declined somewhat and lost its vigor. The reason was that the monks . . . came gradually to combine active life with their ponderings on divine things and their contemplation. . . . It was highly important for the Church that this most holy form of life . . . should be restored to its pristine vigor, so that there should never be lacking men of prayer, who, unimpeded by any other care, would be perpetually besieging the Divine Mercy and thus draw down from Heaven benefits of every sort upon men too neglectful of their salvation. . . .*

*"[Contemplatives] give themselves up to a sort of hidden and silent apostolate . . . we wish that so valuable an institution should spread and increase. For if ever it was needful that there should be anchorites of this sort in the Church of God, it is especially expedient nowadays when we see so many Christians . . . giving rein to their desire for earthly riches and the pleasures of the flesh. . . . But it is easy to understand how those who assiduously fulfill the duty of prayer and penance contribute much more to the increase of the Church and the welfare of mankind than those who labor in tilling the Master's field."*

We cannot fail to see the importance these words ascribe to our cloistered life and the burning desire the late Holy Father had for more and more contemplatives. Obviously Pius XI understood well, as we do in Carmel, the value of the work done by the wonderful priests and religious in the schools and hospitals and missions of the world.

But we who are called to Carmel cannot compromise with the zealous Christ-like work done by these followers of Christ—their vocation keeps them to a certain degree in the world. Carmelite nuns are not teachers, or nurses, or missionaries in the sense that we have any physical contact with students, or with the sick, or with pagans. We must shut out the world, withdraw from the commotion and distraction of the active life, and give ourselves entirely to penance and prayer.

Or again, closer home, one might mention the words of Cardinal Gibbons, former first citizen of Baltimore: "If there be a country in which the contemplative life is needed, it surely is our young and active Republic, where the spirit of action pervades all classes. This action, not to be exclusive and absorbing, must be counter-balanced by reflection and contemplation; and it is from the contemplative orders we must learn this."

We have already mentioned that the first community of religious nuns invited into the territory of what then constituted the United States was a cloistered Carmelite community from Belgium. The early American Church seemed to place high value on the contribution a contemplative order could make to the infant Church here. When eighteenth-century Europe was persecuting and martyring religious with diabolical fury, America opened its door so that they might enjoy here the undisturbed tranquillity of a free and peaceful country.

The patient reader will, I trust, understand that we do not mean to glorify our way of life or to imply that we who have been so blessed with the call to Carmel are in any respect superior to others. God alone knows how far we fall short of our vocation and how many graces are left unused by us. We are aware, let me repeat, that there are contemplatives in the world; there are contemplatives in every active order in the Church—many, no doubt, gifted with true union with God in prayer.

It is only because we in Carmel have been asked to explain the reason for our enclosure and for our solitude in this world, which demands practical productions and tangible results, that we quote what those outside of Carmel think of our contribution to the welfare of the Church and to the spiritual progress of the world.

It is embarrassing at times for us to hear and humiliating to know how much faith people in the world put in our prayers and penances.

It is in the hope that the reader may better appreciate our life and better see the confidence some place in our power to help that the following letter is quoted. The writer is a late New York columnist.

*". . . I know too well how far short I fall of my opportunity. But you hearten me to go on and try harder to keep the light of my tiny, flickering candle alight in a world in which the glow of such radiant spirits as your Carmelite friend shines unseen—though I believe it is lives like hers, hidden and incandescent, that keep us from being lost in darkness.*

*"In all my life I think I have never had a gift to compare with what you have done for me in confiding me and my work to the guardianship of your Carmelite friend. I feel safer, serener and stronger just to know that her prayers go before me. Someday, thanks to the intercession of someone so much closer to the Seat of Wisdom than I can ever be, perhaps I shall be guided to write a word that will make someone think who has power to act. That's all we can do, we who write about the human tragedy of our time —report, argue, explain, plead in the hope that those in position to take action will do something to relieve misery, banish fear and further justice.*

*"With all my heart I thank you and her for your precious gift*

*to me. You have a golden heart to be so lavish in love and gener-*
*osity. I treasure what Sister says about the ministry of pain. Per-*
*haps the world, too, is praying and atoning by the terrible ordeal*
*it is suffering. Perhaps we are moving towards a new moral order*
*by learning what the fruits of the material philosophy really are.*
*I keep coming back to one of my favorite quotations (from Bos-*
*suet)—'when God erases He is preparing to write. . . .'*

*Anne O'Hare McCormick"*

From a letter such as this, from the words of Cardinal Gibbons,
of Pius XI, and of Our Lord Himself, it should be abundantly
clear that our life is an important one.

For those who understand the doctrine of the Mystical Body of
Christ, Carmel's place is clear enough. Since this Body is a spiritual
thing, we can be a part of it and aid it even when we withdraw
from it and outwardly live separated from it. And the more complete our withdrawal from the world, the greater our contribution to its true interests. In our prayers and penances and sacrifices we are hourly conscious of the members of this Body. A Christian in China suffering for his faith is a part of this Body along
with us. We cannot be otherwise but in sorrow when we think of
his great suffering.

Someone has said that in this Mystical Body of which Christ is
the head, "Carmel functions as the heart." Saint Thérèse, the
Little Flower, said that unless the heart of the Mystical Body is
strong, there will not be in the members apostles and martyrs.
Perhaps it would be better to say that all Christians in their contemplation form the heart of the Body and make for better circu-
lation of the spiritual vitality, producing thereby life and action.

It does not surprise us here in Carmel to have priests and bishops
write or call to lay before us plans that they hope to put into action for the spreading of Christ's Kingdom on earth. Mother
Teresa can recall saintly Father Price, the cofounder of Mary-

knoll, coming to the Baltimore Carmel to place the future priests and the future work of Maryknoll under the prayerful protection of Carmel.

And that brings us to one of the most important of all our duties.

The Catholic priest is the spiritual leader of our people. His responsibilities are tremendous. Because his power for good is so great, his holiness is of the utmost importance. The priest, we say, is, through the powers given him in Ordination, "another Christ." He is to take man's prayers and sufferings and bring them to God and in return he brings down God's blessings and graces to mankind. The people are to see in him Christ. They are to know, by seeing him, how Christ looked; by hearing him, how Christ spoke; by beseeching him, how Christ had compassion on the multitude. When the priesthood is as Our Blessed Lord wished it to be, there is no danger that the people will turn from God. Where it is not poor in spirit and zealous for good and compassionate of the poor, then the Church of Christ and the members of Christ suffer and roam about as sheep without a shepherd.

That is why Saint Teresa reminds us often that our chief duty in prayer and penance is to help priests. That is why we pray for priests; that is why priests place such confidence in our interest in their spiritual projects and their own spiritual lives.

We know that the world and satan are waging bitter battle against the priesthood of Christ to weaken it and, if possible, destroy it. Of course, we have no fear, knowing that Christ is with them all days even unto the end of time. And we thank God for the splendid priests he has given His Church.

Still we pray without ceasing for them. We discipline our bodies for them, that they may never give delight to satan by becoming one with the world and its destructive spirit. We pray that they will continue always to be mindful of the vocation which surpasses all human conception. Each Carmelite nun repeats in the silence of her heart before her profession, "I have come to save souls, and especially to pray for priests."

"The vocation of a priest! With what love, my Jesus, would I bear Thee in my hand . . . with what love would I give Thee to souls." Saint Thérèse of Lisieux in these beautiful words shows her lofty regard for the priesthood . . . yet she admitted that she would have preferred to be like Francis of Assisi, the Saint who, through humility, refused the dignity of the office.

It is a source of joy to us in Carmel to have priests request of us some urgent prayers for themselves and their people. We want so much to be a part of every apostolic movement in the Church.

There are many such pleas that come to my mind as these lines are being written. For one priest friend in particular I feel a special duty to pray and suffer, because, at the moment, he is in need, dire need, of prayer.

I was confined to a New York City hospital recovering from one of four major operations undergone during my early years as a Carmelite in the big city and had the supreme consolation of a visit from this pious, zealous, gifted priest.

Many Carmels knew him personally and benefited from his wise direction and his paternal interest. He had directed to the cloister many promising vocations. One of these vocations I know well.

Father was directing Catholic students in a large university. The students felt free to call him or visit him for advice and to have cleared up for them scholastic problems that seemed to conflict with the doctrines of Christianity.

One of these students called Father frequently and met him in the reception room of her sorority to have her doubts dissolved. Her non-Catholic roommate expressed in Father's presence the envy she felt in the good fortune of her Catholic roommate, who could depend on such learned and paternal assistance whenever she needed it.

The priest said understandingly, "You, too, have the same opportunity, if you wish to make use of it. I should be happy to be of assistance to you also."

That was the beginning!

Through the wise philosophy of the priest, she came step by step to the knowledge of the truth, and before she concluded her university studies, she was admitted into the Catholic Church. She did not stop here. She wished to follow Christ completely; today she is a Carmelite nun.

There are many similar stories that might be written about this priest's love for the souls of the students who came under his wise direction.

I remember him best from the visit he made to my hospital sickroom.

My severe pain seemed to cease as he came smiling through the door of my room. What took place then and what our conversation was about can best be reproduced by letting you read the poem which he sent to me a few days later.

### THE FAITHFUL ONE

"The hospital was where I sat beside
That wildly raving fellow till he died! . . .
And then I left him, went across the way
Into her quiet room, 'And will you pray
That I may die with dignity?' I said
'With honor . . . poise . . . in peace?' She shook her head.

"And with that sure-voiced candor she possesses
Which challenges, delights me, and distresses,
Firmly replied: 'My prayer for you will be
That you may die as God may best decree!
And, if bereft of courage and control,
In shame, in terror, whether bruised or whole,
'I promise I shall even still be proud of you,

*Whate'er be whispered or exclaimed aloud of you,*
*Remain the faithful one and come and lay for you*
*My single wreath upon your grave . . . and pray for you!'*

*"And, therefore, I must go, it seems, through gloom*
*Of wreck, disease, asylum, to the tomb,*
*By whatsoever vanquished, or by whom."*

To this priest friend I am still faithful, and for him I still pray. No pain or penance is too much for me; the thought urges me that my friend is in need. That is enough.

Here in our Oklahoma Carmel there is another friend of this same priest. Friendship may demand at times a heavy price. Let me quote for you a portion of his letter to this Carmel in February, 1940. ". . . And now about your little pearl of the Blessed Sacrament, Sister M . . . There is a wonderful destiny attached to the soul of that child. What if she *has* got cancer; what if she has anything? Carmel is her place, her home. Never let her go, will you? Never. . . . Never. . . . If she has to be a victim—the immolation will be brief—she will bring more grace to your community and more support to the whole Church in America than a thousand strong girls ever could. . . ."

As I write these lines, the novice about whom Father wrote is again confined to bed, once more in the throes of cancer pain. But no one would suspect the pain in her body when they look at the cheerful expression on her face. She, too, has a motive in her suffering.

We are always moved deeply by the genuine faith of lay people who come to Carmel and beg for prayers. It makes us constantly mindful of our vocation and our place in the Mystical Body.

It is a common practice for hospital Sisters to call us when a patient is to undergo a serious operation. Here in Oklahoma City we receive frequent requests for prayers from the wonderful nursing Sisters of Saint Francis who conduct St. Anthony's Hospital.

Often we are called to the turn to hear the sad story of some family trouble or illness.

One evening after dark the Turn Sister was called to answer the front doorbell, which was ringing persistently. On releasing the automatic door lock she heard a number of heavy-footed men enter. The voice that spoke first was familiar. The friend of Carmel had chosen this rather late hour to bring a group of his truck-driver friends to Carmel so that the Sister might speak a few words to each man.

They were quite unfamiliar with Carmel, and obviously it was not their idea to seek spiritual advice at that time of night.

The instigator of the scheme told the Sister he would take the men into the parlor and send them one by one to the turn.

It was a humiliating experience for the nun to hear these rough, deep-voiced men suddenly become like little children, quietly confessing that they needed spiritual help to overcome some moral problem in their lives. Several asked prayers for their wives and families.

The truck drivers and their friend had departed only a few seconds when the bell rang again.

One of the men in his anxious, Texas drawl said, "Lady, where's my buddy? He was the last one in here and he ain't outside. Did you see my buddy?"

The Turn Sister explained that from where she was she couldn't see "any buddy."

The man looked around a bit and went out muttering.

God seems to bless those who come in faith to the monastery. The visitors cannot see us; there is nothing personal in the approach. Perhaps, as someone once put it, Carmel is like the hem of Our Lord's garment, and just to touch the hem in faith seems to help the one who makes the contact.

In a vague sort of way I was aware of Carmel's contribution to the apostolic Church before I entered the cloister, but it was not that feature of our life that drew me into the enclosure. Through the years, however, I have discovered that many enter Carmel because of their missionary zeal. They feel that they can accomplish more by their lives of prayer and sacrifice than they could in the mission field itself.

One of the nuns here in our Oklahoma monastery, after receiving her degree from a Catholic college, took a postgraduate course in a large Eastern university where her father had been a professor of history and economics. While there, the feverish zeal of those who were spreading communism began to impress her with their power to do evil. She did what she could to combat this destructive force by argument and by reading spiritual books and spending longer hours in prayer—asking God to make use of her education for His greater glory.

Realizing the menacing danger of communism and watching at first hand the diabolical fanaticism of its followers, she resolved to devote all her talents and energy to combating it. She studied the techniques and propaganda tactics of the Reds, and, whenever able, she attacked their false philosophy openly.

One day Sister attended a lecture on the evils of communism. In the course of his talk the speaker introduced the doctrine of the Mystical Body of Christ. After summing up the devastation that the Reds had already wrought in the world, he asked the question, "Am I my brother's keeper?" When she heard these words, she realized more than ever her responsibility in the struggle against this evil.

After receiving her M.A., she changed to a Catholic university for her doctorate, where she came to understand that her part in the great conflict would henceforth consist not in active works or argument but in the silent prayer and penance of the cloister.

Upon entering the cloister, Sister found the nuns far more conscious of the danger of the Red menace than the ordinary Christian in the world and by their prayers and penance doing all they can to support those who are combating it on the outside.

How similar Sister's story is to that of Edith Stein, who, when told that she might not be able to continue her intellectual pursuits in Carmel, said quietly, "It is not human activity that can help us, but the Passion of Christ. It is a share in that Passion that I desire."

It is possible that some of my readers may be unfamiliar with the life of the remarkable Jewish convert Carmelite. Let me briefly introduce her to you.

Edith Stein, brilliant German philosopher, was an assistant for several years to the great phenomenologist philosopher Edmund Husserl. She was a popular lecturer at the Universities of Heidelberg, Freiburg, and Cologne. She was publicly acclaimed throughout Europe for her translation of Saint Thomas into modern, living German. The Benedictine Abbot, Raphael Walzer, called her "one of the greatest women of our time."

At the home of some friends the Jewess Edith Stein was left alone one day by her hosts. Before departing her friend pointed to her library and said, "All these are at your disposal; take your pick."

Edith wrote later, "I picked at random and took out a large volume. It bore the title, *The Life of Saint Teresa of Avila,* written by herself. I began to read it; was at once captivated, and did not stop till I reached the end. As I closed the book I said, 'That is truth!' "

She immediately sought and devoured other Catholic books; she began to attend Mass regularly and soon was received into the Church, despite the pleading opposition of her deeply devout Jewish mother.

Edith Stein, by her writing and lecturing, was accomplishing great things in the intellectual world and without doubt could have continued to do so if she chose. However, with her great mental equipment, her soul by nature and grace was inclined to contemplation. She accepted Our Blessed Lord's call to be with Him in Carmel's cloister.

Long before she entered the monastery, Edith was a contemplative. Whenever she was at prayer, she seemed completely absorbed in God. She wanted to draw ever nearer to the source of Divine Wisdom, for she felt in that way she could do more and more for mankind, especially for her own Jewish people.

Her mother violently opposed the step that Edith planned to take, and the philosophical world was reluctant to part with one of its brightest lights. But the hesitation and the lingering finally ended, and she was admitted into the Carmelite monastery in Cologne. She was eager to sink herself into the depths of cloistered insignificance. She became just another postulant, and with sweet humility this great soul said, "Carmel is indeed a high mountain and one must start slowly from the base." But she found also that in Carmel's solitude a limitless horizon opened up and there was "music in its silent meditation."

When the Nazi persecution of the Jews reached its height in the early 40's, Edith Stein, then Sister Benedicta of the Cross, was sent from Cologne to the Carmelite monastery in Echt, Holland. There the savage hand of the Storm Troopers sought her out and dragged her from the hidden enclosure of peaceful Carmel to her brutal gas-chamber death in a concentration camp somewhere in the land of hate.

What surprised me most in Carmel was its intense mission spirit.

We were amused one day when a good woman came to the turn and frankly admitted that she could not understand or appreciate the life of a Carmelite nun: "I like Sisters who get out among people and help them; Sisters who take an interest in what's going on—like the Little Flower."

The dear woman was quite surprised when the Sister at the turn explained that the Little Flower never "got out among people" at all, and she was very much embarrassed to learn that Saint Thérèse, the Little Flower, was a cloistered Carmelite nun who lived a hidden life in Lisieux's Carmel.

We are not permitted to forget others, even though physically we are shut off from them. Saint Teresa of Avila said, "Solicitude for the welfare of souls extends itself to every type of apostolate! Always use all kinds of ingenuity and tact to lead souls back to God and closer to Him. Your whole life of prayer has to be lived for the profit of souls."

And in our own day how strange that a Saint, whose life was consecrated to solitude and contemplation in the cloister of Lisieux' Carmel, should have been proclaimed the principal patroness of the foreign missions—equal, in this respect, to the great Jesuit apostle to the Indies, Saint Francis Xavier.

Yet it is not so strange when we understand the mutual help the interior life and the active apostolate for souls render each other. The missionary apostolate, no matter how zealous and brilliant, would be condemned to irremediable sterility if the breath of prayer did not circulate through it; for "Neither he who plants is anything, nor he who waters, but God who gives growth." Prayer and penance are the abiding source of this growth.

The significance of employing prayer and penance as means of propagating and defending the true religion had taken deep root several centuries before Our Saviour came into the world. It was, as we have seen, on Mount Carmel that Elias the Thesbite, the fiery defender of the Mosaic Law, put the theory into practice. This spirit of apostolic action and silent contemplation was passed on by Elias to those who lived with him and to those who followed him, and it has been continuous down to our own day.

Always contemplation was given the preference in the life of the missionaries and scholars of Carmel. Prayers, and the austerities to back up those prayers, constituted the chief work from the beginning.

Without contemplation and penance the active part of our work, or any work for God, would be like a body without a soul. That is why there are always to be found in every Carmel zealous, apostolic nuns who work and pray and deny themselves with tireless determination to extend the Kingdom of Our Lord. The principal effect of contemplation is supernatural love—a love of God, deep and childlike, and a love of neighbor, genuine and universal. For we must love all; otherwise, as Saint John says, "We lie when we say we love God." The more we think of God, the more we yearn for souls to give Him.

Saint Teresa, for all her union of prayer, was supremely apostolic. Virile and with the spirit of an intrepid warrior in the cause of Christ, she gathered about her apostolic souls who would fight a campaign of holiness—a new battlefield, employing new methods. She put her trust in God, and with the spiritual arms of prayer and love she rushed to meet the attack, and God alone can tell the part she played in stopping the spread of heresy.

What Teresa started in 1562 has spread over the whole world. Today there are over seven hundred monasteries of Carmelite contemplatives—indomitable fortresses built to withstand error and to wage a holy war of love by means of recollection and prayer. Here in America, in twenty-nine of our states we have already fifty-three Carmels, housing about eight hundred nuns. At the present time, our Sisters of Indianapolis are making arrangements to open a convent in Reno—"close enough to the dine-dance-and-gamble clubs to see the neon lights," Mother Angela, the Prioress, writes.

The very words spoken by Saint Teresa in the first chapter of her *Way of Perfection* seem directed at the world of 1954 just as poignantly as they applied to the sixteenth century:

*"Aware of the troubles in France I was bitterly grieved. I would have given a thousand lives to save one of the many souls perishing there. . . . My whole longing then was, and it still is, that since He [Christ] has so many enemies and so few friends, the friends should at least be good ones. So I determined to do the little I could, which was to follow the evangelical counsels with all the perfection of which I was capable, and to influence the few around me to do the same, trusting in the great goodness of God who never fails to help anyone who has resolved to leave all for His sake. I hoped that if all of us spend our time in prayer for those who defend the Church, . . . we would be able better to help this Lord of mine who is so grievously oppressed by those for whom He has done so much good. It seems that these traitors want to fasten Him again on the Cross, and to leave Him without a place to lay His head. The world is in a fever; men want to condemn Christ anew. . . . They are seeking the downfall of the Church, and do we have to waste time praying for things of little moment which, if granted, might mean one less soul in heaven?"*

While it is true that we enter the cloister to be near our Beloved and to travel the hidden road of perfection, still this strong personal desire to acquire spiritual riches of the soul would die out in us if we did not, at the same time, feel the impulse to communicate these blessings to others. If we did not try to share our spiritual wealth with others, we would become like miserly, grasping men who take vain and morbid delight in gazing at and counting their money without giving a thought to sharing their wealth for the love of God with those who are in need. Such selfish people, enslaved to their gold, never experience the healthy, uplifting satisfaction which comes to generous souls who share what God has given to them.

It is deeply impressed on every Carmelite nun that she must feel dynamically and at every hour of the day this generous impulse;

otherwise, we, who are the stewards of so much heavenly riches, would not fulfill our mission in the world as we should.

As we grow in the love of God, we realize that this love cannot be idle. It must expand itself and communicate itself to those who do not enjoy it or who do not know about it.

Saint Teresa would shed tears of pity every time she thought of the pagans who had not yet heard of Christ: "Those Indians are costing me not a little."

Listen as the great missionary heart of Teresa pours forth its love for souls in her *Book of Foundations:*

*"After four years—I think a little more—there came to see me a Franciscan friar, Father Alonso Maldonado, a great servant of God, having the same desires that I had for the good of souls. He was able to carry his into effect, for which I envied him enough. He had just returned from the Indies. He began by telling me of the many millions of souls there perishing through the want of instruction, and preached us a sermon encouraging us to do penance, and then went his way. I was so distressed because so many souls were perishing that I could not contain myself. I went to one of the hermitages, weeping much, and cried unto our Lord, beseeching Him to show me, when the devil was carrying so many away, how I might do something to gain a soul for His service, and how I might do something by prayer now that I could do nothing else. I envied very much those who for the love of our Lord could employ themselves in this work for souls, though they might suffer a thousand deaths. Thus, when I am reading in the lives of the saints how they converted souls, I have more devotion, more tenderness and more envy, than when I read all the pains of martyrdom they underwent; for this is an attraction which our Lord has given me; and I think He prizes one soul which of His mercy we have gained for Him by our prayer and labor more than all the service we may render Him."*

It is the same in Carmel today; we plead for those who do not yet know they have a Saviour, and we rejoice whenever the frontiers of Christianity are pushed back and new souls enter the true sheepfold.

The love we have for God and the love we have for our neighbors are inseparable virtues. Each Carmelite monastery is founded for the same reason for which Saint Teresa founded the first of her reformed convents at St. Joseph's in Avila: "That through solitude, penance and prayer it might increase the Catholic faith and procure conversions of non-Catholics; and in order also that God would deign to give the Church holy, learned and zealous priests."

The Carmelite vocation is missionary.

It did not surprise us when the foreign mission society at Maryknoll set up at its Center a cloistered branch of Sisters. These nuns, on fire to bring Christ to pagan lands, understood that there must be dedicated missioners spending themselves in prayer and penance; and all this in solitude, in order that those on the field of battle may be well supplied with the spiritual strength and courage so necessary for the accomplishment of their difficult task.

These selected Maryknoll nuns can say with our Carmelite nun, Sister Elizabeth of the Trinity: "Apostle, Carmelite, it is all one. While you carry Him to souls, I, like Magdalen, will stay close to the Master in silent adoration, asking Him to render your word fruitful in souls."

Among the priests of Carmel there have always been those who have carried Christ to distant corners of the world. Only death prevented Saint John of the Cross, the great mystic and founder of the Reform, from coming to America. His last assignment was to the missions. Here in Oklahoma there are Carmelite Fathers who have left for the time being their life of seclusion in order to aid in the establishment of the Church in these remote areas. They carry into their active ministry not only the apostolate of prayer

but also, like their saintly founder, the apostolate of high spirituality and missionary zeal.

Here is how Saint John of the Cross felt about bringing souls
to God: One day at Granada, during recreation, he made little
piles of gravel and then took away one little stone and said to his
fellow monks, "In all those parts of the world [he pointed to the
piles of stones] our true God and Lord is not known." Then he
pointed to the little stone and said, "He is known only in that
tiny part of the world, and, even there, only 'few are chosen.' "

The Little Flower of Lisieux did not leave her beloved cloister
for even one minute; yet she has been acclaimed by the Church
the greatest contemplative and the greatest missionary of modern
times.

I did not intend to dwell so long on Carmel's missionary character, but because today there is such an inspiring resurgence of
missionary zeal—particularly in our own country—I trust my enthusiasm may be forgiven.

It would be presumptuous of me to attempt to suggest anything
to our admirable missioners enduring untold hardships in the face
of overwhelming obstacles. It is merely in the hope that they may
better understand the deep interest we have in every step they
take that I speak at all of missions.

When I write of Carmel's share in those missionary activities, it
is not to imply that we could withstand the climate and hardships
of those primitive countries—although there are Carmelite nuns
in most mission countries, and in my heart there has for years
burned the desire to imitate them. I mention our part to remind
every missioner, at home and abroad, that we are one with his
plans and hopes—we are in the cloister, he on the field.

You will not mind, I trust, if I quote a paragraph from Saint
John of the Cross which expresses so loftily the feelings of all of
us in Carmel. In his *Spiritual Canticle* he says:

*"Hence, when a soul has any of this degree of pure love, great harm would be done to it and to the Church if, even though for a short space of time, it should become occupied in external activities, however profitable they might be. After all, it was for this purpose of loving that we were created. Please, then, let those who are very active and who hope to hold the world in their hands because of their preaching and their external activities understand that they would do more service to the Church and would please God more—to say nothing of the good example they would give —if they would spend even half of that time in being with God in prayer, even though they did not experience it in such a high degree as contemplatives. Indeed, they would accomplish with one work of this kind more than with a thousand of the other kind, and with less trouble; for their prayer would have merited it and would have given them all kinds of divine assistance. In any other way their work is reduced to beating the air and to doing little more than nothing, at times nothing at all, and at times even harm. . . ."*

The missionary apostolate is the communicating of the supernatural life to the soul.

Saint Francis Xavier is regarded as a perfect missionary, Saint Thérèse a perfect contemplative. I think it would be safe to say that, according to sound theology, the two parts are inseparable. Saint Francis Xavier would not have been a great missionary if he did not have a deep interior life; nor would the Little Flower have been a perfect contemplative had not the torrential flood of her love for God watered the huge field of apostolic labors throughout the world.

It is needless to say that for each of us in Carmel, the great Saint Teresa, our Mother, and Saint Thérèse are the models after which we try to fashion our zeal for the missions and for souls.

"I will spend my heaven doing good upon earth . . . there can be no rest for me till the end of the world." These apostolic words show so clearly Carmel's missionary heart.

"Patroness of the Missions"—that is the title Holy Mother Church has seen fit to give the Carmelite nun of Lisieux. Her apostolic spirit is the reason for this; the spirit of love and penance, without which any apostolate is doomed to die. She had an exceptionally apostolic soul, developed in the solitude of Carmel. She desired to be a missionary "from the creation of the world to its consummation" and above all to die a martyr. This dream of martyrdom increased to tremendous proportions as she grew in the perfect love of God.

It is, of course, this missionary ideal that has prompted Carmelite nuns to establish foundations all over the mission world. There are Carmelite monasteries in India, Indo-China, Hong Kong, Japan, Borneo, Singapore, Africa, and throughout the Middle East—one even in Iceland.

In October, 1949, our Baltimore convent sent nuns to found a cloister in the Philippines, and the Cleveland Carmel in the summer of 1951 sent nine of its nuns to Nairobi in Africa, where today there is so much fierce antagonism against Christianity among the native Mau Maus. And in this glorious Marian Year of 1954 our nuns of Santa Clara have opened a house on the island of Formosa.

Missionary bishops in many parts of the world have written to ask for nuns of Carmel to establish monasteries in their territories, and it is a very great joy to the nuns when they are able to comply with such wishes. The bishops want, as they put it, "to let the natives see and be edified by a life that is devout and striving for perfection."

It is a cause for rejoicing, as well as an incentive to greater love and penance, when we receive letters from missionaries in foreign lands. One wrote recently, "There was great consolation in reading that you keep me in your daily prayers, without them the past half year would have been far more difficult than it was. We need Our Lord's help constantly so that the people will see Him in us."

Another says, "Your prayers are earnestly solicited. It is your prayers that bring us safely through."

A Jesuit Father in the Orient wrote, "I am consoled with the thought that while I am assisting in an active way, you will be 'behind the scenes' storming heaven for someone whom we are trying to reach and bring to God." And he pleads, "Help me to face the trials, hardships and disappointments of this life."

We do indeed pray for him and for all those who labor in the vineyard of the Lord. May we be worthy of the vocation whereto God has called us, and may we fulfill as perfectly as possible our solemn function in the Mystical Body of Christ.

# Chapter 13

# All Things Were in Quiet Silence † WIS. 18:14

I HAVE already confessed that for me the most difficult feature of Carmel's Rule was silence. It is not only that I like to talk; I like to listen, too. Just recently one of the postulants, in considerable embarrassment, acknowledged to me what she called a "horrible thought." The even temper and the constant self-control and the perfect silence of the nuns were getting on her nerves. She wished someone would "blow her top" once in a while, as some people do in the world.

It was impossible for me to repress a smile. It was as though I were listening to the very words I might have used when I myself was a postulant. "I know just how you feel, dear," I said, "but don't be disturbed by the lack of noise. Thank God for it. As time goes on, you will appreciate and love it."

The New York City Carmel, where I entered, seemed to me a veritable desert of silence. In the midst of the busy, crowded city of noise and pleasure, Carmel was a mysterious citadel of silence and penance. Lay people have told us of the comfort they derive from their short visits to our quiet Chapel. They long to escape for a few minutes from the needless noise outside, the blaring radios, the senseless excitement.

We don't mean to imply in any way that all noise is sinful, nor do we intend to imply that all silence is virtuous. However, I think you will agree that much of the disturbing noise in the world can be traced to confusion, turmoil, or despair. Apart from the disquieting effect this pandemonium has on the nervous system, there is still a more serious effect on the soul. The constant chatter of people and the din of mechanical monsters have a way of filling the mind with sounds and confusion from without. The soul cannot hear the still, small voice within; nor can it recollect itself in the midst of the bedlam of its own mind.

From my own experience in the world, I know it is possible, despite the external noise, to listen and hear God in the silence of one's own heart—but I also know it is not easy. People in the world can and do become oblivious of the turmoil; many rise above the turbulent restlessness of created things and spend some time each day in silent prayer.

The young, crippled scrub woman who visited me at the time of my reception was not by any means unique in her prayer life. There are countless others who feel strongly at times the need for silence, and they yearn to rest, like Magdalen, at the feet of the Master, eager to hear all He has to whisper to them. Despite the press of business and family obligations, despite the conspiracy constantly waged against their privacy and solitude, they manage to find a quiet corner where they may go to rest in silent recollection and draw down the strength and nourishment their souls require.

"But the mind," as Edith Stein says, "is occupied with many things; so much so that one thing is always crowding on another in a constant state of movement and of tumult and uproar."

Much of the high tension and neurosis, all too common in our day, could be eliminated if each person in the world were to spend the first hour of the day in silent prayer. Persistent problems and duty's dull routine would not seem so overwhelming if the torrent of the world's affairs could be held back for an hour before one faces the day. Surprisingly, there are a great many people who faithfully do this, and they find a solemn stillness enters their hearts that stays with them throughout the day. That hour in touch with the divine Life gives them the courage and strength they need. The din of the factory, the pressure of office business, the exhausting routine of conducting classes become less irritating and distressing. They have made room in their hearts for God, and with His presence come peace and quiet. Senses dead to the world's discordant din are better able to recognize the divine Voice when it whispers in their hearts. It is possible, we know, to achieve this recollected interior silence, wherein one hears the Word; but, we repeat, it is very difficult. The noisy, nervous world ceaselessly conspires to disturb the silent cloister of the heart and drown out the whisperings of the Eternal Word.

The early solitaries fled from contact with men. They knew the havoc noise could cause in their interior life. In the desert they were relatively free from all exterior distractions.

And so in Carmel the rule of silence must be kept with scrupulous exactitude. When once the signal has sounded, ending the period of recreation, a nun even in the midst of a story, as we have mentioned, may not presume to utter an additional word. Difficult though the rule may seem in the beginning of one's convent life, it is not long before we appreciate the value the rule of silence has in our monasteries; for we realize that without silence our recollection and our solitude would be constantly disturbed and ultimately rendered impossible. Pope Leo XIII once said, "Without silence there is no prayer, without prayer there is no Carmel."

While I found the observance of silence trying at first, and while, frankly, I broke the rule occasionally (as when I tried, in a moment of vanity, to exhibit a painting at the cell doors of several nuns), still from the beginning there was a deep desire within me for Carmel's solitude. I wanted the seclusion of a cell where I could pour out my heart to my Beloved. Every Carmelite finds her delight in isolation; she never tires of being alone. Silence and solitude—these are, I have discovered, necessary elements of the purest spirit of Carmel.

Each Carmelite monastery has a special devotion to Elias, the saintly prophet who was the first to lead the eremitical life. God commanded him to flee from the dwellings of men and hide himself in the desert far from the multitude. "Get thee hence," God ordered him, "and go towards the east and hide thyself by the torrent of Carith. . . ." Elias taught the holy hermits of Carmel to detach themselves from all that was not God. And it was the dearest wish of Saint Teresa of Avila to restore to Carmel this pristine spirit of silence.

It is said that the one thing needed to reform any house of religious that has fallen into lukewarmness is to enforce rigidly the rule of silence. Lack of silence and failure to control one's tongue can ruin a monastery in short order. Charity quickly diminishes, and recollection and fervor decline. In the cloister, as in the world, one is apt to fail in speech more easily than in any other way. "If any man offend not in word, the same is a perfect man." So once a nun has become master of her tongue, she has advanced a long way on the road to perfection.

In Carmel every possible step has been taken to assure the absence of noise. Besides the holy Rule, which forbids talking at all times outside the recreation periods, we silence the distracting tumult of the world by excluding from the enclosure all radios, newspapers, and novels and all picture magazines and "movies." Our feet shod in soft sandals make no sound as they move about the silent corridors. The parlor grille and the monastery wall—everything in our life—tend to protect us from the world's turmoil and guarantee us solitude of spirit.

We may never, according to our Rule, enter the cell of another nun—except, of course, that of the Prioress or Novice Mistress. The reason for this, again, is to protect our solitude. One of the postulants, charged with the duty of distributing clean laundry, naïvely interpreted quite literally the instructions of the Mistress of Novices. Told that she might, in the execution of her assignment, put a foot in the nuns' cells, she hopped in and out of the rooms depositing the laundry on the cell tables instead of leaving it at the doors!

Only one nun, the Turn Sister, is ordinarily permitted to converse with lay callers. She is forbidden to talk of worldly matters, except in so far as she may offer a few words of advice or consolation or a promise of prayers. Salesmen who come to the turn find talking to the unseen prospect on the other side of the turn taxes all their sales technique. To close a sale without getting inside the enclosure is not easy. Just recently a man selling floor wax displayed monastic patience as he demonstrated his product on various convent articles, including the shelf of the turn itself, and had the Sister show the shining results to Mother Prioress piece by piece. One deliveryman was obviously frightened by the eerie mystery of the turn and stuttered, "L-l-lady, do I gets out o' here the way I got in?"

The office of Turn Sister does cause some distraction for the nun assigned to answer the calls from outside, but the nuns regularly relieve one another of this duty, and no one is disturbed for long.

Each Carmelite monastery has always been likened to a mountain; in silence and in solitude each nun lives as though she were already in Heaven. In this pure, precious silence for which she hungers, she is able to listen to and penetrate ever more deeply into the Infinite Silence and possess God.

It should not surprise anyone to hear that a cloistered nun rejoices in being alone and in silence. That is precisely what we had in mind when we left the world and entered the enclosure. To be undisturbed and alone in each other's company is why lovers in the world seek solitude and silence. Any noise or intrusion disturbs the joy they find in each other's presence. It is the same with a nun and her Beloved Spouse, Jesus. We know that Our Lord is to be found in the silent depths of our souls, and in solitude we are able to enjoy Him and plead with Him for the people of the world.

Any one who desires to belong to God will hear His voice; whether you are in your factory or office or in your kitchen, you can, if you will try, rise above the restlessness of created things and enter the silent desert of your heart and there hear the calm, consoling whisper of Our Lord. Again I repeat, this is not easy; but I know it is being done.

Is it not the desire for silence that has made the "week-end retreats" for men and women so popular in our own times? As Our Blessed Lord suggested, people are seeing the value of going apart and spending some time in silent recollection. They find peace returns to their souls and strength to their hearts, enabling them to face more calmly the world and its problems. After a few days in relative silence, they realize more than ever before that talk does not necessarily mean thought. They are better able to listen after this period spent in solitude, away from the unbearable din of the busy world.

We learn early in Carmel that God's life is a silent one; we are to model our lives on His. Sound belongs to matter—sometimes it is senseless, often it is irrational, and not infrequently it is sinful. That is why in Carmel—in union with the Mystical Body everywhere—we plead with the God of silence to forgive the sins of the tongue, to silence the words of hate and quiet the noise of war's madness. If only those who control the power of government and direct the alarming preparations for universal suicide would seek rest for their souls, go apart and listen to the plea of the Prince of Peace!

I hope that all this insisting on silence has not given a wrong impression. Our monastic silence is not due to any morose anti-social disposition on the part of the nuns, nor is it due to a dumb taciturnity that finds nothing about which to talk. Most Carmel-ite nuns, much as we appreciate the silence of the enclosure, find pleasure in talking during our two recreation periods permitted by the Rule. And most of us like conversation so much that we would never enjoy passively listening to a radio or watching tele-vision, even if such modern "necessities" were permitted in Car-mel. But we are not alone in finding it difficult to curb our tongues —Saint Teresa, the gifted conversationalist, had to force herself at times to keep silent.

It is wonderful to watch the young postulants and novices gradu-ally acquire control of their speech at recreation time, though at first they are apt to monopolize the conversation or to introduce topics of a worldly nature. This control, in great measure, is learned and perfected during the long hours of silence, when the novice is taught the meaning of Saint James's words: "If anyone think himself religious, not bridling his tongue . . . that man's re-ligion is vain."

Since useless talk leads to dissipation, we admonish the novice never to speak merely for her own sake or for her own gratifica-tion; or, as Edward Leen says so forcefully, "never [to] speak to satisfy an impulse, but solely for the glory of God, for the right accomplishment of duty, for the promotion of truth, for the exer-cise of charity, for the comfort of the sorrowful and for the pur-pose of brightening the lives of one's fellows."

To reduce the necessity of any "emergency" for breaking silence, Carmel has a set of signs by which we are able to communicate mes-sages. We are not able, like the Trappist monks, to carry on a con-versation with our sign language, but with our hands we are able to express many thoughts. For example, if we wish to speak to or about Mother Prioress, we touch the veil; in referring to the Mis-tress of Novices, we touch the scapular; if we are looking for the

Turn Sister, we form a circle in the palm of the hand. When we join the fingers of the right hand turned upward, we indicate a cup; bread is requested by forming a circle with the thumbs and forefingers. The novice has no difficulty learning the signs and for some time rather enjoys putting them to use.

Like the "long river," Carmel flows ceaselessly and in silence. Perhaps nowhere on this restless earth is there a calm repose equal to that which settles on a Carmelite monastery in the evening. It is a stillness that nothing may disturb. Not only may we not speak, we may not *do* anything that might cause a noise. Sweet silence wraps us round with its soft mantle, and each nun withdraws into her own interior silence.

While Carmels are called the "sanctuaries of silence," there is far more to solitude than the negative aspect of no exterior noise. To be completely silent, something else is vitally needed.

Silence is not an end in itself; it is a means, along with solitude, of being recollected. It is an aid to concentration and to love. To be recollected, ordinarily, means that one is silent, and one must be recollected in order to pray. Despite the unavoidable noise in a factory or an office or a home, a person could be momentarily recollected and could, in the midst of the din, be in prayer. It is *interior* silence that matters most. The imagination, the emotions, the memory, and, most of all, the desires can speak also, and unless they are silenced there is no real recollection.

Within the cloister of Carmel, as our good friend Monsignor Middleton once said so beautifully, "there is another cloister—the enclosure of each Carmelite's heart."

It was new to me when, as a novice, I first heard about the silence of the soul. But it didn't take long before I realized that this silence is the most important of all. Not thinking of anything but my Beloved, immolating my imagination, my memory, and all my desires, *there* is the precious Great Silence so difficult to achieve. Saint John of the Cross says that only one desire does

God allow in the soul: the desire to do the will of God and carry the Cross of Christ. It was a relatively easy thing to reduce the tumult raging on the outside, but it was quite another to still the constant distracting din in my heart.

The first time I heard the Novice Mistress speak of the "silence of the eyes," I thought she was making fun. Then she went on to explain about the disturbances caused in the soul by the confusing and useless images that enter through these windows of the soul. "Silence of the imagination" was another of Mother's pet themes: guard against those interior sensations and feelings that disturb one's recollection and take possession of the heart.

Nothing that has been impressed on the mind through the eyes or ears is ever lost. The memory records everything irrevocably. I can recall still, and quite vividly, incidents that happened to me when I was a child of two or three. And it is these crowded memories of one's whole life that try so viciously to haunt and distract the soul striving for silent recollection. It is only by a constant effort of the will that they are kept deep down in the bottom of the soul's storeroom.

Silence must reside in the will if it is to persist for any length of time, because it is in the will that each human act begins, and only human acts can add to our sanctification. In the will reside the powers to love and to obey and to be silent.

Sister Elizabeth of the Trinity, the great Carmelite mystic of our day, pleads with us to let a "deep silence reign in the soul." And she adds, "If my desires and fears, my joys or my sorrows are not completely ordered to God, I shall not be solitary; there will be turmoil within me."

Silence is a lovely thing, and if it can exist anywhere in our noisy world, it will exist in Carmel, and we must do nothing to disturb it. Silence of the tongue and heart and mind, all are absolutely necessary for our life of prayer and contemplation; we can do nothing for the souls of others if it is destroyed. Our Blessed

Lord advanced in wisdom and in grace in the silent, hidden obscurity of Nazareth.

And so, if a Carmelite nun is to remain recollected, she must keep herself in that great interior silence. She must retain a silence of judgment, never bitterly critical; she must guard the silence of her intellect, never uselessly dwelling on vain or worldly thoughts; she must keep the silence of her will, wishing for nothing but the accomplishment of God's will, loving no one but her Divine Spouse, and only through Him loving the souls of all mankind. Like Mary, she listens silently to the Silent Word and becomes immersed in the abyss of the Silent Triune Love. She lets the Holy Spirit breathe in her so that she may experience the peace and quiet joy of His silence.

In this, as in everything else, the Carmelite nun tries to model her life on that of her Beloved, Who was born in the silence of midnight in the quiet of a cave, Who lived in the silence of Nazareth, and Who died while His silent mother looked on. My Spouse is the Word Whose noiseless power produced the universe and guides the course of the silent stars; I belong to Him Who placed the fragrance in the rose and the warmth in the silent sun, the light of which is darkness compared with Him.

The Carmelite nun has another perfect model, too—"the Woman wrapped in silence." Mary is the inspiration and the teacher of the solitaries. She shows us how to live the recollected silence which is gathered up into God, a silence wherein no fear enters to destroy the calm of the soul living intimately with God. She teaches us how to treasure the sacred secrets of her Divine Son in the holy silence of a tranquil soul.

In the secret cloister of each Carmelite's heart, we try to let the deep silence of love reign; we try each day to increase our love in order to approach more closely the God of silence and there plead with Him for the needs of a suffering world.

While I was preparing these few disjointed thoughts on the

Silence of Carmel, someone asked me, "Reverend Mother, how can you speak of silence the essence of which is quiet?"

My reason for attempting to tell you about our silence is simply the hope that you may know, in a general way, why we insist on hushing at the enclosure door the noise and tumult of the world; also the hope that some word of what is written may help you in your busy day to seek and find the solitude and quiet so necessary for finding God. Saint Gregory says, "A person given to much talk will never make any great progress in virtue." That principle applies just as much to you in the world as it does to me in the cloister.

Whatever progress we who lead the contemplative life make is made in silence; whatever spiritual growth is made in the world is made in silence also. As the *Imitation of Christ* says, "in silence and quiet the devout soul goeth forward and learneth the secrets of the Scriptures." "In silence . . . shall your strength be."

Naturally, it is much easier for us in the cloister to be silent. We are freer to converse with God, we do not have the distractions or the responsibilities that torment the soul in the world. But even so, much effort is needed for us to discipline our tongues and our imaginations that we may keep all our faculties at all times for God alone. When we scatter our strength and our energies by thinking of useless matters, we do not have the power to recollect ourselves and to lead our life of contemplation as we should.

In surroundings of deep peace high on the towering peak of Mount Carmel, the Carmelite spends her days. Every needless sound of human life is hushed. Only the low-murmured syllables of our office prayer sweep over the monastery. The whisper of the wind and the soft, soothing cadence of the psalms. Carmel is a good place to "wait with silence for the salvation of God."

*Chapter 14*

# Works Worthy of Penance

† ACTS 26:20

ON HEARING about the fasts and penances practiced in Carmel a friend of mine once asked, "Did you know, before you entered, that you would have to deny yourself so much?" I admitted that prior to my entrance I did not know the details of Carmel's penances; but I quickly added that it would have made no difference if I had known. I knew that closing the cloister door behind me did not mean the end of all struggling, and I recalled reading Saint Teresa's wise words about comforts having "no value for our inner life." I knew, too, there was to be a constant fight ahead against my selfishness and self-assertiveness and self-centeredness. I could have told her that frankly I did not come to Carmel to escape the miseries of life.

All the rigorous discipline and monastic austerity in Carmel are ordained for two reasons: to make reparation for the past, and to aid those who have not yet cooperated sufficiently with grace to amend their own lives. We try to make up in our penances for their debts.

When I chose Carmel, I chose the type of life I thought God

196

wanted me to lead. Like every nun in every religious community, I chose the whole of the life.

When I applied for admission in Carmel, I did not ask whether or not I might be permitted ever to listen to a radio or whether I might continue with my painting and music. I did not ask how appetizing the food might be, or if the habit would be rough and coarse, or if the sandals would be uncomfortable. I did not inquire about the rule of silence or whether or not I might see my relatives and friends frequently. I did not ask about the furnishings in the cell or the softness of the bed. I asked only for the privilege of sharing in the life of Carmel and in everything Carmel's life entailed. I wanted to do that for the sake of my vocation, for the glory of God, and for the good of mankind everywhere.

After all, what would a military recruiting officer think of a young man who volunteered to assist his country in an hour of great distress if the young man began by inquiring about the food and lodging and the material of his uniform and the softness of his cot? A soldier volunteers for the Cause, and he accepts his tin plates and metal cups, his foxhole bed and coarse garments, as part of the life he freely undertook. Nor does a soldier look for sympathy because he has slept in mud and fought vermin and filth along with his country's enemy. All this is his glory.

It is much the same in the army of Our Lord. One should not be amazed to see a young woman voluntarily enlist in this spiritual army. She wishes to conquer herself in order that she may be able to make amends for the outrages committed against her Master. She deprives herself of all comforts and luxuries—even seeks out additional ways to add to the discomfort of her body—in order that these vicarious sufferings, deliberately sought, may be united with those of her Blessed Lord's and bring good to others.

While it is true that the girls who come to Carmel today are from homes where cars and radios and television are considered quite indispensable, and where there is no problem about food for the table, still they are reminded that there are hundreds of millions of people who do not have any of the things many Americans consider essential, millions who are rarely able to eat as much as they want.

We do sleep on a bed made up of two planks stretched across two trestles, on top of which is a sack of straw. This is a quite different arrangement from that to which we were accustomed in our own homes. Still we know that the majority of the people on earth have no innerspring mattresses and many do not even have a sack of straw on the boards that form their bed. Frankly it is quite easy to accustom oneself to the hard bed and rough straw and even the lack of linen sheets. As a matter of fact, I have always been so tired when I go to bed that I'm sure I could sleep quite well on a concrete slab!

The same is true of our monastery diet. Our Rule states, as I have mentioned previously, that we may never eat meat, except in case of illness or infirmity. Here again we are aware of the fact that for many of the world's millions meat is a rare luxury; and by many others (vegetarians, for example) meat is shunned completely.

We are well aware also that many homes, not only in the so-called "backward" areas of the world, but here in America, have no plush easy chairs and reclining couches. Why then should we expect them? In Carmel there are no soft padded chairs—either in our cells or in the recreation room. When we sit, it is on a straight-backed wooden chair.

We know there are millions of barefoot poor and shoeless refugees throughout the world; so we must not give our homemade rope sandals a second thought, should we feel that they are a source of penance.

Many homes throughout the world are bare of pictures and ornaments; they have no musical instruments or works of art; that is one additional reason why in a Carmelite monastery it would seem incongruous to have our cells or common rooms luxuriously appointed. We do not need these things for the edification of guests, as some convents do, because we are not permitted to entertain visitors within the enclosure of Carmel.

In speaking this way, I am sure you will understand that we do not in any sense mean to condemn all these modern comforts. There is nothing wrong with soft beds and easy chairs, good food and works of art. We wish merely to say that in our monasteries they would be out of place and would be a distraction in the type of life we are called to live. The cloister is not meant to be a quiet, comfortable haven.

I mention these things merely to show you that we are deserving of no sympathy because of the way we live, nor do we wish to elicit your pity in any way because we may lack what you think are essentials. Should you be impelled to laud us for depriving ourselves of luxuries that are far from commonplace in most of the world, we would have to beg you to refrain, lest Our Lord say to us, "Behold you have received your reward."

The important thing is not that we deny ourselves certain conveniences (when possibly we could have them): it is the *motive* for which we deny ourselves that makes the difference. What we do is done not from necessity, but voluntarily; not for a few weeks, but for life. What we do is done for Our Blessed Lord.

Actually there is little material difference between a somewhat overweight fashionable woman of the world voluntarily forcing herself to follow a rigorous diet, so that she can rid herself of ten or twenty unsightly pounds of excess flesh, and the fasting of a Carmelite nun. When a nun, for example, requests special permission to undergo a bread-and-water fast for nine days for the soul of an unrepentant sinner who is at the hour of death, her diet may not be any more severe than that of the fashionable lady. However, there is obviously a tremendous difference in the motives prompting the self-denials, and a great difference also in the effect the fasting has on the people involved. The one is done for the sake of the body and could very well be vain; the other is done for the sake of the soul and is, we can presume, in every way selfless.

As I have mentioned, the penances which I expected would be difficult and trying have never really caused me much concern, and that is the usual observation of the postulants and novices today. The bed, with its coarse bedclothes, the fasting, the rough habit, the absence of radios and musical instruments, the lack of mirrors and cosmetics—these are quite minor problems, and each nun adjusts herself quickly to them.

Every nun in Carmel seems to agree that the most difficult penance is fatigue. There is never a moment, from 5:30 in the morning until she retires at 11 at night, when a nun can "completely relax." Except during the summer months, when we rise at 4:30, a nun may never use her bed during the day. In the summer we are permitted an hour's siesta at noon. In our cell we must use the straight-backed wooden chair. I cannot tell you how many times during my early years—yes, and my later ones, too—I longed to throw my exhausted body across the straw sack on our bed. In chapel we must kneel without the support of a kneeling bench and hold our office book always in the proper manner. Once when I was observed leaning against the wall, I was reminded that "a Carmelite leans on nothing but God"!

Fighting back this constant feeling of fatigue is the most difficult of penances.

Besides the thought of my Beloved which should make everything easy, I had the heroic examples of Saint John of the Cross, the bright star of the Dark Night, and Saint Teresa, the tireless reformer of Carmel. When I recalled all they accomplished in their busy, fruitful lives and when I reminded myself that they never averaged more than four hours' sleep, it was difficult to pity or to pamper myself.

It is true, as Saint Teresa tells us, "God prefers your health to your penances—and that you obey." Still, we must admit that God does not want us to indulge our bodies in any way; and He doesn't like to see us too long in bed.

Saint Lutgarde, the Cistercian mystic of the twelfth century, was ill once with fever. She thought it more prudent to remain in bed. Suddenly she heard a Voice: "Get up quickly, Lutgarde; why are you lying there? At this very hour sinners are wallowing in their vices, and you ought to be doing penance for them. . . ."

Another unexpected, and, for me, rather trying penance was the rule that forbade eating or drinking anything between meals. (With permission a nun may drink water at any time.)

Postulants coming from homes where there is access to well-stocked refrigerators or who have had the habit of dropping into a drugstore on their way home from school find it hard to curb their appetites between meals. Individual tastes are not consulted in the cloister; one must eat what is served; and since the day in Carmel is long and the life strenuous, one must eat sufficient. We don't come here to die as quickly as possible; nor may we do anything to hasten the end. Carmel is not a planned, slow suicide; its austerity is tempered by prudence. I repeat, we do not condemn food nor the body, in Manichaean fashion, as intrinsically evil.

Keeping our holy Rule exactly is a far more acceptable penance than fasting on bread and water. Monastic regularity is just as trying at times as insufficient sleep. To stop instantly one's work and to cease abruptly one's conversation and to repair immediately to the next scheduled duty is a daily source of penance, for to be late is a fault and to rush is a fault; one who acts promptly is always on time.

Our life, obviously, is not designed to afford pleasure to our sensible appetites. We are asked to forgo every claim to all things that might give enjoyment to the senses, for these are the source of the most powerful passions of the heart. In order to love God perfectly, a nun must have no other good but Him. To be too cautious about her health is like creeping to meet her Beloved; to long for sensible pleasures is like having one foot still in the world.

Girls love comforts. In America they love the movies, dances, ice cream, and dainty food; they like fashionable clothes, late sleeps, and late nights. Yet in America the life of Carmel with all its discomforts and penances is growing more and more popular with the modern girl. Our American youth, despite its strange restlessness and its reputed mania for pleasure and ease, is overflowing every monastery of contemplation and solitude. There is the mystery and there is the fact.

We have received letters from friends in which they have asked us what we mean by "taking the discipline."

Well, before I attempt to answer that rather delicate question, let me first tell you why we do it.

A mother might, in a physical way, discipline her child should he become unruly. She does this, of course, for her child's training. An athlete undertaking rigorous exercise in preparation for a contest might—and, I presume, not infrequently does—inflict bodily punishment on himself to harden his muscles and discipline his body. A surgeon once told us he lifted many times each morning a fifty-pound weight to strengthen and steady the muscles and nerves of his right hand. No one gives these matters a second thought.

Saint Paul puts the problem this way: "I chastise my body and bring it into subjection, lest while preaching to others, I myself become a castaway."

Chastising one's body has nothing at all to do with the Fifth Commandment—unless, of course, it were done in excess and thereby impaired the health of the body. Our primary purpose in using the knotted cords of the discipline on our bodies is to keep them always under control.

Never, of course, is this penance inflicted upon oneself with the severity of, say, Saint John of the Cross.

One evening Saint John of the Cross, exhausted by fatigue and illness, asked the Prior's permission to take his evening meal a little earlier. But as soon as he had eaten, he was grieved at having given in to himself and for perhaps having disedified the brethren. He went to Padre Antonio and asked permission to accuse himself of his fault in the presence of the Community. When the hour for the meal arrived, John entered the Refectory with bared shoulders and holding a discipline in his hand; he advanced to the center of the room, knelt down, and scourged himself. He then accused himself. The discipline whistled again, and its blow fell like hail on his flesh. Only a Saint who has felt the purity and holiness of God could be so moved to strike himself for what seems to us a very minor imperfection.

In Carmel, when we are inflicting this penance upon ourselves, we have more than our own bodies and our own souls in mind. It is true that we accompany the flagellation with the chanting of the psalm *Miserere* for our own sins; but we also recite prayers at this time for the exaltation of the Church, for peace and concord on earth, for our benefactors, for the souls in Purgatory, for those in the state of sin, and for those in captivity.

This exercise is performed in the choir, in common, in every Carmelite monastery of the world; it is done at the time of night when possibly the spirit of the world is running most rampant.

Our vows also are a penance. By our vow of poverty, we deny ourselves those goods which might otherwise be legitimate for us to enjoy; by our vow of chastity, we deny ourselves those goods which are the pleasure of the heart; by our vow of obedience, we deny the greatest good of all—our own wills. Most people try to avoid taking orders, being poor, eating tasteless food, being thirsty, being uncomfortable. We try to make up for all this by our life of penance.

It is clear, I trust, that we take our vow of obedience, not because we don't like to do as we wish, or because we have anything against liberty: we take it because we want to give something very precious to Our Blessed Lord. We take the vow of poverty, not because we don't like to have things of our own, or because we think it is sinful for anyone to own things: we take it because we wish to give everything to God. We take the vow of chastity, not because we think marriage and human love are wrong, but because we prefer to be the virgin spouses of Christ.

We take the vow of obedience to atone for the pride and self-will that cause so many to disobey; we take the vow of chastity because some abuse marriage; we take the vow of poverty because some sin against property by avarice and greed. We try in some small way to make up for those excesses.

A Carmelite nun denies herself food because some people make food the aim of their lives and end up eating more than they need. We do not drink between meals, not because we think it is healthy to do without drinking, but because there are many who drink to excess and end up being drunkards.

When a person is deeply and truly in love, he finds there are a great many things he can get along without. When a nun is really in love with her Divine Lord, she finds out the same thing and she never misses anything. For the sake of the Beloved, she can more easily discipline her body and curb her natural desires.

And all this brings about a self-control and strength that is immediately noticed by the new postulant. There is nothing of softness in the life of Carmel.

Let me insist, I am not condemning those in the world who may occasionally indulge themselves too much; even He who was Innocence did not do that: "He that is without sin among you, let him first cast a stone at her." I am simply saying that someone has to make amends for these abuses, and in Carmel—in a feeble way —we try to do that.

The first step in the religious life of Carmel—as indeed it is everywhere—is to rectify the past, to purge out the old habits and worldly inclinations, to burn out every stain, every blemish of the soul. We call this the "purgative way." The most effective way to do this is by purifying penance and daily mortifications. For most of us the past has become a deep-rooted part of our being, and only hard work can rid the blood and brain and heart of it.

So in order to strip ourselves of all self-will and self-love—which are irrevocably opposed to the love of God—we need to do penance and mortify the senses. It is not enough to be sorry for our past offenses; it is not enough to try to forget them—once a person has discovered the infinite beauty and holiness of God, he wants to make up, not only for his own sins, but for every sin that has ever been committed. Love has been wounded, and reparation must be made.

Carmel is a desert to which we come to make amends for ourselves and, in so far as we are able, for others. Carmel was never meant to be a playground; it is, in a sense, a battleground; and many a nun undergoes the fierce struggles of the anchorites of the early Christian Church. Saint John the Baptist had a bitter struggle in the desert, as did Our Lord Himself. By definition an ascetic is one who exercises himself, one who exerts himself in the struggle, and one who trains to prepare himself for that struggle.

Discipline is necessary for the body, as well as for the impulses, just as medicine is necessary to repair sick members. Medicinal remedies may be bitter; penance and mortification are often bitter too.

Our self-discipline is not an end in itself, but a means we use to reach the real end—Love. For no matter what we do, if we do not have charity, it does us no good; "even if we deliver our bodies to be burned," unless we do it for love, there is no meaning to it. We come here to die for Christ and for souls, not to pamper or to indulge ourselves. As Saint Teresa says, "The more you give in to the body, the more it requires. It is very fond of comfort."

However, Carmelite nuns, as we have said, have, besides self-discipline, a further reason for penance. We are always conscious of our unity with all mankind everywhere, and we are aware that there are many who do not have the courage or the love necessary to do penance for their sins; so we have taken upon ourselves the task of satisfying for the guilt of their souls. We plead and deny ourselves in order that these people may turn from sin and approach their Merciful Father humbly and repentantly.

Nothing in our entire life gives us the joy that comes to us when we hear of a wayward soul's return to God: "There is more joy in heaven over one sinner doing penance than over ninety-nine just who need no penance."

It is the unrepentant sinner that causes the nun to multiply her penances, deny herself, and plead with Our Heavenly Father.

In all this we try to emulate Our Blessed Lady, who, though she had no personal guilt, did not spare herself but accepted her share of the world's guilt and suffered sorrowfully to appease the justice of God.

That is the great mission of Carmel, to save not only our own souls but the souls of all mankind by our sacrifices and our prayers. We wish to atone for those who will not atone; we wish to stay the arm of God's justice, which might strike down those who defy Him and blaspheme Him.

If we had a medicine that would cure all the ills of man, we should wish to send the panacea to all in need of it, even though we might never see those whom the medicine saved; and even though those helped would never know from whence came their salvation; and even though many might not even wish to taste the medicine. There is such a cure, and the cure is penance.

To hear of an offense committed against God is to want to do penance for that sin. And when reparation is made, those in

Heaven rejoice, and we on earth will be at peace, all unworthy though we are ourselves.

We should like to be able to say with Saint Catherine of Siena, "Lord give me all the pains and all the infirmities that there are in the world to bear in my body; I am fain to offer Thee my body in sacrifice and to bear all for the world's sins that Thou mayest spare it and change its life to another."

It is for love of God that we leave the pleasures in the world in order that we may bring all mankind to Him.

Our Blessed Lord loves the sinner who repents. His most beautiful parables tell of repentant sinners: the prodigal, the woman taken in adultery, the story of Magdalen, the Good Shepherd. There is more joy in heaven over one of these repentant sinners because God loves His children and He knows there is always danger that one might be lost.

It is at the foot of the Cross that we learn the depth of God's love: "God so loved the world that He sent His only begotten Son. . . ." The cross in our cell can show us what sin can do to God and what we can do for sinners. We are not viewers of the Crucifixion; we are participators. Sin matters so much; how can anyone be indifferent to it once he has knelt at the foot of the Cross?

The Carmelite nun does penance that the sinner who refuses to turn to God may acknowledge his guilt and discover peace and the love of God. No one who has the habit of sin or who lives in the occasion of sin can appease God's wrath—only one who loves Him. Just as blood can be transfused from one body to another, so our penances can help, because of our oneness with the Mystical Body of Christ. Just as we are bound up with the sufferings and joys of the members of the Mystical Body, so we are united with their faults and must be also in their reparation. That is our great consolation. We are able, in part, to cover the cost of a soul when the owner will not or cannot cover the cost himself.

Let me quote here Bishop Fulton Sheen's kind words about

contemplatives: "These hidden dynamos of prayer, the cloistered men and women, are doing more for our country than all its politicians, its labor leaders, its army and navy put together; they are atoning for the sins of us all. . . . They have not become less interested in the world since leaving it; indeed, they have become more interested in the world than ever before."

"Greater love than this no man hath that a man lay down his life for his friend."

When we receive the veil of profession, we are covered with the symbol of total surrender.

There is only one way we can secure grace for someone in need, and that is through personal sacrifice. Carmel's life is, as someone once said, a "holocaust." It is only by offering ourselves for others that we can be in any way like our Spouse.

Closely allied to our life of penance and self-discipline is Carmel's custom of public correction of external infractions of the Rule. We call this the "Chapter of Faults."

At first blush this is, I'm sure, a hard practice to appreciate. Yet there is no way superior to this in aiding a nun along the path of virtue. It is one of the most essential aids for the maintenance of the perfect observance of the Rule.

Here is how it works.

A professed nun is appointed Monitress, or Zelatrix, for the week. It is her duty to observe and report infractions of the Rule and to admonish those at fault: anyone who came late for community exercises; anyone who was careless about choir ceremonies; anyone who ignored the rules of religious decorum, who failed to keep silence, or who broke any other regulation of the house.

This is done publicly, not only because it is an opportunity for the nun accused to practice humility (and we know there is no other way to practice this virtue unless one is occasionally humiliated), but also because a fault of which we are accused publicly is soon corrected. We may hear conferences on the various virtues and the Rule of the Order, but these words never leave the impression on a nun that a public correction does.

The Sister Monitress upon being interrogated rises at her place in the Chapter Room and says without exaggeration or comment simply this: "In charity I accuse Sister So-and-so of the fault of doing such-and-such. . . ."

A penance is then imposed by the Mother Prioress, and the nun accused silently thanks the Sister Monitress and prays for her.

Does that sound strange? Well, it really isn't so unusual. Might it not be the same among a group of actors who are eager to perform in absolute perfection? Might not one say to the other, "Watch every move I make, and stop me if it is not perfect"? We are the same; we are striving for perfection in the spiritual life, and anyone who is able to aid us along that difficult road is our friend and benefactor. We are grateful that someone is really interested in our improvement.

Unless asked to do so, the accused nun is never permitted to reply or excuse herself—even when the accusation may seem unjust. She is to have this additional opportunity to resemble her Innocent Spouse, Who was so unjustly accused in public for crimes He could not commit.

The nuns may also accuse *themselves* of their own faults—there are times when even the Prioress may take part in this. And, as one young nun has said, one definitely recalls the fault one accuses oneself of in public; something quite positive should be done to correct it.

Once the Chapter of Faults period comes to an end, the matter discussed there may never be mentioned again.

It is a strange fact that during the hour of recreation which follows the weekly Chapter of Faults, the nuns are gayer and happier than at any other recreation time. All nuns have observed that.

Even the severe Chapter of Faults has its humorous moments. I recall the nervous young novice who once caused a ripple of laughter throughout the austere Chapter Room when she shyly confessed that through carelessness she "broke her skull on the floor."

For the average American girl, "Chapter" is not, in the beginning, easy. Most nuns confess a certain repugnance at first toward these public confessions. Yet each one admits that after she has been accused, or after she has accused herself, a great peace comes over the soul.

To some people much of what I have said about our life of penance will make no sense at all. Only those who realize that we must pass through suffering and tears to get home will understand in part. Only those who look on life upon this earth as Saint Teresa did, "a night spent in a wretched inn," will understand it completely.

But after all wasn't my Beloved's folly far more foolish than mine? Look at what He did! What happiness to be called foolish and unreasonable by the world! As the Little Flower said, "it is the world that is insane because it heeds not what Jesus has done and suffered to save it from eternal damnation."

## Chapter 15

# As Needy, Yet Enriching
# Many
†2 COR. 6:10

A CARMELITE nun should be, by the very nature of her vocation, a specialist in prayer. Or, to give it a more modern twist, she is a career woman in the field of prayer and contemplation. Prayer is our profession, our first occupation. Besides the time we spend in private devotions, each day seven hours are spent in formal, community prayer, the greater part of which is devoted to the recitation of the Divine Office, the official prayer of the Church. Each one of us tries to substitute herself for those who have no love for God, or very little; for those who do not pray, or pray very badly.

We are not in Carmel long before it becomes clear that we have a responsibility to perfect ourselves in prayer if we are to be faithful to our vocation. It is taken for granted by everyone—Bishops, priests, religious, and lay people—that we must pray for the needs of others.

Recently a Bishop wrote, "May I beg prayers and sacrifices for the success of our priests' Retreat next month? . . . As the priest, so the people. . . . There must be more saints in our ranks."

Seldom a day goes by without a letter from a priest begging us to pray for some project he plans or for some soul he wishes to help. "Request your obedient Sisters in Christ to pray most vigorously and most vehemently for my intention." A very young priest wrote shortly after he began his parochial duties, "I would ask your prayers and the prayers of all the Sisters for these two intentions: first, that I will be faithful always to my spiritual exercises; and, secondly, for the help to get up in the morning two hours before I celebrate Holy Mass, regardless of what time I retire the night before."

A chaplain wrote during World War II from Algeria, "I know full well that it is your prayers that have so far protected me and the men from sudden and unprovided death and I shall continue to count on them heavily for our safe return."

Carmel, from the first week of postulancy, impressed me as being a spiritual headquarters far up in the battle area. The nuns seemed almost to "stand at attention" whenever the Prioress read an urgent request for prayers. Prayer seemed like a sort of warfare —silence was our fortress—penance and mortification were our strategy.

Let me, at random, jot down just a few such bulletins; you will understand something of the martial atmosphere by these announcements; you will see that women who are silent within cloistered walls can strive for peace and assist their fellow men.

*"Terrible automobile accident . . . recently ordained priest, not expected to live. Beg God to spare all who are involved."*

*"Holy Father's health failing—all should increase their private prayers."*

*"Non-Catholic just called requesting prayers for a little boy kidnapped in Kansas."*

*"Doctor Starry 'phoned. Very delicate operation at 10:30."*

*"Keep in mind priests who are on Retreat this week."*

*"It is Saturday—remember those who may be having difficulty making a worthy confession."*

*"Mission at Sacred Heart Parish. Pray especially for those longest away from the Sacraments."*

*"Oklahoma's ex-Governor Trapp has only a few hours to live —Mrs. Trapp just called from the hospital bedside."*

*"Five men to be executed at midnight. Pray that they may be strengthened and consoled. All who are able may make a Holy Hour from eleven to midnight."*

*"Unemployment is increasing—anyone who wishes may ask permission to go on bread and water."*

*"Word received that a marriage is threatened with divorce— pray hard that God may save the marriage for the sake of the children."*

*"Be mindful of the refugees streaming into Hong Kong and those seeping through the Iron Curtain."*

*"S.O.S. from Father Keller requesting prayers for new Christopher project."*

It is obvious that everyone's problems, trials, and aspirations are the concern of Carmel; and the explicit confidence placed in the power of our prayer terrifies and humbles us. Perhaps it is the faith others have in our prayers that enables us to pray with greater confidence. All weakness though we are, we like to feel that our prayers from the high mountain of Carmel pour down and overflow the busy streams of life, that they overflow into every hospital and across every battlefield and everywhere that grace and help are needed.

Occasionally we receive requests for prayers for an intention that is incompatible with Christian charity. One evening after visiting hours an unusual caller came to the turn. At that time Joseph Stalin was still alive, and our visitor was not pleased about it. He said he had an urgent request. He wanted the nuns to pray that he might get an opportunity to "bump off" Joe Stalin. The nun at the turn tried patiently to explain that we simply could not pray for anything like that. "But," she added, "we will continue to pray for his conversion." The militant visitor would not hear of prayers for Stalin's conversion—he wanted prayers desperately so that he could "bump him off."

Actually when word did come that Stalin had died, there was a feeling of sorrow for him expressed by several nuns, even though there was great joy in the hope that communism would be weakened by his death. We prayed for his soul because it was terrifying to contemplate a soul that had "compiled such a record" going before the Eternal Judge.

It may surprise some people to know that we, too, have need of prayers for ourselves. Priests often write and assure us of remembrance in their Masses; lay people occasionally promise us a share in their rosaries. We need this spiritual help in order that we may fulfill our vocation as perfectly as possible.

This will amuse you. One evening a noisy group of people carrying out, rather vociferously, a missionary enterprise of their somewhat boisterous sect, gathered in front of the monastery. After a well-sung hymn or two, they started to shout, "We're a-praying for you sinners in there; we're a-praying for you." We thought that was very good of them because we feel that all too few people pray for us.

In Carmel each year we divide up the whole world geographically, and each nun is responsible for a portion of it. (The Little Flower, for example, prayed especially for America the year before she died.) So, in a general way, I might offer my prayers and sacrifices this year for Africa, next year for Europe, and so on. The areas are written on slips of paper (called billets) and chosen on the Feast of the Epiphany.

Besides the large areas of the world we make everyone and every plan for good an object of our prayers.

We pray for those who may die each day, that they may die in the state of grace; we pray for those in mortal sin, that they may have the stain removed. We pray for those who zealously work for peace, and even for those who foolishly try to bring about disharmony in the world, that God may change their hearts.

Some deserve our special love and prayerful attention. How moved we were when a priest who attends disabled veterans wrote to us, "I beg an inclusion in your prayers and good works, not for myself, but for over 131,000 'forgotten men,' War Veterans, disabled for life, in scores of our government hospitals . . . at places like Valley Forge and Deshow, one sees the horrible effects of modern war—thousands with no arms, no legs, or only parts remaining; hundreds blind for life, hundreds of the extreme paraplegics, the pitiable 'basket cases!' " The chaplain went on to tell us that many of these men are rebellious and blasphemous toward the Crucified Christ. Many are in deep despair.

We assured the sympathetic priest that we were not forgetting these disabled heroes of our country's great victory. We pray for them because we know they need great strength and courage and faith. They need faith to turn their suffering into profit for themselves and for the world. They are so near to great sanctity. Once, they gave their all in a great Cause; now their physical deformity must not bring on a spiritual deformity. Our constant prayer is for these poor men, to whom our hearts go out in deepest sympathy and sorrow; it is our prayer for those who are despondent and in despair that they may remain courageous now as they were once in the teeth of bitter battle on the field. They need our prayers. They need the visits and letters and gifts and prayers of every American for whose freedom they were wounded. Don't let these men complain, as the man by the pool of Bethsaida did, "When the waters are moved there is no man to put me in."

It is true, as the chaplains assure us, our government has given these men every physical help; but there is a need for something more. They need the faith and courage that come from prayer. And it is hard for a man, as ill as many of these men are, to pray— even should they wish to pray—that is why we have special prayers at Carmel for wounded veterans and particularly for the saddest of all human cripples, the basket cases. I dare say there are few places in our country where our heroes—both living and dead— are held in greater esteem and more loving memory than in Carmel. The world is so busy about many things—it is our business to remember.

During World War II, I was still in our New York City Carmel, which overlooks the Harlem River. We could see Medical Center across the river, reflected in the sparkling silver stream; and we would pray for those suffering there and for their grief-stricken loved ones everywhere.

Often as I opened the breviary to begin our Office prayers, I would take within my praying hands all the boys in our armed forces. Sometimes I would picture a ship full of young uniformed Americans falling into the cruel, cold sea, and in tears I would go down into their watery graves with them as they made the supreme sacrifice. My prayer, as I tried to prepare their souls, was that not one of them would be lost—Catholic, Protestant, or Jew. Many a night I sobbed myself to sleep in prayer for those thousands facing the maniacal mass murder of modern war.

So we pray for those who are in danger and for those who are sick. We pray not only that they may get well quickly, but, what is more important, we pray they may have courage to see in their illness the hand of God and use their suffering for the purification of their own souls and the good of mankind.

We pray for the virtuous and devout in offices and factories who are mocked and ridiculed for no other reason than that they are trying to follow the delicate dictates of their conscience.

We pray for students, especially for those whose faith is exposed to the poisonous insinuations of godless professors; we pray that all searchers for the truth may find it and, finding it, may face it squarely and accept it completely.

We pray for those suffering behind the Iron Curtain—for the children who may not know Our Lord's name or that there is a Christmas still in the rest of the world—those poor children, more sinned against than sinning, from whose eyes the limpid look of childhood has long since disappeared.

We pray for all those who have strayed from the path of virtue and are stumbling blindly along the alleys of sin; we pray that they may return to their Father's house, where alone they can find peace and rest. We pray that all those who have habits of sin may not only know but *do* what is right. How our hearts go out to the man or woman who has become the victim of alcoholism; how their dear ones must suffer to see them lowered beneath the level of beasts! We pray that they may control this vicious urge and use in moderation what they now use in excess—or better still, for such as these, that they may get the strength of will to see its danger for them and refuse to let it pass their lips. And prayer alone can accomplish such a feat.

Sometimes our prayers are not answered in the way we think they should be. Sometimes they are not answered as quickly as we should like them to be.

A good example of heroic patience in prayer is the story of our Mother Teresa's brother, Mike.

Mike left home to seek his fortune in the world when he was twenty-one. In his wanderings all over the country, he had wandered away from the Church. Mother Teresa heard only once from Mike in forty-three years and had not seen him during all that time. Down and out, suffering from asthma, and rejected by the world, he had come to the end of his rope in the little town of Pitcher, only two hundred miles from the Oklahoma City Carmel just founded by his sister, who was offering her prayers for him. Miraculously it was discovered that he was Mother Teresa's brother, and with great charity saintly Monsignor Garvey brought him to the Old Folks' Home here, comprised at that time of just two small cottages. Today the beautiful new St. Anne's Home for the Aged, established by Bishop McGuinness and staffed by our Third Order Sisters (Active Carmelites), is said to rank second to none of its kind in the entire country.

When he recovered sufficiently in health, Mike came to Carmel to visit his sister. Mother suggested he visit Our Lord in the Chapel. Mike did. He returned in tears to Mother in the speak room: "That is the first time I have been inside a church since I last saw you, forty-three years ago."

A few days later in our chapel Mike made his "First Communion"—the first, in almost half a century—and there was great joy in the hearts of the nuns. Within two years Mike died in peace in Oklahoma City's St. Anthony's Hospital. He was attended at the end by Monsignor Garvey and also a Carmelite priest; several of the hospital Sisters also knelt about his bed as he breathed his last.

It is abundantly clear, I'm sure, *why* we pray. "We try," as Saint Teresa puts it, "to assuage the anger of an offended God." This is why we live here together: prayer is the mortar that keeps us together. God has brought us here for that purpose; it is our work, the object of our longings; our tears and prayers beg for this, not for any worldly matters. The first point of our holy Rule states that we are to "pray without ceasing." This is our most important duty. Penance and mortification will follow easily; for we shall not be self-indulgent when we are on our knees pleading for others. The saintly Teresa warned all of those who were to follow her, "If ever we should fail to offer our prayers and sacrifices for souls we would cease to be Carmelites." And she added, "Indeed, all I cared for . . . was that as the enemies of God are so many and His friends so few, these latter might at least be devoted friends of Jesus Christ."

A Carmelite cannot let her soul be shut up in the narrow confines of her cloister. Her thoughts are those of the Redemption, and we try to cover the world with our co-redeeming prayers. Nuns in a monastery are often thought of as one person in the role of Moses, raising his arms to Heaven, interceding for the people on the plain, and singing, in the name of mankind, the glory of God.

To say for whom we pray and to try to indicate why we pray are relatively easy chores. But now, in as simple a manner as I am able, let me attempt briefly to tell you *how* we pray.

"Lord, teach us to pray. . . ." That was the pleading request of the disciples who followed Our Blessed Lord and watched Him absorbed in prayer.

Following the instructions and suggestions of Saint Teresa, our first requisite in prayer is to *love* and to *think* when we pray. We must consider who God is, to Whom we are talking, and we must consider who we are. Then we shall be reverent and humble. If we do not keep in mind the dignity of the Person to Whom we speak—nor our own insignificance—no matter how many prayerful words our lips may utter, we cannot call that prayer. We must be reverent when we address God; we must be careful to speak humbly to Him and have our minds on what we are saying. It is not enough to say the words, no matter how distinctly pronounced; we cannot speak to God and listen to the world.

"Lord, teach us to pray. . . ." Listen again to the words of the Master as He instructs us: "When thou prayest, go into thy room, and closing thy door, pray to thy Father in secret; and thy Father, who sees in secret will reward thee. But in praying, do not multiply words, as the Gentiles do; for they think that by saying a great deal they will be heard. So, do not be like them; for your Father knows what you need before you ask Him. In this manner therefore shall you pray: 'Our Father who art in heaven, hallowed be Thy name! . . ."

Picture Our Lord beside you teaching you how to pray. And as He slowly speaks the words to you, you repeat them slowly and deliberately, thinking of their inexhaustible meaning and beauty. Our Lord makes Himself one with us: *"Our* Father." Then He teaches us how to address the Heavenly Father.

I think all will agree that an indispensable aspect of prayer for everyone is recollection. Recollection is not, of course, the same as contemplation, about which we shall say a few words in a moment.

In its negative aspect recollection is primarily the opposite of distraction. When we find it difficult to concentrate our attention on the matter of our prayer, we say we are distracted—we cannot "collect ourselves"; we are fitfully flying from one image to another or from one thought to the other, never giving much attention to any image or any thought. This state of mind obviously is the antithesis of recollection; there is no concentration, no attention given the object we set out to think about.

When we are recollected, we are wide-awake to the essential object of our prayer, we are unhindered by any superficial diversion, we refuse to dwell on any trivial matter. Engrossed in the one thing that matters, released from all surface interests, we deliberately set our minds and hearts on God. Most often this requires a strong effort on our part. When we begin the Divine Office, we pray first for recollection: "Open, O Lord, my mouth to bless Thy holy name: cleanse also my heart of all vain, perverse, and distracting thoughts. . . ." We wish to empty ourselves and awaken to the one thing that really matters.

Our memory and our senses combine to make it difficult to collect ourselves as we should wish. This should not discourage anyone from making the effort. No one finds it easy. Saint Teresa, mistress of prayer, confessed that she found mental prayer so

difficult at the beginning of her religious life that there was no
penance she would not have preferred to the penance of trying to
recollect herself. She would even shake the hour glass to make the
time move more quickly! I was comforted when I read about Saint
Teresa's difficulties. I would say that it is quite unusual for anyone to go through an hour's meditation and remain completely
recollected for the entire hour—at least, I think it safe to say that
I have not yet, after twenty-five years in the cloister, been able to
do so. And so I try to make the most of my distractions, should
they persist.

This is what I mean: suppose I'm meditating on the text, "Unless you be converted and become as little children you shall not
enter the Kingdom of heaven." Picturing Our Lord taking the
little child and affectionately pointing to the child as the model
for all of us, I become distracted and my imagination skips back
to my school days. I'm on a picnic at St. Joseph's Orphanage at
Peekskill. . . . I sadly watch the little ones who will never know a
mother's love or feel a father's warm embrace. . . . I am about to
take one of the children in my arms, when suddenly I "come to."
I'm back in the choir of the monastery. Let me see, I was meditating on "spiritual childhood" and Saint Thérèse's Little Way.

But before I can get very far along the Little Way, I'm off again
to the orphanage at Peekskill. This time I deliberately stay there.
I start talking to my Beloved about those little ones, and I beg
Him to father and fondle them and keep them free from harm. I
ask Our Blessed Mother to strengthen and console the self-sacrificing Sisters who supply the mother's love these children need. I
then pray the Lord of the harvest to send more Sisters to assist
these tireless nuns in their long hidden hours of difficult work. . . .
I thank God for the wonderful Sisters who have dedicated their
lives to these children. . . . I thank God for my own parents. . . . I
thank my Beloved for staying with us, and for not leaving us
orphans.

So instead of being upset by my distractions, I try to make the best possible use of them. I repeat, even the Saints had difficulty in recollecting themselves; but the reason they succeeded in reaching the heights is that they never became discouraged; they put forth a serious effort at all times to rise toward God and put as much distance as possible between their present material concerns and Our Blessed Lord. Once we have, with deliberation, taken the first step, the next step will be that much easier. We shall have more light as we advance.

This effort to be recollected we try gently to carry over throughout the whole day in all our activities, all our prayers, all our thoughts—we try never to separate ourselves from God, the ultimate center of our being. We give to each scheduled act that place which it can rightfully claim in the eyes of God; we look at everything from God's point of view. The awareness of God's presence continues to resound in our soul; it forms the background for all our external acts and interests. The soul then never becomes dull, nor is the voice of the Beloved ever silenced in the depths of our soul. We never allow ourselves to become submerged in external objects, no matter how essential or valid they may be.

Closely connected with the idea of deliberate recollection is the state of *contemplation*.

In contemplation, as Saint Teresa says, we are "like babes in God's arms; we do not know what we are enjoying, nor how; we know only that it is good, and good for us."

It would be rash of me to attempt a scientific explanation of a state that even the great mystic could not explain scientifically.

"Mary hath chosen the best part." Our Blessed Lord in these words indicates the primacy of contemplation. He does not mean that we are to spend all our time in contemplation, nor that everyone is called to spend more time in contemplation than in action. He merely wants to point out that contemplation is the higher of the two, the goal at which ultimately all of us who will be numbered among the elect are to arrive.

Supernatural contemplation is not merely *thinking* about an object, nor does it have anything to do with "contemplating" a future action. It is the conscious dwelling on a truth, dwelling in the bliss derived from the light of beauty and goodness. Contemplation is *absorption* and *enjoyment*. Mary Magdalen not only listened to the words of Jesus; with deep love, she immersed herself in the beatific presence of her Master, in Whom she saw her God. As Saint Teresa puts it, "Contemplation is a divine union in which Our Lord takes His delight in a soul, while the soul rejoices in Him." It is the science of love, calm and peaceful.

In contemplation, I "abandon" myself to God, I "commune" with Him—through "dark glasses" I look up at the face of God. When I am in a "contemplative attitude" I am relaxed and restful —but, of course, not every relaxed and restful attitude is contemplative! It is the relaxed and restful *soul* we speak of here. I do not mean by this to imply that contemplation is not activity. It represents the highest form of spiritual activity. It is "a simple gaze at truth," as Saint Thomas Aquinas says, adding "under the influence of love."

The object of a Carmelite's contemplation obviously is the Triune God.

When I am not only truly recollected but also in an attitude of contemplation—as I might be, for example, at the Elevation of the Sacred Host during Mass—time, for a moment, seems to halt. This is a momentous moment, a "now," in which the rest of the world fades away. Lost in God, like Magdalen I look up into the face of my Beloved. "My Lord and My God . . . how admirable is Thy name in the whole earth."

Perfect infused contemplation is a pure gift of God. Our part is to prepare for it by making our vocal prayer and our mental prayer as perfect as we can possibly make them.

How essential it is, then, that I first get rid of everything that cannot be held up before the face of my Beloved! "Who shall ascend into the mountain of the Lord; or who shall stand in His Holy place? The innocent in hands, and the clean of heart."

Here again is where our religious vows help to fit us for our role of contemplatives: by our vows of poverty and chastity we rid ourselves of all preoccupation about material things—we "empty" ourselves of everything; by our vow of obedience we renounce our own will and give that, too, to God. Now we are ready to face the Divine Reality; now we belong entirely to God; now we are able to love and praise the Beloved unmindful of all else—for it is in contemplation that the central theme of our whole existence, our union with God, is realized. Seeking the presence of God in all circumstances might be said to be the very essence of our Carmelite life.

To arrive at the goal of contemplation spiritual writers and the experts in prayer, like Saint John of the Cross, Saint Ignatius, and Saint Teresa, suggest that, at least in the beginning, we follow carefully a method. Thank God, I was able to overcome my repugnance to using a system—otherwise I might still be beating the air and wasting my time.

We repeat, the first and most important step in our prayer or meditation is to recall to whom we are speaking; we thereby recall to mind the presence of God. We think of an attribute or aspect of God or Our Blessed Lord, and in this way we recollect ourselves. We then dwell on the subject of our meditation, turn it over in our minds, and draw from it sentiments or affections of love and praise. From these affections we may enjoy moments of contemplation, losing ourselves in adoration of the Beloved. We end by resolving to remain close to Our Blessed Lord, to please Him and do something special for Him that day.

When asked what she did when she finished her prayer, Saint Teresa replied, "Imagine a person so deeply in love that it is impossible for him to live apart from the object of his affection for a moment. Yet his love could not be compared with that which I feel for Our Lord, which prevents my quitting Him for an instant, either rejoicing in His presence, or speaking with Him or about Him."

As we have seen, this ideal condition in which the soul is always in a state of recollection is not easy to achieve; yet a surprising number of people—outside as well as within the cloister—do experience it. Contemplatives can be found, even in the din of our factories. However, even in Carmel we do not let this recollected attitude interfere with the assigned duties of the nuns. Jokingly we say, "Sister, if you can make the soup and at the same time keep in the presence of God, that is wonderful; but if in striving for recollection you let the soup burn, better for you to keep in the presence of the soup."

Of course, work can be a great help to recollection and prayer. Saint John of the Cross says, "Work and silence recollect the soul in God." "Ora et labora" (pray and work) indicates that even for us in Carmel, whose primary purpose is contemplation, work is not to be wholly forgone.

I repeat, in the enclosure we have the advantage. We have fewer distractions; our seven hours of scheduled community prayers give us the practice and the atmosphere that is needed. But I plead with you who do not have our advantage to make a place in your life for contemplation. You do not have to be in vows to be a contemplative. Refuse to let yourself be dragged into the whirlwind of exterior activities, driven incessantly, as so many are, from one task to the other with never a pause to reflect on God and turn a glance of love or gratitude toward Our Blessed Lord. Don't, we pray, let the uninterrupted tension of modern living sap the spiritual life from your soul.

Consecrate even a small part of an hour each day to mental prayer, to thinking about Our Blessed Lord, Who loves you so much and has done so much for you, and in Whose company you are to spend your Eternity. Separate yourself for this short interval of silence from all the "weighty concerns" that seem to demand your attention. Forget them for this moment, and think rather of the one thing that really matters, your soul, and its relationship to its Creator.

Don't, I plead, don't permit your daily obligations to make you forget your chief purpose in life; don't be "troubled about many things," like Martha, and be unmindful of the one thing that is necessary.

The world needs the perfume of your prayers as much as it needs the help of cloistered nuns; the unwholesome air of lust and avarice cannot be purified in any other way. One faint spark from your heart burning with love could set the world on fire.

## Chapter 16

# Walk in His Ways and
# Love Him     †DEUT. 10:12

W<small>HAT</small> a glorious sunrise this morning! The sky was turquoise, overlaid with a sunburst that reached to the middle of the heavens. It was like waking up in paradise. God seemed very close. Sunlight has always been for me a nearly perfect symbol of God's love—"who maketh His sun to shine upon the just and the unjust."

Most Carmelites find the life of the cloister exacting and tiring, but no true Carmelite ever finds the life dull or tiresome. No one who is in love is ever bored in the presence of the beloved. If there are boredom and emptiness in modern life—and we have reason to fear that there are—we know that it could come from many sources, even from something similar to love; but it can never come from love. Like people in the world, nuns want life, life in all its fullness; we want knowledge, knowledge in all its purity; we want love, love in all its sweetness.

It is a source of great sorrow to me whenever I hear of married people who cannot find happiness in one another's company. They seem to feel that an evening without a party is an evening a year

227

long. They must be constantly "going someplace." I say, it is hard for me to understand how that state of mind can exist in people who are deeply and genuinely in love.

Carmelites are in love with Jesus; and we are never happier than when we are alone with Him. With the bride in the Canticle, we can say, "In His company there is no tedium."

Here, I hope you won't mind if I repeat something already mentioned. We do not give up anything when we enter the cloister: we merely make an exchange. We have substituted the love and happiness of God for the love and pleasure of creatures. This love, like human love, does demand sacrifice; it inspires, as human love does, a giving of self. We are watchful lest we offend that love. The more ardently one loves, the more one shrinks from offending the beloved; and whenever, through thoughtlessness, one does give offense, one grieves instinctively and quickly seeks to make amends. Saint John of the Cross says that "perfect union takes place when there is naught in the one that is repugnant to the other."

Whether it be divine love or human love, the greatest proof of love is to be willing to give one's life for the one loved: "Greater love than this no man hath, that he lay down his life for his friend." A Carmelite gives her life to her Lord that He may do with it as He wishes. And "life," as used here, includes all that we are and have, as we saw when speaking about the vow of obedience.

We enter the cloister because we love Our Lord; we enlisted in His service to do something for Him and for souls. That is why superiors in Carmel are always concerned about the genuineness of the vocation when a girl says she wants to enter Carmel to find peace and quiet. One should not enter the cloister to receive anything, but rather to give all. The search for personal peace is far too selfish a motive to survive for long the austerity of our life. It is like contracting marriage mainly for personal security or some other selfish advantage; when sickness and misfortune and misunderstanding have to be faced, the marriage is not likely to stand the test, whereas the deprivation of material things is no insurmountable hardship if the sole motive for conjugal union is love. The same applies to the nun in the convent.

The love of Jesus, rapturous beyond one's most extravagant desires, is the only motive that should prompt a girl to leave the world and become His spouse; it is the only motive that will enable her to take up her daily cross and persevere to the end. When a nun loves Our Lord, she will automatically love all mankind at the same time, and in the same way as He does. We must love everyone in the way that Christ has first loved us: "By this shall all men know that you are My disciples."

In the monastery our human affections are not stifled. We love others with a far more universal love and far more ardently than ever we did in the world. Now we are at the service of everyone. We try by our prayers and sacrifices to help all those who are hungry and homeless, all those in despair and near death, all those who are in sin and in sorrow. We wish to envelop all mankind, as Our Lord does so tenderly, in one single embrace, and we wish to love unto the end and forever. We wish to exclude no one, as He excludes no one. We wish to imitate Him whose arms stretch out to heal and comfort the entire human race, including even the most abandoned, repulsive, and criminal souls on the face of the earth. We wish to imitate Him Whose love overflows into the irresistible cry, "Come to Me *all* of you." His heart is big enough to hold us all.

We are instructed in Carmel to model our love for creatures after the example of Our Divine Spouse, Who proved His love by sacrifice. He did not love with any thought of recompense, or self-interest, or pleasure. Although He was disappointed when the affection He showed others was not returned, nevertheless He continued to serve and love even the ungrateful. His was a true love, ever more eager to give than to receive.

A Carmelite has only one thought, one desire: to respond as perfectly as possible to God's love. Ardently she yearns to give herself completely and continuously to Our Lord, Who gives Himself wholly only when we give ourselves wholly to Him. At the beginning there is much of the "natural" in her manner of acting; her likes and dislikes almost unconsciously influence her in her relations with others and even with God Himself, but as she grows in the spiritual life, a change imperceptibly takes place; the Holy Spirit gradually takes possession of her mind and heart and will, and there comes a time when she is aware that she is no longer loving merely with her limited human heart but with the very love of God Himself—"for the charity of God has been poured abroad in our hearts by the Holy Spirit who has been given to us."

In meditation God reveals Himself to the one who earnestly seeks Him. To Our Holy Mother Saint Teresa, Jesus once said, "Gladly would I reveal Myself to all men; but the world makes so much noise in their hearts they are deaf to My voice."

It is beautiful to watch the young girls who come to the cloister respond with glowing countenance to the grace of God as He warms their hearts with the sweet breath of His divine love, making sacrifice easy and penance a joy.

Is it not evident that we find our greatest happiness in loving Our Blessed Lord in the silence and solitude of Carmel? This, I repeat, is the meaning of our whole life, this is the secret of our apostolate—the love of Jesus. Oh, when will the fire He came to cast upon earth become a great conflagration and a sweet enkindling in the hearts of all men? Our Divine Master does not need our deeds—except as a manifestation of our devotion. He thirsts only for our love. Without that, nothing else we give has any value in His eyes.

As a Carmelite nun I have shut myself off from the world, not out of indifference towards my fellow human beings—still less out of scorn for them—but in order to lead as many as possible into the loving arms of God, that ravishingly attractive Being Who is resisted only when He is not known. I wish to know Him better, to honor and love Him more and more and come as close as I can to Him and thus be in a better position to help my fellow man. It is only the quality of my love for Jesus that matters, not the quantity of my penance and my prayers; and as I grow in that love, so do I increase my power to help save and sanctify the world.

Let no one think that a Carmelite nun is unmindful of those in the world who are in need. She tries to model her love upon that of the Heart of Jesus, which knows no frontiers and overflows the universe. She, too, would love all classes and all races. She knows her Spouse ate with and consoled the rich, even though He was one of the poor. She knows "there is no distinction of Jew and Greek; for the same is Lord over all, rich unto all that call upon Him."

I recall one of our young chapter nuns telling me of her feelings after World War II when our soldiers were called to Korea and so many of them were being wounded and killed. She spoke of the extra prayers and penances she was offering for the safety of their bodies and the salvation of their souls. "Many of these young boys are only eighteen years old," she said; "some have never been away from home before and some will never come back to their homes again. And there is many an only son among them. It is easy to appreciate the dangers and temptations to which they will be exposed and, alas, to which many will succumb. . . . Our concern for them and for their families must be very great; we cannot forget them."

It is when we have pity on those in misery and in danger that we are most like Our Blessed Lord, Who had compassion on the multitude because they were as sheep without a shepherd, and Who had pity on the adulterous woman because no one but He could purify her sin-stained soul. Jesus lets one ray of His light fall on a sinful woman at His feet, and she begins to weep and to rise. He speaks one word of love to her, and she is encouraged to dream of perfection, and to "dream of perfection is to go higher."

Sister Elizabeth of the Trinity reminds us, "In the evening of life only love remains. We must do everything for love. We must constantly forget ourselves." We wish, in every act of the day, to please Our Blessed Lord. Like a faithful spouse, the nun tries to do everything she can to please her Beloved. She does not live her life for herself, but for others through her Blessed Lord, Who spent Himself completely for us, Who was never concerned about a place to live or about His honor or His dignity, Who was concerned only about the honor and glory of His Father and about us and our eternal salvation.

It is only when we approach the Source of all charity that we begin to appreciate the great love Our Blessed Lord has for us. "He loved *me* and delivered Himself for *me*." Knowing this makes my own sufferings bearable—even a joy. Love is no deeper or more genuine than our willingness to suffer for the one loved. As Saint Teresa puts it, "The measure of our love is the measure of the cross we can bear."

Saint Thomas says, "The perfection of the Christian life is none other than the perfection of charity, for the Christian life consists specifically in love." All other virtues are, in a sense, secondary and are perfect, in the supernatural order, only in the measure in which love inspires them. The reason Christian perfection consists in charity is that the goal of everyone should be union with God; and only love—humble after the manner of Our Lady's love—can unite us with God. "He that abideth in charity, abideth in God, and God in him."

Nothing can be truer than Truth Itself. Then why is it that more people do not heed Christ when it is He, the Truth, Who gives them the words of life and the Way of life, especially when He speaks of His love for us and of His desire that we all be one in Him? Sometimes it seems as though He had never spoken to the world.

For meditation this morning, I used this Scripture text: "We are sons of God even NOW, and what we shall be hereafter has not been made known as yet." Oh, if only man would use his fine mind to penetrate these great truths!

The night before His death, Jesus, praying for His disciples, said, "Not for them only do I pray, but for them also who through their word shall believe in Me, that they all may be one, as Thou Father in Me, and I in Thee, that they also may be one in Us: that the world may believe that Thou hast sent Me. And the glory which Thou hast given Me, I have given to them; that they may be one as We also are one. I in them and Thou in Me, that they may be made perfect in one, and the world may know that Thou hast sent Me, and hast loved them as Thou hast loved Me."—That is, by communicating to them the same love as to His Son, though not, of course, in the same way: not actually but by way of union and transformation in love. "Nor," says Saint John of the Cross, commenting on these words, "are we to suppose from this that Our Lord prayed that the Saints might become one in essential and natural unity, as the Father and the Son are: but that they might become one in the union of love as the Father and the Son are one in the oneness of their love."

"O souls," he goes on to say, "created for this, and called thereto, what are you doing? What are your occupations? Your aim is meanness, and your enjoyments misery. Oh, wretched blindness of the children of Adam, blind to so great a light, and deaf to so clear a voice; you see not that, while seeking after greatness and glory, you are miserable and contemptible, ignorant and unworthy of blessings so great."

So my perfection as a Carmelite nun will consist not in my contemplation, not in any work I may do in the cloister, not in my penances, not in my sufferings—I shall become more and

more perfect only as I grow in love. That is why all obstacles to
this love must be removed, not only sins, but even legitimate affections for created things which could impede my approach to
and possession of God. It must be an active, practical love, one
that gives proof in sacrifice of self.

In order to safeguard this love, which is increased by loving, I
have made a vow of chastity—I promise God in this vow to consecrate voluntarily my body and guard its inviolability for life. I
made my vow of chastity, as every nun and religious does, not because I thought the marriage state was evil or of doubtful moral
value; not to avoid marriage. I desired lifelong virginity in the
religious state because I thought God wished me to give myself
entirely to Him in this way. I renounced the love of an earthly
spouse solely out of love for Our Blessed Lord, Whom I wished
to serve with an undivided heart.

I have found that the Carmelite's love has no horizons, no
boundaries of home or family to restrict it and that our cloistered
love has an "apostolic fertility." When our love is strong and our
readiness to sacrifice is always present, we may be worthy, to some
extent, of these words of Pius XI: "Those who devote themselves
to a life of mortification and prayer do more for the extension of
Christ's Kingdom on earth and the salvation of souls than those
who labor in active works in the Lord's vineyard."

Saint Thérèse of Lisieux, in explaining her vocation to Carmel,
said:

*"As I meditated on the mystical Body of Holy Church I could
not recognize myself among any of its members described by St.
Paul; or was it not rather that I wished to recognize myself in all?
Charity gave me the key to my vocation. I understood that since
the Church is a body composed of different members, she could
not lack the most necessary and most nobly endowed of all the
bodily organs. I understood, therefore, that the Church has a*

*heart—and a heart on fire with love. I saw, too, that love alone imparts life to all the members, so that should love ever fail, apostles would no longer preach the Gospel and martyrs would refuse to shed their blood. Finally, I realized that love includes every vocation, that love is all things, that love is eternal, reaching down through the ages and stretching to the uttermost limits of earth.*

*"Beside myself with joy, I cried out: 'O Jesus, my Love, my vocation is love! I have found my place in the bosom of the Church, and this place, O my God, Thou hast Thyself given to me: in the heart of the Church, my Mother, I will be Love! . . .' "*

It should be clear that no young woman takes the step toward the enclosure of Carmel without having in her heart an intense longing for Our Blessed Lord and a burning desire to please Him. It should also be clear that no novice takes the step toward the vow of virginity without first understanding all it implies. She does not embrace perpetual chastity unmindful of the dignity and the beauty of the married state. To make sure that the novice understands what she is renouncing, the divine institution of marriage is explained thoroughly.

The vow of chastity is next explained—its physiological, emotional, and creative renunciation. The religious life and our vow of chastity are then given their proper spiritual meaning. The Carmelite nun is told that she will attain rich treasures in her religious life—treasures far surpassing those which the most promising human marriage offers to men and women in the world. When all this is thoroughly understood, there is no danger of any nervous disorder; for it is not continence that causes disorders, but the absence of the complete love-gift generously given. All of Carmel's Saints have been seraphs of love—models of self-surrender and self-oblation.

In her more than forty-five years in the cloister, Mother Teresa, who founded two Carmelite monasteries, has seldom—almost never—seen a nun troubled with neurosis. The reason may be that Mother Teresa exercises more than scrupulous care about admitting doubtful girls into the cloister; or it may be her constant motherly care and vigilance over the young nuns; or it may be the thorough manner in which the life of Carmel and all its implications are explained—or it may be a combination of all these. At any rate, thank God, we have had very little nervous trouble in Carmel.

In Carmel I have never had to suppress my instinct to love: Jesus is my Spouse. I have never had to suppress my mother instinct: all mankind are my spiritual children. The relationship between a nun and her divine Spouse is difficult for a worldly person to understand; but for all its spiritual and mystical significance, it is nonetheless real.

Let me quote a paragraph from Saint Augustine's *Confessions*, for he can express so much better than I who this Spouse of ours is:

*"But yet when I love Thee, what is it that I love? Not the beauty of any body, not the order of time, not the clearness of light that so gladdens our eyes, not the harmony of sweet songs of every kind, not the fragrance of flowers, or spices of aromatical odors, not manna, nor honey, nor limbs delightful to the embrace of flesh and blood. Yet do I love a kind of light, a kind of voice, a kind of odor, a kind of food, a kind of embracing when I love my God, who is the light, the voice, the odor, the food, the embracing of the inward man, when the light shineth into my soul which is not circumscribed by any place, when the voice soundeth which is not snatched away by time, when that odor pours forth which is not scattered by the air, when that food savors the taste which is unconsumed by eating, when that embracement is enjoyed which is not divorced by satiety: this is it which I love when I love my God."*

Can you not see my joy in longing for and possessing this love? He will always come to anyone who in holy, silent solitude yearns for Him. He always permits us to find Him. In the evening of life He is going to judge me by love, for "GOD IS LOVE."

"If anyone loves Me, he will keep My word, and My Father will love him, and We will come to him and make Our abode with him."

This love, as Saint Augustine tells us, is strength and beauty, and he urges us to pursue it, for "without it the rich man is poor and with it the poor man is rich." Whether in the cloister or in the world, love is patient in misfortune, moderate in good fortune, strong in suffering, glad in toil, secure in temptation.

If we have this love, we have everything, and then nothing else —absolutely nothing else—matters. Saint John of the Cross was speaking from experience and from an overflowing heart when, in the *Living Flame of Love,* he wrote these burning words: "The heavens are mine, and the nations are mine; mine are the just and the sinners are mine. Mine are the angels and the Mother of God; all things are mine; God Himself is mine and for me, because Christ is mine and all for me. O sweetest love of God, too little known, he who has found Thee is at rest. O my love, all for Thee, nothing for me: nothing for Thee, everything for me!"

If only everyone would *believe* in God's merciful love and in His eagerness to lift us up and even make us partakers of His divinity! Great Saints have to a degree sounded the depths of God's unfathomable love. They understand best His great love for every single soul, and they can speak best of that love. The Little Flower understood how much Our Lord wants everyone of us: "His love of us," she says in her *Autobiography,* "makes Him actually blind. If the greatest sinner on earth should repent at the moment of death, and draw his last breath in an act of love, neither the many graces he had abused, nor the many sins he had committed, would stand in his way. Our Lord would say nothing, count nothing, and without delay He would receive him into the arms of His mercy. But to make Him thus blind and incapable of reckoning the number of our sins, we must approach Him through His heart—on that side He is defenseless."

It is a pity that so many people in the world confuse love, which is a spiritual thing, with attraction and pleasurable sensations, which are physical things. There is no question about it: our age is disordered in many ways, but principally it is disordered in its understanding of love and of suffering and in its incessant search for pleasure. People seem to feel that they must gratify their senses. Their desires and yearnings for self-satisfaction are limitless.

So many confuse pleasure with joy. Pleasure gratifies the senses. Joy is in the quiet of our will and is profoundly spiritual. Joy is deeper, surer, nobler, and more constant. And here is the wonder of joy: it can coexist with physical suffering, with privation, anguish, and even spiritual desolation.

Christian joy is a gift of God flowing from a good conscience, through contempt of earthly things and contemplation of things divine. It is the fruit of real love.

No doubt it would be a cause of great surprise to some people to know that in Carmel there is a distinct inner jubilation, despite the extraordinary spirit of penance. Great penance and great joy. Now this, I'm sure, doesn't make much sense to the worldly wise. Yet there has always been a definite connection between the two. We see it in the life of Our Blessed Lord Himself. We see it in the Saints: Francis of Assisi, John of the Cross, and Teresa of Jesus —all had great suffering and deep joy.

Saint Teresa once said, "Nobody who does not know it by experience will believe the joy we have in these monasteries when we find ourselves within the enclosure." Saint Teresa had in mind the joy that comes from fraternal charity and from serving Our Blessed Lord and listening to Him in the silence of our hearts.

"I have spoken thus to you in order that My joy may be in you and your joy may be complete."

The monastery, I soon learned, was a "holy family" where each one sacrifices herself for the others. We have been told that charity begins at home and that if we possess fraternal charity we will certainly attain to union with Our Lord. If we are lacking this charity, we are far from pleasing to God. Serving others in love may at times cost much—very much—in sacrifice, as it did Our Divine Saviour.

My first year in Carmel taught me the truth of Saint Augustine's beautiful words when he described how sweet it became for him, of a sudden, to lack the sweetness of vain pleasures: "It was now a joy to renounce what I had dreaded losing. Thou . . . didst set me free from them. As Thou wast ridding my heart of them, so didst Thou enter in their stead, more delightful than any pleasure —though not to flesh and blood; brighter than any light, but deeper than any secret, loftier than any honor, but not to men lofty in their own conceit."

Like Saint John the Baptist, I rejoiced "with joy because of the bridegroom's voice." Saint John leapt with joy on that day when, within his mother's womb, he heard Mary greet Elizabeth. He thrilled at his Lord's presence; and later, in penance and solitude, he gave up all pleasures for the joy of hearing the voice of Christ. He cut himself off from all creatures.

The Carmelite nun does the same; she is set apart for this one joy—to hear the voice of the Beloved. No other passing pleasure can satisfy me. That is why John fled to the desert; that is why I fled to the enclosure of Carmel. My joy is to be near my Beloved, Who has loved me with an everlasting love; my desire is to hear His voice—all other sounds are drowned out in the desert.

*Chapter 17*

# Delighted in Abundance
# of Peace

† PS. 36:11

I N the speak room just recently, a visitor asked me to what we in Carmel attribute our sense of deep, abiding peace. The answer I gave could, I think, be true of anyone anywhere who enjoys peace of soul: It is of primary importance that a person know the purpose of life, that he conform his actions to the manifest will of God, and that he interpret the events of life in the light of faith, I told him.

But we must not seek after peace directly—and the same holds true of happiness—or it will evade us. These things are always by-products. They follow in the wake of right conduct, and their degree always corresponds to the degree of our perfection.

It is so tranquilizing to be continually aware that we came FROM God, that we are here FOR God, and that we are going TO God. And it is such a joy to live in the friendship of our sweetest Jesus. For, as Saint Paul says, "To them that love God, ALL things work together unto good"—disappointments, reverses, illness, misunderstandings, difficulties of all sorts—yes, even our sins—all these things work for the good of those who love God and who know well that He Who is all-powerful "ruleth mightily from end to end, ordering all things sweetly."

It is not surprising, when we consider how earnestly mankind longs for it, that the first promise made at the birth of Our Lord

240

was *peace:* "Glory to God on the highest, and on earth peace to men of good will." Nor is it strange that in His parting words to His disciples the night before He died, Jesus said, "Peace I leave with you: My peace I give unto you."

For centuries before the birth of Our Saviour, the chosen people were longing for the Messiah, the bringer of peace, Who would heal the strife of the world. He was to be called the Prince of Peace. Every Carmelite nun spends long hours daily praying for peace, for concord among nations, for an end of discord and disunion and dissension. We try by our prayers and penances to be peacemakers, that we may deserve to be called "the children of God."

A true spouse of Christ gives little thought to herself. A person who constantly thinks of himself is rarely at peace, nor is a person who has no control of his desires, who yearns for material things beyond his means. Whoever has more concern for his body than he has for his soul, who insists on his own will instead of God's will, who is more anxious about time than he is about eternity, more conscious of the absence of comforts than he is about the presence of God, more anxious to be loved and pampered than he is to love and suffer, more interested in receiving favors and being consoled than he is in aiding his neighbor and comforting others—there is a person who seldom knows peace.

Some years ago, when I was experiencing a temporary loss of peace, I was given this beautiful prayer of Saint Francis of Assisi: "Lord, make me an instrument of Thy peace; where there is hatred, let me sow love; where there is injury, pardon; where there is doubt, faith; where there is despair, hope; where there is darkness, light; and where there is sadness, joy. O Divine Master, grant that I may not so much seek to be consoled as to console; to be understood, as to understand; to be loved, as to love; for it is in giving that we receive, it is in pardoning that we are pardoned, and it is in dying that we are born to eternal life." Many times, through the years, I have passed this prayer along to others.

Dante's line, "In His Will is our peace," speaks volumes to me.

Very early in our religious life we are warned not to set our hearts on anything outside the will of God. We are told to restrain our eager desires to have or to do until we find out clearly what Our Lord wishes us to have or to do. This attitude, called "holy indifference," prepares the way for unalterable peace; it must not be confused with a lack of feeling; we are referring here to an attitude of the will. We try not to desire a long life rather than a short life, health rather than sickness, honor rather than dishonor, consolation in prayer rather than aridity, until it is evident what God prefers in our regard.

In connection with this, I often think of an incident one unforgettable day when we had a fire within the enclosure. Three or four of the firemen, equipment in hand and straining to get at the flames, nevertheless stood perfectly still, their eyes riveted on the captain, without the slightest inclination to move in one direction rather than another until he surveyed the scene and issued the orders. Then they plunged ahead with all their might.

The old nuns tell about a postulant in Carmel who couldn't get this principle straight even after it had been repeatedly explained to her. Eventually they had to send Cynthia home. Her "indifference" was really nothing more than apathy. Even when something was manifestly the will of God, Cynthia would look up shyly, then lower her eyes, purse her lips, and say, "It makes no difference to me," whereas it should have made a tremendous difference to her. We must be indifferent only until we find out what God wants—and we must take means to find out what He wants. After that, we must be enthusiastic.

As I said, this indifference is in the will and not in the feelings. Although it is a great blessing to be able to feel deeply, feelings are dangerous unless they are guided and controlled. Emotion is a good servant but a bad master. The reaction of our Lord in the Garden of Gethsemane is a perfect example of holy indifference. Faced with His Passion and Crucifixion, a mortal fear came over Him. He sweated blood. He said, "My soul is sorrowful even unto death." In fact, He begged His Heavenly Father to save Him from it all: "Father, if it be possible, let this chalice pass from me . . ." but He added, "Yet not my will but thine be done!" . . . And you may be sure no infant in the arms of its mother ever rested as peacefully as Christ dying in agony on the Cross of His Father's Will.

In the cloister, little by little we are led along this path of holy indifference which leads to perfect peace—as far as it can be attained on earth. The ability to control our desires and hold them in abeyance until we know the will of God gives us liberty of spirit which frees us from the tyranny of pride and sensuality.

Souls that are caught in the nets of competition and rivalry cannot be free. A soul that is bound by the petty domination of jealousy, envy, and human respect cannot be more than a slave. Even the more pardonable bondage of fear makes it impossible to attain peace. How many people there are whom you know who fear *something!* Unreasonable fears, oppressive fears, paralyzing fears have no place in Carmel because we know that nothing happens but by the loving will of God, and we are at rest in His will.

I think it is a hopeful sign that so many of our troubles can be traced to a lack of enlightenment rather than to a lack of good will. "Father, forgive them for they know not what they do." I have often been astounded at the sudden change in myself after a confused idea had been set right. One of the many blessings of religious life is the help that is offered us—through spiritual directors, superiors, companions, and good books—to keep from confusion.

Not so long ago a terribly upset woman came to the turn to tell us of a serious misunderstanding she had had with her husband.

She was extremely wrought up; she was angry, and apparently all charity had gone out of her. What she felt in her heart, she expressed in bitter words. She said she hated herself; and because she hated herself, she hated everyone else.

We tried to bring back some charity and peace to her agitated heart. We pointed out the evident and deep-seated suspicion in her own character and told her what Saint John of the Cross says: "Where there is no love put love and you will find love." After she had spent some time in the Chapel with Our Lord, she became calm.

How often peace returns to those who seek it at the feet of the Prince of Peace! "Come to Me all you who labor and are heavily burdened and I will give rest to your souls."

As the poor woman bade good-by to the nun at the turn, she quietly remarked, "It was really my fault, Sister. . . . How I wish I were one of you nuns, free from all the problems of the world!"

In a sense she was right. God has chosen us out of the turbulent world, and He has set us apart, undisturbed by the cares of a family or of business. We are indeed blessed, and we are conscious of this fact. But it would be false to think that we are free completely from all problems. We have difficulties, also—economic, as well as spiritual—but we know how to keep them from disturbing our peace of soul.

My married sisters have urgencies and emergencies from which I am free. They have more than themselves to consider in illness or in death—others depend on them. In Carmel I do not have that concern. It is true that I must do all I can to preserve my health and not become a burden to the Community; but I know that I can be replaced very easily.

In the cloister we are in most ways old-fashioned. We refuse to let inconsequential things disturb us. We do not have to be concerned about our social prestige, except to become as humble and low as we can; we need not be anxious about our complexions or the smoothness of our hands, for no one among us pays any attention to these things. Changing styles in dress and shoes pass us by, for our habit is the same today as it was in Saint Teresa's time, and no one ever sees our loose-fitting, flat-soled sandals. We are spared many anxieties here that might disturb us were we still in the world.

I think I can say that since I have entered the cloister, except for the fear that I might not be worthy of Carmel and the dread I used to have of death, I have had no real fears. Early in my postulancy I heard the words of my Beloved: "Why are you fearful? . . . Behold I am with you all days. . . ." That was enough for me. Even should enemies—real or imaginary—gather against me (as they did against Edith Stein), what have I to fear? "Though I should walk in a dark valley, I will fear no evils, because Thou art with me. Thy rod and Thy staff, these comfort me."

Of course, a Carmelite does have, like everyone else, a certain apprehension about death. Even though the thought of dying and of being united with God in endless bliss delighted me, a mortal terror used to come over me at times when, in the infirmary, I'd dwell on the thought of that final wrench of soul and body. I tried to overcome this but couldn't. Then I learned that what I was experiencing was a perfectly natural reaction, that God never intended the soul and body to be separated; death was inflicted as a penalty for sin only after the Fall: "Thou shalt die the death." Now I look forward to it as a most efficacious—and my final—act of penance.

True and lasting peace of heart is a gift of God and should be prayed for. But it is a part of wisdom to keep in mind that in this life our peace is to be found in patient endurance rather than in freedom from conflict. Peace can deepen and mellow even in suffering and sorrow, but it cannot exist in a troubled conscience. It is when the soul is detached from sin and has become attached to God that it knows real peace. It possesses a conscience that is still and quiet. That is the reason one so often hears from the lips of a person who has made a good confession, "I feel a peace that I haven't had for a long time."

Another reason for Carmel's peace is the fact that we put ourselves in the loving care of our Heavenly Father—not by halves, but entirely. We are for that reason never inordinately anxious about anything—present, past, or future. Like a child in its mother's arms, we lie quietly in His embrace, having no will but His.

Nothing can destroy one's peace of soul more quickly than inordinate anxieties. There is no peace in the heart that is constantly agitated by worries or by fretting about things beyond one's control.

People with nervous disorders are apt to be unduly anxious about many things. Our Blessed Lord warns all of us: "Do not be afraid . . . you are of more value than many sparrows . . . do not be anxious for your life, what you shall eat; nor yet for your body, what you shall put on. The life is a greater thing than the food, and the body than the clothing. Consider the ravens: they neither sow nor reap, they have neither storeroom nor barn; yet God feeds them. . . . Consider how the lilies grow; they neither toil nor spin, yet I say to you that not even Solomon in all his glory was arrayed like one of these. . . . And as for you, do not seek what you shall eat, or what you shall drink; and do not exalt yourselves (for after all these things the nations of the world seek); but your Father knows that you need these things . . . seek *first* the kingdom of God, and all these things shall be given you besides."

This confidence in God accounts for our genuine and unalterable peace of mind. We are children living in God's house. Every moment of the day we are aware of His loving providence and His paternal love. Before me on the table is a bookmark on which are written these words: "Providence CAN provide, Providence DID provide, Providence WILL provide." Those who do not know this

Providence and this love are like orphans, uncared for and un-loved. Some are orphans through no fault of theirs; others have deliberately abandoned their Father's house to seek their pleasure in created things and to feed on the husks of swine.

We have a wonderful example of confidence and peace of mind in the life of our Holy Mother, Saint Teresa of Avila. She was a perpetual invalid, suffering intense physical pain. She was called an impostor, threatened with excommunication, shunned as an apostate. In Andalusia Teresa was treated as an undesirable per-son, abused, and brought before the Inquisition. In the midst of this surface tempest she was calm and her soul was at peace. She still could laugh: "Let them say what they will." She had com-plete confidence in her Divine Master. To serve, to suffer, and to love, this was her life, her martyrdom. Because her heavenly Spouse was with her, she was invulnerable, her peace of soul was never disturbed. She had learned the joy of suffering for love of His Divine Majesty, and that is true peace indeed.

Every Carmelite nun commits to memory Saint Teresa's beauti-ful words of trust:

> *"Let nothing disturb thee,*
> *Nothing affright thee,*
> *All things are passing,*
> *God never changeth.*
> *Patience gains all things,*
> *Who has God wanteth nothing,*
> *Alone He sufficeth."*

From the letters we receive and from the troubled souls that often appeal for prayers, we sense an increasing agitation in the hearts of modern people. We feel also that there is much uncer-tainty and disquiet in the hearts of those who direct the destinies of nations. It would seem essential for those who are attempting to effect world peace to experience peace first in their own hearts.

Of course, if the Prince of Peace is excluded from the plans for peace, it will be impossible for the world to live in harmony. Men and man's science cannot very well bring about peace, which is a spiritual thing and a thing of the soul.

Peace in the individual's soul is unquestionably a most vital factor in the realization of peace among men; for how can I be at peace with my neighbor if I am not at peace with myself?

That person has found peace who, as we have said, lives for God and for others and not for himself or for the things of this world (which are less than self). It is only when we look at this world and the things of earth in their proper light—when we compare them to the soul and to God—that we can find peace. "Peace is the tranquillity of order," says the Angelic Doctor.

There is no Carmelite nun who has not been deeply impressed by the intimate union of heart and the true harmony of peace that pervade the cloister. And it is quite evident that this harmony is produced not by a similarity of tastes—for there are no two of us alike—but by a spirit of self-abnegation.

There is a very definite connection between peace and humility, which someone has defined as "the silence of self." Our Lord has said, "Learn of me because I am meek and humble of heart and you shall find rest to your souls." Isn't it true that the humble person is not easily disturbed? The truly humble man has perfect equilibrium, for God is his center of gravity. He is below being puffed up and above being cast down; in all things he recognizes and loves the truth that "we are what we are in the eyes of God, neither more nor less."

Our custom of being accused publicly of external faults does much, I suspect, to rid us of any touchiness. Many times we hear things that are unpalatable to our pride; but it is a matter of Rule to pray for those who do us good—and one cannot pray in charity if one is sullen or embittered. If we are blamed for something we did not do, Saint Teresa suggests that we think of the many imperfect things which we did do and which no one knows about.

Most agitated and upset people—"neurotics" as they are called today—seem always overabsorbed in themselves. Saints, on the other hand, like Saint Catherine of Siena, Saint Teresa, Saint Paul, though highly nervous, spent themselves in serving others in complete forgetfulness of themselves.

Saint Teresa, along with her utter unselfishness, had a marvelous sense of humor; this great gift often saved her from breaking under the constant strain of her continual illness, work, writings, and direction. Few neurotics, I should imagine, are quick to see the funny side of things. New arrivals in the cloister are delighted with the nuns' keen sense of humor. At recreation periods we are always quite ready for a laugh. Edith Stein said that she laughed more during her recreation hours in Carmel than she ever did while she was in the world.

Doctors tell us that it is our severe discipline of mind and heart and body that favors both our good sense of humor and our peace of mind.

In his book, *Religion and Health,* Doctor James Walsh says, "I am brought into contact with a great many religious women every year . . . and it is a never-ending source of surprise to find how few of them suffer from the nervous symptoms so common in our time. . . ."

Important as are humility and a sense of humor in setting one's heart at rest, silence—interior and exterior—is equally important.

All spiritual masters admit that silence is a great help to spiritual peace. Our solitary and cloistered life gives us, it is true, an advantage in this regard. How few persons can maintain a lengthy conversation without saying something which might better have been left unsaid! And how often it is a heedless remark that sets in motion a train of thought which stirs up the emotions and cools charity! The spirit of peace never comes to a soul that is in agitation or frequently troubled by the turmoil of its passions and strong feelings. In Carmel, through long hours of prayer and meditation, we try to cultivate the spirit of recollection which continues throughout the day, and gradually we acquire a peace of heart seldom experienced by people in the world. With our motto "In silence and hope shall your strength be" as a guiding principle, one's whole being is enveloped with love, peace, joy, and a heavenly calm.

Even those who do not understand our life feel that somehow we have attained a degree of peace in the convent that few elsewhere can hope to know.

Parents seem to sense this, also, and even non-Catholics often wish to place their children under the convent care of dedicated nuns. I recall Mark Twain's beautiful letter from Europe to his wife on the subject of sending their daughter to a convent school. The letter appeared in Clara Clemens's biography, *My Father, Mark Twain.*

*"I am glad, very glad, Jean is in a convent. I was astonished at myself that I had never thought of a convent. And away down deep in my heart I feel that if they made a good, strong, unshakable Catholic of her, I shall not be in the least bit sorry. It is doubtless the most peace-giving and restful of all religions. If I had it, I would not trade it for anything on earth. If I ever change my religion, I shall change to that."*

While we in the enclosure of Carmel are blessed with a calm, deep, sure peace—a peace that comes from faith and trust in God and a heart set free from inordinate desires—still we are at war for the kingdom of God. We cannot make a truce with evil.

We are to fight the evil, but we are to love the one who errs. We are never to lose our charity and our concern for the sinner; we pray and make sacrifices for his soul. Our battling for the kingdom of God is a striving for true peace. When men in the world fight battles, they but sow the seeds of future strife and disharmony. Our Blessed Lord's peace is different. . . . "My peace I give you: not as the world giveth, do I give unto you." Christ came to give us an *inward* peace. And we have this inward peace only when we are united with God, when we act in a way that is pleasing to Him.

I know that it is possible for some who are far from God to possess a false peace. They are so absorbed in their own prosperity and selfish pleasures that they never stop to think about the transitoriness of earthly life; they are in a sort of daze and are too dull to think clearly. For these souls also I pray. Once they begin to sense an insufficiency in themselves, a little insecurity in their future, a disturbance in their conscience, then there is some hope that they will attain true peace, some hope that they may reach out for the hand of God before it is too late.

Before World War II, a retreat priest in one of his conferences said to us: "We will not have peace until the world goes down on its knees and adores Almighty God. . . ." And he exhorted us at that time to increase our fervor and to do all we possibly could in the way of prayer and penance in order to keep back the avenging hand of God.

It might seem to be oversimplifying the solution to say that the peace of the world depends on the answer to the question, "Are you for God, or are you against Him?" According to Pope Pius XII, this is the question of supreme moment for the future of the world. The Pontiff, speaking to all the nations, said, "The world must be converted from the empty, turbid cisterns of selfish gain, back to the clear, living fountains of the moral law." Conferences for peace, meetings for brotherhood, books on "the freedoms" are meaningless unless we first admit the sovereignty of God.

The great prophet Saint Elias saw the problem in its proper light when, from the slopes of Mount Carmel, he stood up like a fire and cried out to the people below, "How long do you halt between two sides? If the Lord be God, follow Him!" There is the secret of peace; and unless He be followed, the heart of the world will remain sick and cannot be cured.

The peace we wish the world to know is the peace of silent Carmel, peace "as an overflowing torrent," yet as deep as the soundless sea, a peace that no storm is able to disturb. A deep, sweet peace fills my soul. Even when wild winds rage over the upper ocean of the world, far beneath the surface roar there is within me a peaceful stillness, like the flow of a deep, silent river. This is Carmel, where my Beloved has called me.

AUTHOR'S NOTE

Before the day is done, this manuscript will be on its way to the publisher and I need not give it another thought. But if I forget the book, I assure you I shall not, nor could I, forget a single one of my readers. Indeed, if you be found "in Christ" you are my Beloved. And there will always be a very special bond between us, carrying over even into Eternity. From my solitude of Carmel, prayers and sacrifices will ascend to the throne of God for you day and night. Even my Heaven—if I get there before you—shall be a prayer for you. And I hope you will remember to pray for me, too.

May we all become exactly what God has destined us to be!

Carmel of Saint Joseph
Oklahoma City
Oklahoma